The Complete
Book of
Witches and
Wizards

THIS IS A CARLTON BOOK

Text and design copyright © Carlton Books Limited 2007

This edition published in 2007 by Carlton Books Ltd
20 Mortimer Street
London W1T 3JW

First published in separate volumes, *The Book of Wizards*
(2001) and *The Book of Witches* (2005) by Carlton Books
Limited.

A CIP catalogue record for this book is available from the
British Library.

ISBN 978 1 84442 395 8

Printed in China

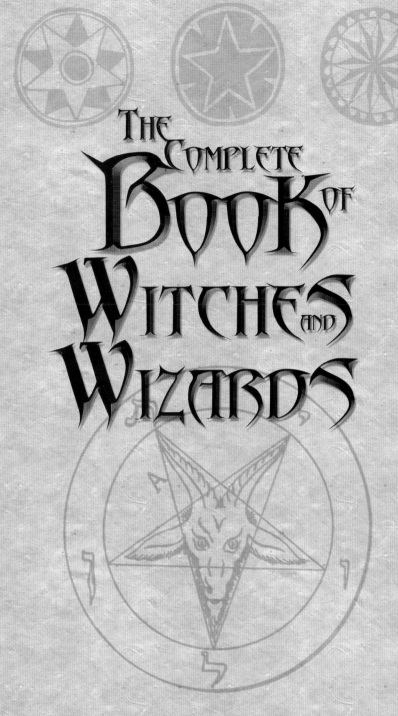

THE COMPLETE BOOK OF WITCHES AND WIZARDS

Tim Dedopulos

CARLTON
BOOKS

Contents

Part One

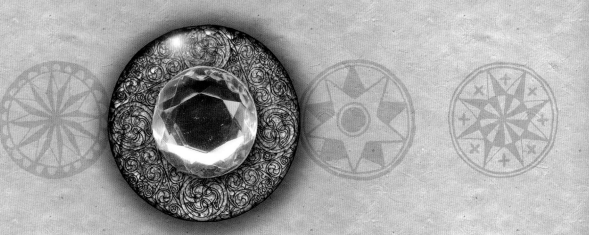

Witches

1
"Round About the Cauldron Go"

"Round About the Cauldron Go"

An Introduction to Witchcraft

Beware the night! Darkness is when the witches roam, safe from discovery and identification. They lurk in the shadows, their powers hidden from the world, and reach out to blight or bless with no more than a pinch of herbs or a muttered spell. They can ride the winds on their broomsticks, take on the shape of an animal, destroy crops, ruin livelihoods and miraculously bring the sick back from the very edge of death. They are anonymous, anyone and anywhere... but, most of all, they're an expression of our need to master the elements and forces of nature – and a cruel legacy of the male fear of feminine power.

Almost every culture on Earth frightens itself with legends of witchcraft. The forms change, but they have much in common. Typically, witches work secretly, in darkness, harnessing natural forces to sow illness and calamity out of a sense of sheer malice. The widow next door could be one, or the quiet woman on the corner, or the midwife who understands the uses of herbs… It's as true of rural African tribes as it is of medieval Europe. At their core, tales of witchcraft are about the fear of the outsider in our midst. It is as if we believe, on some deep, primitive level, that being apart from the normal flow of society makes a person dangerous, granting them access to dark powers and urges.

Like nature, witches are thought of as fickle, dangerous and frequently cruel. Their powers can dominate every element of everyday life: health, weather, prosperity, fertility, love, wisdom, luck and more. As with life itself, they are said to be quicker to take than to give. Witchery is a calling rather than a talent, a craft that can be learnt, should any be dark-hearted enough to seek the knowledge – well, that's what the propaganda says, anyway. Plenty of people believe that witches were always wise and benevolent, a way for local people to have access to healing and some power over their lives. The idea of learned women providing help and solace to the masses outside of a religious framework was horrifying to the men who ruled the lands and churches. Greedy and jealous of their own power and influence, they demonized anyone who possessed the old wisdom.

Whichever view you subscribe to, there are examples from fiction, myth and even real life. The gingerbread witch from the "Hansel and Gretel" story was so evil that she ate children, while the Celtic witch Bechuille supposedly dedicated herself to finding and destroying the goddess of black magic, Carman, and her three evil sons. The White Witch from *The Lion, the Witch and the Wardrobe* ruled the land of Narnia savagely, keeping it in eternal winter, while Hermione Granger has frequently risked her life (and her exam results!) to help her friend Harry Potter.

Whilst the stereotypical view is that witches are old, ugly women who live alone in out-of-the-way places and keep strange pets, there have always been

exceptions. For example, the North Berwick witches were a Scots group burned to death in the 16th century, and included several men amongst their number. Many other men were killed as witches during the times of the infamous trials. More recently, television has developed a noticeable inclination for witches to be young and pretty, as *Sabrina, the Teenage Witch*, *Buffy the Vampire Slayer*'s Willow and Tara, and the *Charmed* Halliwell sisters all demonstrate.

This book will take a detailed look at witches and witchcraft. It will examine all of the most famous witches of history, myth and fiction, looking at their lives, powers, inclinations and the periods or settings they lived in. It will also investigate the sorts of places that witches can be found and the equipment they collect with which to work their will, the organisations they form, and the animals they bind to themselves. First of all, though, we are going to look into what being a witch involves, how to identify a witch from other similar magical types, and what general sorts of witches can be found.

φ *Macbeth first encountered the three witches on a blasted heath.*

Reasons to be fearful

ᚾᛗᛖᚷᚱᛏᛁᚾᛗᛟᚾᛟᛚᚠᚱᛏᛁᚠᚠᚷᛟᚾᛟᛗᚾᚺᛗᚠᚺᛗᚾᛟᚾᚠᚠᛗᛏᛁᛚᚱᛗᚺᛖᛗᛗᚺᛁᛗᚠᛟᚾᛗᚷᚱᛏ

The greatest weapon in the witch's arsenal is her mastery of **magic**. Often defined as the art of changing the world through direct application of will, magic comes in many forms. There are as many different styles of magic as there are people to use it, but witches typically restrict themselves to a few different ways of working their will. Different types of magic-user have different methods available to them of course, and in many senses, it is the *style* of magic that a person uses that really defines them as witch, wizard, shaman or thaumaturge. As a rule of thumb, **vulgar magic** breaks the laws of reality, while **subtle magic** works within them. Turning someone into a toad and flying through the night on a broomstick are vulgar magic displays, while causing bad luck or making someone feel love towards you would be subtle. Almost everyone believes vulgar magic to be impossible in the real world, while opinion is divided regarding subtle magic.

Spells are the most famous form of magic, and one that is very powerfully identified with witchcraft. A witch's spells are subtle and dangerous, and can be turned to almost any effect. They almost always take the form of snatches of rhyming verse, simple doggerel, usually in the witch's native tongue. There's often no need for powders or complicated gestures or other action, unless the spell is bound into an object as a **charm**, in which case the "spell" might be as simple as just hanging a toad in a chimney. Usually, however, gazing at the victim and muttering the words is enough – coupled with the witch's fierce will forcing the desired result.

Some of the traditional spells that rumour and hearsay have preserved for us were frankly bloodcurdling, as this excerpt from a book-protecting spell shows:

> *Let it change into a serpent in his hand and rend him.*
> *Let him be struck with palsy, all his members blasted well.*
> *Let him languish in pain, crying aloud for ending,*
> *Let there be no end to his agony as he sinks to the pits of hell.*

A nineteenth-century illustration depicts spells being cast.

Almost as notorious as spells, witches' **potions** have been feared for centuries. All sorts of the most disgusting, peculiar, abstract and mythical ingredients have been said to be used, almost always tossed into cauldrons and boiled – for as long as five years, in some cases. Sometimes, just brewing the potion was enough to make magic; in other instances, the target had to drink some.

The most famous potion of all is described at the start of Act 4 of Shakespeare's *Macbeth* – fictional, obviously, but also written so as to sound entirely plausible to the people of the time. The material that Macbeth's witches throw into their cauldron reads like a shopping list from hell: everything from the infamous but comparatively innocent "eye of newt and toe of frog, wool of bat and tongue of dog", up to hemlock root dug up in darkness, the liver of a Jewish blasphemer, poisoned entrails, the finger of a still-born baby delivered in a ditch, and, impossibly, dragon scales.

It was commonly thought that witches had secret cupboards containing jars of all sorts of repulsive and abominable potion ingredients, but there must have been times when the witches had to go on special quests (or killing sprees) to track down harder-to-find ingredients. It was long thought that witches would steal unbaptized male babies in order to use the baby's fat in flying potions.

The most frightening style of magic at the witch's disposal was probably the **evil eye**. This is a type of magic that requires no ingredients, formulas or tangled spells, and takes no time at all to cast. It's the pure expression of the witch's will and malice, free of any other complications that might make it harder or slower to bring about. All that's required is that the witch be able to see the victim – and even then, she is free to make use of magical scrying to peer in from a distance. Any ill, disease or misfortune could be the result of the evil eye, and people with unusual eyes of any sort – deep-set, misaligned, different colours, even piercing blue or green – were often immediately suspect.

The most mysterious of the witch's magical styles is the phenomenon that fantasy humorist Terry Pratchett jokingly names "**headology**". Simply by being a witch, she can cause magical events to happen. Although Pratchett uses the term to make a point about the psychological aspects of the supernatural, there is something deeper behind what he's saying – that a symbol is itself powerful over a person who recognizes it, regardless of any intent or virtue placed within it.

Early anthropologists, observing witch-doctors cursing victims who then sickened and died, suggested that this was the force behind these experiences. The opposite side of the coin is the medical placebo effect, which allows doctors sometimes to cure incurable, even fatal, illnesses through the use of dummy medicines with no treatment value whatsoever. Doctors have estimated that the placebo effect – the magic of headology – accounts for as much as 40% of all medical cures. Sometimes merely going through

♦ *A witch's potion was always brewed in her cauldron.*

the motions is enough to produce genuine magic. Whether that magic is produced by the victim's mind, or whether something even more mysterious is happening, headology is a very real and powerful part of life. Terry Pratchett himself has often been asked in interviews about the occult secrets that he works into his books – a fact which gives him endless amusement.

Magical effects

As we've just seen, there is a certain range of magical styles that are typical of witchcraft. The same is true of the sorts of areas (known as "**domains**") that witchcraft has power over – in other words, a witch's magic tends to be powerful in certain areas. Unlike wizards, witches are very firmly grounded in the here and now. They are part of society, working within it and upon it in ways no isolated wizard could ever really know. Witches are close to the real world, to rain and leaf and dirt, with a deep understanding of natural rhythms and cycles, and a good knowledge of people and what makes them tick.

⬦ *In Wales, witches were thought to be able to turn themselves into large hares.*

The type of magic that witches are most famous for – the reputed power which has been turned on them the most frequently – is the **curse**. In its most general form, a curse condemns the victim to bad luck, often spectacularly bad. It has been well known for thousands of years that if you angered a witch, things would start to go wrong. Sickness, deformation, broken bones, destroyed relationships, lost wallets, ruined crops, spoilt milk… a witch's curse would cause all sorts of misfortune, possibly even hounding the victim to his grave.

Lots of anecdotes of curses in action have survived from the medieval ages. But think on this. When things go wrong, particularly lots of things in a short time, it is very human to look for a reason, to vent your anger: a god to placate… a witch to blame… a lonely old widow on the edge of the village to burn…

A domain closely linked to the witch's curse is that of **transformation** – the power to change a person's shape. Fairy tales are full of people being turned into toads and mice by evil-minded witches as a very specific form of curse. That wasn't the extent of a witch's power, though, impressive as it might be. A strong witch could take other forms herself – most commonly a hare, a big black dog, or a raven. Some witches, moreover, were able to take on the shape of any living thing, even vegetable.

Victims didn't just have toadhood to fear, either. The famous Rollright Witch of central England is said to have confronted a Danish challenger for the English throne as he stood on a hill looking over the village of Long Compton in Warwickshire. She challenged him to take seven paces, and if he could still see the village, he would be sure of becoming king. The pretender agreed, and took his steps, but at the last moment the witch made a mound of earth rise up in front of him. For losing, she cursed him:

As Long Compton thou canst not see,
King of England thou shalst not be.
Rise up stick and stand still stone,
For King of England thou shalst be none.
Thou and thy men hoar stones shall be,
And I myself an Elder Tree.

He promptly turned into a tall standing stone. His men, camping some distance off, were turned into a stone circle; even a group of his knights conspiring against him a quarter of a mile away were caught in the spell. Her work done, the witch turned herself into an elder bush next to the pretender, to watch over his punishment. The Rollright Stones remain a beautiful and eerie sight today, and the witch/tree is still there guarding the pretender and his men.

Less destructively, witches are also known for their control over other people's **emotions**. Witches had all sorts of tricks for altering what their victims were feeling. Unsurprisingly, most people thought that this ability was used to sow chaos and destruction in a local area. However, there are also plenty of stories of villagers turning to a local witch for help in this area. The emotions most commonly conjured by witches are the strongest: love, hate, terror and fury.

We have all heard tales of the famous witches' love potion – and probably wished for one once or twice ourselves. Just like bad luck, though, serious social problems in small villages were often blamed on witchcraft meddling with feelings. If Tom and Ned, say – decent neighbours who'd known each other these 40 year gone – suddenly started trying to rip each other to shreds… well, people thought that must be a witch causing trouble, rather than the long-repressed irritations of over-familiarity finally erupting. Who knows?

The domain of **weather** is another of the witch's strengths. Like their control over emotions, witches were best known for causing the strongest, most dramatic freak weather conditions. Violent storms at sea, blazing periods of drought and withering heat, crippling cold spells… witches were able to reproduce the harshest, most unpleasant weather patterns. These normally seemed to coincide with disastrous effects on a village's crops or stored food supplies, or – in the case of storms – with a catastrophic shipwreck. The assumption remained, as always, that witches delighted in causing as much death and misery as possible.

But not everyone always assumed the worst. As another critical aspect of life, **fertility** was also an area where witches were well-known to have power. While there were accusations of evil deeds levelled at witches in this area – particularly with regard to barren livestock or a childless couple – this sort of mischief more normally fell under the idea of a curse.

There was much more interest in the idea of a witch as a facilitator of pregnancy. Witches were said to have all sorts of charms and remedies to help women become pregnant – and to help them stop being pregnant, too. They had spells to decide the sex of a baby, to bless it with health, strength and beauty, even to help it meet a good fate later in life. Of all of the domains of a witch's power, fertility was the one most likely to be thought of favourably – possibly because it was the one area that such people could not easily turn to their own purposes.

Of course, it was well known that witches could offer **healing** potions, salves and charms for just about any illness or ailment, if it suited them. Legends are full of tales of injured or diseased heroes collapsing in the woods, and waking up days or weeks later to find themselves in a witch's hut, completely cured. It was also known that most witches would sell remedies for assorted problems, either for cash, produce, or, more sinisterly, unspecified favours.

We know for certain that there were women in medieval Europe and America who had knowledge of herbal medicine and other forms of received folk **wisdom**. It is possible that a lot of these Wise Women were rooted out and killed by zealous witch-hunters; certainly the "cunning" men and women (the word comes from the old English kenn, to know) had all but vanished by the turn of the eighteenth century. Whether the "kenning" women and men had a secret formalized structure or society, or dabbled in darker arts, is now lost in history.

All manner of herbs and spices were used in witchcraft.

terms, it's the difference between being gifted with the prodigious ability to work out the square root of a 26-digit number in your head, and knowing where to find a computer program that can do the calculation for you.

Many of the real witches that we remember today were particularly renowned for their gift of **prophecy**. There's nothing quite like foretelling doom to give yourself a bad reputation, even if you mean well. The Greek legends of Cassandra are all about a woman who was cursed by the gods always to tell the truth about the future, and always to be ignored for it. She was swiftly forced into a miserable existence, laughed at wherever she went, driven from town and village alike by complacent people, who simply didn't want to hear that it would ever happen to them.

But it's worse for a prophetess who is still there when she is proven right. Foreknowledge, of course, is automatically suspicious. If she knew it was coming, the "logic" runs, that can only be because she caused it. Even when the prophecy is just blindingly obvious common sense – such as "Keep harrowing that one field, and it'll go barren" – it's still the prophet's fault.

The witches we remember, like Mother Shipton, who we'll meet later, were careful to keep their prophecies distant, abstract or both. The ones who gave out the bad news they saw never lasted long enough to become famous… and that remains just as true for professional psychics today.

The power of **clairvoyance** (or **scrying**) is distantly related to that of prophecy. The biggest difference is that while prophecy looks at what might be happening in the future, scrying looks directly at what is happening, right now, in different places. It's the ultimate voyeurism, every spy's

Dark powers

ᚾᛗᚠᚷᛈᛏᛃᚾᛗᛩᚾᚱᛈᛖᛈᛏᛃᛈᛈᛈᚷᚦᚾᚦᛗᚾᚼᛗᚠᚼᛗᚾᛩᚾᚾᛈᛖᛈᛗᛏᛃᛈᚠᛗᛗᚼᛃᛗᚠᛩᚾᛗᚠᚷᛈᛏ

In addition to their magical abilities, witches traditionally had access to a range of other supernatural **powers**. The difference between a power and the use of magic is fine, but important. A power is something inherent, a skill or ability in its own right. Magic, by contrast, is a force used to produce specific results – an intermediary. Even when the end result is very similar, the difference lies in the journey taken to get there – not least because it often takes different methods to defend against magic from those needed to be safe against the use of a malicious power. To put it in modern fondest dream – the ability to see any place on Earth as if you were there. The power allowed witches to learn all sorts of unsavoury secrets, which could then be spread to cause trouble, or used as blackmail material.

Unlike wizards, who use crystal balls for scrying, witches traditionally looked afar by gazing into liquids, usually in their cauldrons or in special scrying bowls. Being spied on is bad enough – particularly when you're doing something private – but the real danger was that a witch could cast spells or make use of the evil eye through her scrying bowl. She didn't even have to come into the same village to infect your cattle or blight your crops. So much for alibis.

The most famous power, of course, is **flight**. No self-respecting legendary witch went anywhere without her broomstick. A long, tatty besom brush made out of a thick bundle of twigs tied to a staff, the broomstick remains the defining symbol of witchcraft right across Western culture. When we depict a witch, it's almost always mid-air on her broomstick. Her pointy hat and black cat familiar are optional extras; the broomstick is the visual badge by which we sum up everything unnatural about witches and their powers. It was seen as the most indispensable witch's tool, allowing the witch to get about the countryside to work her evil, and to meet up with other witches at their dark sabbats.

The irony, of course, is that the broomstick was a vital tool of everyday medieval life, and no woman would ever be without one. The supposedly greatest tell-tale sign of witchy evil was the one household tool that you would be guaranteed to find in every woman's house.

Sometimes considered a power and sometimes an unfortunate side-effect of harbouring so much evil, witches were also prone to cause minor **corruption** effects wherever they went. If you had a witch in your house, fresh milk would curdle and go off, ale would turn cloudy and sour, and other fresh foods might spoil, too. You might notice an increase in insect life and other vermin in the immediate area. Small plants, both inside and outside the house, would wither and die. Pets would be scared to stay in the building. Productive animals outside would yield little produce, if any – hens wouldn't lay, cows would dry up. Religious statues and icons might even weep small tears of blood.

Presumably, witches were able to turn off these effects when they were in their own homes. Otherwise, they may well have had a hard time keeping any food around. The patches of blighted ground surrounding their houses would have been a clear give-away as to their location, too.

Being able to **commune with spirits** was probably a more useful power for most witches. The types of spirit that a witch could talk to depended a lot on the religious and mythological history of the area that she lived in, it seems. In Celtic-influenced areas, witches were in contact with the sidhe or fairy folk and their kin – from fairies and pixies through to boggarts, trolls and hobgoblins. Where memory of other old ways lingered, witches might be in touch with the spirits of stream and forest and field.

As far as zealous Christianity was concerned, witches were able to communicate with Satan and his demons, and that was all there was to it. Less paranoid regions allowed for the possibility that a witch might be able to open a link to lesser angels, long-deceased relatives and other comparatively benevolent forces. A witch had no inherent control over the spirits she could talk to, whoever they were. While they would often do things for her, such favours had to be purchased, or pacts entered into at the very least.

Less commonly, some witches were also said to be able to **control vermin** in the local area. Covering everything from fleas up to rats – and even rabbits, according to some farmers – vermin were generally any creature that was considered harmful or unwelcome. Some witches were thought to have conscious influence over such pests, being able to plague a house or barn with rats, mice, flies, toads, ants or just about any other unwelcome visitor.

Rival spell-casters

ᚻᚹᛖᚷᚱᛏᛁᚾᛗᛟᚾᛏᛚᚻᚨᚱᛏᛁᚠᚱᚷᛟᚾᚯᛗᚾᚻᚹᛖᚻᛗᚾᚯᚾᛄᚹᛗᛏᛄᚹᚻᛗᚻᛖᛗᚻᛋᛁᚹᚨᚯᚾᚹᚨᚷᚱᛏ

As we've seen, witches have a wide range of powers at their disposal. They are not the only naturalistic magic-workers, however. There are all sorts of different types of individual capable of casting spells and using strange powers, who have, over the centuries, appeared in one way or another to be similar to the traditional witch. They are very different breeds, however.

The first obvious possibility for confusion is with the **witch-doctors** of African legend. Although there is a similarity in name, the two serve very different roles in their societies. Witches, as we have seen, are outsiders, usually distrusted and blamed for all sorts of ills and misfortunes. Witch-doctors were tribal magicians, working for the good of the village, and, though often feared, were still appreciated and respected.

A typical witch-doctor would share many of the witch's domains and powers – curses, fertility, transformation, healing, even prophecy – but tended to be male and to cast his magic through complicated tribal rituals. Often most relied upon for help in tribal battles and food hunting, the witch-doctor would bless the tribe's warriors, curse enemies (sometimes to death), treat diseases and injuries, dispense his wisdom and learning on all sorts of subjects, and use his powers to seek out good

✦ *A witch-doctor shares his wisdom and advice with his tribe.*

hunting grounds. Witch-doctors are normally pictured in the popular press as tall and imposing men prancing nearly naked around a fire, clutching gruesome skull-topped magic staffs, with a bone set through a piercing in their nose.

Shamen are found worldwide, and have quite a lot in common with both witches and witch-doctors. Like witch-doctors, they are tribal magicians, working for the good of the group; like witches, they are natural outsiders, in touch with spirits, not entirely part of the real world. The defining characteristic of a shaman is that he has special access to the spirit realm, granted through a patron spirit, or totem. While other types of magician may be able to communicate, the shaman goes on voyages into the world of spirits, using his power there to heal the sick, foretell the future, discover lucky places to hunt, and even to draw animals to the tribe for eating.

In many cultures, a shaman would have one particular spirit guide, a spirit that acts as protector and guardian over a particular species of animal. Each species has its own 'totem' spirit, a being with superhuman intelligence and abilities that represents the ideals and greatest potential of that species. Each shaman would be adopted by one totem when he first learnt how to visit the spirit world, and it is from that relationship that he would gain all his powers.

Many **alchemists** were accused of witchcraft in the sixteenth and seventeenth centuries, but without much real cause. Just possessing esoteric depths of knowledge was often enough. Alchemists sought the methods and techniques by which ordinary objects could be turned into gold. The ultimate goal of their research – a substance called "The Philosopher's Stone" – was supposedly also able to grant eternal life. As part of their ongoing quest, alchemists typically made many discoveries and accumulated huge bodies of odd knowledge. Some became skilled at healing, and all were known to concoct all sorts of potion-like brews as part of their experiments.

At its heart, though, alchemy was about purification rather than about control or wreaking havoc. Alchemical laboratories typically had more chemical apparatus in them than a witch's lair would do, and the alchemists themselves were often considerably wealthier than the average witch was thought to be. Even so, their astrological knowledge and their interest in herbs were enough to get them into trouble with the Inquisition if they weren't careful enough with investigators.

Wizards are a different type of being entirely. Aloof and mysterious, they tend to live out of the reach of lesser mortals, devoting their time and energy to strange research and arcane spells. The masters of magic, their interests are very different from those of the earthy witch.

Typically, wizards devote themselves to trying to understand the most esoteric details of the universe itself, concentrating on abstruse facts and types of knowledge in their research. They accumulate vast libraries, and are frequently to be found absorbed in books. Their magic powers are fearsome, as direct as a hammer-blow or as subtle as cobwebs – but without great application to the everyday world. Wizards may be expert on the hidden lore of Aldebaran or the secrets of quartz, but tend to know very little of crops and pregnancy and how to prick a farmer's pride to set him against his neighbour. For the most part, wizardly magic involves complex rituals with all sorts of very particular actions and requirements to complete, and hardly any wizard would dream of being seen without his wand or staff. If witches are tied to the forces of nature, then wizards are definitely linked to the principles that led to science.

Finally, some of the beings thought of from time to time as witches are actually **spirits** of one form or another. It can be difficult to tell the difference between a bona fide witch and a dark sidhe (fairy folk) crone living in a near-derelict hut in the woods. Fairies, wood spirits, lesser demons, half-humans and even troubled ghosts have all been known to take on the guise of rural semi-hermits – and the wide range of powers that they have access to can make them seem quite witchy indeed.

In general, spirits don't need to do magic, they can achieve the supernatural ends they desire entirely through their own innate powers. Some of the sidhe have ability with spells, but most fairy magic is more ethereal than that, and concentrates on illusion, deception, charm and meddling with

time. Few spirits are known to use cauldrons for anything other than cooking in, and they keep themselves as isolated as possible from the human communities around them. Even the most reclusive witches, by contrast, like to make sure they know what's going on in the villages around them, and have frequent dealings with some of the braver (or nastier-minded) individuals from the area. The best way to tell the difference, however, is the presence of a broomstick. Even the sidhe don't use brooms to fly – the only time a spirit will be riding a broomstick is when it is deliberately pretending to be a human witch.

◈ *You couldn't be an alchemist without chemical apparatus, some skulls, and one or more stuffed crocodiles hanging from your roof.*

Which witch?

ᚺᛗᚨᚷᛏᛜᚺᛗᚩᚾᚦᛏᚠᚨᛏᛃᛈᚠᚷᛜᚦᚾᛗᚻᚺᛗᛃᚺᛗᚾᚦᚾᛈᚠᛈᛗᛏᛃᛈᚠᛗᛃᛗᛗᚻᛃᛁᛗᚦᚾᛗᚠᚷᛏ

With the range of different abilities and domains at a witch's disposal – and the wide assortment of ways that her powers can actually be used – it should be no surprise that there are a number of different types of witch, and they are not all evil. Despite the best efforts of certain historical factions to label all witch-like activity as the work of the devil, some types of witch are interested only in helping soften life's hardships. Others, of course, are rotten to the core – even if they don't actually know it.

The **Classic Witch** is fairly hostile to the rest of the world. This is the stereotypical type of witch, as seen in gift shops and Hallowe'en displays right across the Western world. She is aging and ugly, all skin and bones, with wild hair, craggy cheeks, a pointy chin and a huge, beaky, wart-covered nose. She keeps a black cat as her familiar, and lives somewhere out of the way – near one or more villages for sure, but never closer than the edge of a village, and often out in the middle of nowhere.

The classic witch demands respect and obedience, and if she is defied or insulted, she will stop at nothing to get her revenge. She can – and will – cause sickness, bring down horrible curses, wreck ships with sudden storms, blight fields and cattle, and generally make a destructive nightmare out of herself. She occupies her time in all manner of malicious plots aimed at everyone from the ruler of the land down to the local villagers. She is jealous and spiteful, and may curse a pretty young girl just for being attractive while she herself is now old and ugly.

Despite all this evil, the classic witch is not completely dark-hearted. If approached correctly and sympathetically, she will sometimes sell her services and blessings, provide healing or help with pregnancy issues, agree to lift a curse, and otherwise be surprisingly helpful. She has been consistently scorned, hated and driven out all her life, and she has become extremely bitter, resentful and distrustful. Her better nature remains, however, and if you can get past her towering cliffs of cynicism, she can prove to be a powerful ally. In our scientific age, the great majority of people doubt that any classic witch ever actually existed – magic, surely, just isn't strong enough to turn a boy into a toad or to make a broomstick fly – but medieval folk believed it without question.

The **Wise Woman** is at the opposite end of the spectrum. Although she starts along the same path as the classic witch, her innate sweet nature and desire to help mean that she uses her powers and abilities to help cure and bless the folk of the local area as much as possible. Where pride, vanity and the use of power inspire people to fear and hate the young classic witch, driving her out, the young wise woman is accepted into the community. Although typically born and trained in a village, she'll often move to the nearby town so as to be able to help people from all the surrounding villages. Her special skills lie in herbal medicine, basic surgery and other forms of healing, particularly of women's issues, but she also knows how to ward off evil and defeat curses and other malicious spells.

As the name suggests, the wise woman has a

good understanding of human nature, local politics and issues and basic psychology, and so she is often called in to help arbitrate disputes or settle other thorny problems that may be troubling the community. Despite her kind nature, though, the wise woman is no doormat. Quite capable of being matronly or even sternly forbidding, she does not react well to insults or attempts to cheat her.

People who think they can take advantage of the wise woman would do well to remember that she has all sorts of tricks up her sleeve – she just chooses not to use them… most of the time. Wise women are also known as white witches. Several real historical wise women are known to have existed, and most people nowadays assume that there were many more of them, serving as early doctors and healers for the rural communities. It's thought that many, even most of them, were murdered during the witch-hunts.

Another type of witch in the popular imagination is the **Satanic Dupe**. The model of witchcraft favoured by religious zealots and witch-hunters, the satanic dupe gets all her powers directly from the devil himself. She is invariably part of a coven of thirteen members from the local area, and they get together to meet on the night of the dark moon (the day before new moon). At these gatherings, they engage in perverted orgies, sacrifice babies and virgins, and eventually call up Satan himself to join in their sick sex games. Satanic dupes are also known as **warlocks**, a term often mistakenly applied to male classic witches. In fact, "witch" is a gender-neutral term.

These witches can be male or female, of any age or temperament. Their link to the devil is usually maintained through a familiar, a pet that acts as a conduit to the forces of hell. The witch has to feed the familiar her own blood regularly, and in return

Occult rituals were a favourite fantasy of all frenzied witch-hunters.

the creature will carry out evil deeds at her command. Satanic dupes keep their witchcraft secret, and take part in the normal everyday life of the village, using the evil eye and secretly casting spells to bring death and agony to their friends, families and the people they grew up with.

Although they have invariably been promised some sort of specific benefit – wealth, influence, eternal youth, the love of a specific person – satanic dupes typically are just turned into soulless vessels of evil demonic hate, and given a range of powers linked to cursing and blighting with which to work their master's will. Each has a "witch mark", generally a spot on their body which is mysteriously numb to the touch. Satanic dupes exist only to spread death and agony in the name of Satan, and cannot be redeemed. The witches killed during the period of the witch trials in Europe and America were invariably accused of being satanic dupes rather than classic witches. Like classic witches, however, it is doubtful that any have ever actually existed in the real world.

A rarer kind of witch altogether, the **Involuntary Witch** can cause as much damage and panic as a satanic dupe but, tragically, knows nothing about it whatsoever. Like the "Jonah" passengers so feared by superstitious sailors in the past, some otherwise perfectly decent people were in fact terrifying witches. Sometimes, involuntary witches are nothing more than magnets for bad luck. Like lightning rods, they attract disaster, calamity and pain, but rather than channelling it safely into the Earth, they themselves are unharmed while the bolt strikes someone very nearby.

It would be easy to assume that this sort of witchcraft is the result of an unconscious use of dark powers to lash out at people that the involuntary witch resents or fears, but that's missing the point that involuntary witches are capable of harming anyone, regardless of their personal links to the victim. In some parts of the world, particularly Africa, the idea is taken a step further. A perfectly normal person can become infiltrated by a parasitic form of witchcraft, becoming a witch. Their power

manifests only when they sleep, lashing out at other people in the village and eating portions of their soul to make them ill. Such witches typically have an extra parasite organ inside their stomachs – a large black, spotted sac. Diagnosis is only possible for a dead witch, of course.

These cases are particularly tragic because they are often tracked down to someone totally innocent of any malice or misdeed in their normal, waking life. There is no way an involuntary witch can be cured, however, only killed.

Last, but not least, the most recent addition to the ranks of witchcraft are the practitioners of **Wicca**. The great witchcraft revival took place in the 1940s and 1950s when an occultist named Gerald Gardner talked openly about the witchcraft training he had received from a mysterious old woman of his acquaintance. She in turn had supposedly received the craft from a previous witch High Priestess, and so on, back through the ages to the time before the witch-hunts and the great suppression. Gardner declared that this form of witchcraft was called

Wicca, and all modern witchcraft and Wicca practices have been developed either directly from Gardner's work, or as a response to it. Despite Gardner's claims, it seems highly likely now that he invented Wicca himself, working from general occult principles.

Wicca is now a recognized religion in most countries where that is legally possible, and its practitioners claim that the magic teachings within the craft – which run the entire gamut of subtle magic – are genuinely effective. Wiccan magic may fall short of transforming people into toads, but modern witches claim to be able to manipulate probability and luck, influence people's emotions one way or another, bring about specific twists of fate, peer into the future, communicate with spirits, and promote healing – much like the White Witches of old. Wiccan magic is, of course, a lot less showy than legend and rumour suggested vulgar medieval witchcraft could be.

Things we now count as physically impossible – flying spontaneously, transforming one object into another, causing dramatic instant physical change and so on – are beyond the power of Wicca. It is a subtler craft, one that works by supposedly changing the intangible aspects that help to make up our world. Rather than suddenly turning your old bike into a flashy new car, Wicca might be able to bring you the promotions and bonuses that would let you buy the car for yourself. Instead of yielding a potion that would make a specific person fall in love with you instantly, Wicca can offer you ways of making love grow gently.

There is plenty of scope within Wiccan magic to turn it to the dark ends of medieval legend, of course – to sow heartbreak and misery, curse people with bad luck, ill health or an evil fate, even theoretically to set evil spirits upon them – but Wicca teaches how much damage that sort of spell also does to the caster. Few people are stupid enough to want to hurt others for no good reason, knowing that they would hurt themselves far more in the process. Accordingly, while there are plenty of White Wiccans out there, almost none are prepared to work with the darker side of witchcraft. Even discounting the fact that it is simply wrong, the cost is just too high.

2
"Weird Sisters, Hand in Hand"

"Weird Sisters,
Hand in Hand"
Witches from Book and Screen

◆ *You can spot
Russian witch
Baba Yaga by
her bone legs and
the pestle she
sits in.*

The best-known witches today are the ones we've grown up with – our companions through the years, from television, films and books. They run the entire spectrum from friendly Wiccans through to grim classic witches. Free of the constraints of reality, our fictional witches are free to explore the very limits of what it means to be a witch. In this chapter, we'll look at a selection of the best-loved witch characters from the last few decades.

Willow Rosenberg

ᚾᛗᛖᚷᛉᛏᛁᚾᛗᛟᚾᚱᚲᛇᛉᛏᛁᛎᛇᛉᚷᛟᚾᛟᛗᚾᛉᛗᚠᛉᛗᚾᛟᚾᛈᚠᛈᛗᛂᛉᚲᛏᛗᛉᚠᛗᛗᛉᛁᛗᚠᛟᚾᛗᚠᚷᛉᛏ

Buffy the Vampire Slayer's best friend and main sidekick, Willow is the creation of Joss Whedon, the mastermind behind the hit television show. Over the course of the programme's seven-series run, Willow developed from being a nerdy, slightly gauche teen hacker to flower as an incredibly powerful witch. Firmly on the side of good – most of the time, anyway – she has played a key role in saving the world on a number of occasions and, once, came within a whisker of destroying it.

Biography

The daughter of Ira and Sheila Rosenberg, Willow was born in 1981 in Sunnydale, California. Her parents, brilliant in their own fields, were somewhat distant, and she grew up to become a socially awkward teenager, shy and bookish. She had a superb intellect, however, and made up for her social shortcomings by concentrating on school studies, quickly becoming one of the top students at her school and high school. She was particularly interested in computers and became an expert hacker as a means of expressing her fledgling rebellious edge.

When Buffy Summers relocated to Sunnydale during the first year of high school, Willow and her childhood friend Xander Harris befriended the new arrival. It was a fortunate new friendship; Buffy was the vampire slayer, the one chosen to hold back the forces of darkness, and she arrived just in time to stop the 16-year-old Willow from being turned into a vampire herself on an ill-advised first date. From that moment on, Willow and Xander joined forces to help Buffy in her quest to keep the world safe.

Initially, Willow was satisfied just to offer Buffy her assistance as a hacker and research expert. After a year or so, however, the group became friendly with the computer teacher at the high school, Jenny Calendar, who eventually revealed that she was a technopagan. Jenny clearly inspired Willow, and first brought the idea of witchcraft to her mind. Willow soon started practising some simple witchcraft. When Jenny was killed trying to help a mutual friend, Willow took it on herself to complete the complex restoration ritual Jenny had left behind. It took some effort, but she was finally successful, cementing her fascination with the field.

Over the years that followed, Willow dedicated herself to studying witchcraft, slowly gaining the power first to cast simple spells, and, eventually, to become an extremely formidable witch. At the same

◊ Willow (Alyson Hannigan) looks concerned – but then, in the background, so does vampire Spike (James Marsters).

time, she came out of her shell significantly to flower as a confident, attractive young woman. She was helped immeasurably in both these processes by her girlfriend Tara, herself a minor witch who had been studying for some years. The path was difficult, though; eventually, Willow was drawn in by the darker side of witchcraft and became addicted to the rush of the power. Her behaviour destroyed her relationship, and almost cost her all of her friends too. When Tara was murdered, Willow gave in to the dark side entirely, destroying first the murderer, and then trying to wreck the whole world in her grief and pain. Fortunately, her friends managed to stop her, and helped her rehabilitate.

Willow remains an extremely powerful witch, with the force and knowledge to genuinely change the world, but she keeps magic at arm's length out of fear of relapsing into her addiction. She currently lives in Brazil with a new girlfriend, a vampire slayer named Kennedy, where she works part time in an art gallery. She also studies at a local university.

World

The *Buffyverse* – the name that fans have given to the universe that the television show is set in – is a darkly dangerous place. The powers of evil are close at hand, taking an active interest in society and its affairs. The forces of good, on the other hand, seem distant for the most part, choosing to act almost exclusively through a small number of ordained champions. Vampires and demons are littered across the Earth, ranging from ancient slumbering evils of almost unbelievable power right down to sleazy back-alley devils lurking about on the fringes of society. Vulgar magic spells are no harder (or easier) to cast than subtle ones within the Buffyverse; one of Willow's earliest practice spells is making a pencil float into the air. While some Russian researchers might claim that such a feat is within human capabilities, no one would claim it's a simple, beginner-level trick.

As is so often the case, the lords of evil in the Buffyverse are stuck in a range of alternate hells and dimensions, but remain close to affairs on Earth. They meddle directly whenever possible, and always seek a way through to take control. They even run a major law firm in Los Angeles, as detailed in the spin-off series *Angel*. By contrast, the powers of good are distant and aloof, hard to contact and largely withdrawn from the real world. Heaven demands much and offers little, while Hell is eager to offer all sorts of gifts and riches, and asks just for allegiance.

Magic

For the most part, magic in the Buffyverse is the province of evil. Witchcraft is frequently referred to as "The Black Arts", and most of its practitioners seem temperamentally better suited to evil than to good. Willow is a sweet, kind-hearted young woman, but even she finds herself drawn towards the darkness inherent in the magic that she is learning. It is much like a drug, addictive and corrupting, and her journey down that route parallels a lot of real-world teachings about drug-abusing teenagers becoming deceptive, selfish liars. When she finally regains control of herself, it is at the point where she is about to destroy the world itself. Ultimately, Willow's magic abilities extend to the full range of powers typically ascribed to the most powerful of vulgar witchcraft and then beyond, to feats like teleportation, suspending time and shifting dimensions.

Name: Willow Rosenberg
Age: Twenties
Description: Slim and pretty, with mid-length red hair, green eyes, and a ready smile. Often appears a little distracted or concerned.
Dominant abilities: Spells, computer hacking, research
Traits: Intelligence, kindness, determination
Nature: Good
Power: Very strong
Type: Wiccan
Domain: General-purpose witchcraft
Goal: To help Buffy and save the world
Key equipment: Apple notebook
Creator: Joss Whedon

Granny Weatherwax

ᚾᛗᚠᚷᚱᛏᛋᚾᛗᚩᚾᚱᚠᛈᚱᛏᛋᚠᚠᚷᚩᚾᚩᛗᚾᚼᛗᚠᚼᛗᚾᚩᚾᚠᚠᛗᛏᛋᚠᚱᛗᚼᚠᛗᚾᚼᛋᛗᚠᚩᚾᛗᚠᚷᚱᛏ

The second most popular of all Terry Pratchett's literary creations – after the laconic figure of Death himself – is the Discworld's most formidable witch, Granny Weatherwax. Tall, forbidding, and relentlessly on the side of *right* without ever really approaching the side of *nice*, Granny stomps an indomitable path through half a dozen or more of Pratchett's novels.

Biography

As old as the hills, and every bit as grim on a cold winter morning, Esme "Granny" Weatherwax is a witch in every sense of the word. She lives in the kingdom of Lancre, a small flyspeck of a country lost in the wilds of the Ramtop Mountains. The Ramtops cluster around the Discworld's central spire, Cori Celesti, the home of the Gods. Close proximity to all that magic makes the Ramtops strange – strange even for a flat, disc-shaped world dragged through space on the back a giant turtle – and the area is famous for producing the Disc's best wizards and witches.

Esmeralda Weatherwax and her twin sister Lily were born into this heritage as part of a normal Lancre family – numerous siblings, cousins, aunts, great-aunts, goats, sheep and chickens included – but quickly discovered that they were meant for greater things. From an early age, the twins understood that they were destined for power, and to keep balance they were supposed to sit on opposite sides of the moral scale. While Esme was quickly recognized as a potential witch and taken into training, Lily discovered a calling to become a fairy godmother. Esme was supposed to be evil, and Lily to be good, they both knew it… but something went wrong. Convinced that she knew what people wanted – and that the greatest good was to give it to them, and make sure they enjoy it – Lily rapidly spiralled away from virtue and into cute, fluffy evil. Esmeralda, with her power as a witch already mounting, found herself duty-bound to put aside her instincts and inclinations, and take the opposite position: stern, menacing virtue, forcing people to take what they needed.

With her innate strength and laser-sharp powers of insight bolstered by her utter refusal to acknowledge rules or restrictions, Esmeralda Weatherwax quickly became the most respected and feared witch in the Ramtops and, by extension, the rest of the Disc. It is a position that she has held for years, and she seems unlikely to allow something as petty as age to loosen her grasp. Recently, she has taken a young witch called Agnes under her wing. Of all the other Lancre witches, Agnes is the first to show any signs of the iron-hard strength of character that really defines Granny's role.

Deep down, Granny Weatherwax knows that she was supposed to be the evil one, and that she has had to give up all the fun by moving into the place of virtue, and she's never been particularly happy about it. But she is absolutely determined and thoroughly pragmatic, and wastes no time in self-pity or bitterness. There's far too much to be done. Granny is a firm believer in rules and regulations, although it would never occur to her that they might apply to *her*. She's a witch, after all. She's there to do what's needed, not to fool around with what other people are told to do. As she herself says, "Being Good and Right doesn't make you Nice, and I ain't."

World

Saying that the Discworld is magical is a little like saying that the Atlantic Ocean is a touch damp this time of year. Every form of magic and supernatural creature has a home here, from werewolves and vampires right up to the most ancient, lurking evils. The night is full of things that go bump – and clank, and whoosh, and *aaaargh* too, for that matter. Granny Weatherwax's home kingdom of Lancre is a quiet, traditional, conservative land of farmers, craftsmen and magically powerful individuals.

Technology in Lancre means having wheels to put on the cart, or finding a way to sharpen your ploughshares. Granny and her coven fill a vital place in the tiny kingdom's social structure, regulating social behaviour on a level that the king and the miniscule army would never want or be able to do. The witches of Lancre make sure that the populace respect the social structure, treat each other decently, and look upon their elders with esteem. Without the witches, things would quickly fall apart. As such, they represent a force largely absent from modern society – one that we are starting to miss.

Magic

Granny Weatherwax is an immensely powerful witch. Her mastery of witchcraft is prodigious, and she knows spells, charms and remedies for just about any situation. She is assisted and frequently accompanied by her coven-mates, the drunken, lecherous matriarch Nanny Ogg, and kind, concerned Magrat Garlick, Queen of Lancre. Between them, the three very clearly embody the mythic triple goddess, with Magrat as the soppy, romantic maiden, Nanny as the eternal domineering mother, and Granny as the perfect embodiment of crone. Not that anyone would dare utter the Cr-word in front of her…

Despite her skill at transformations, curses, weather, healing and control, Granny's greatest

talent is in "headology", the art of achieving her ends by manipulating beliefs, expectations and symbolism. She is a lethal expert in analysing the underlying structure of a situation and turning it to her advantage. It's important to highlight the distinction between headology and psychology, between understanding minds and understanding people and stories. To quote Terry Pratchett, "It has been said that the difference between headology and psychology is that a psychologist will convince you that there are no monsters, whereas a headologist will hand you a bat, and a chair to stand on."

Granny Weatherwax is the very image of a stereotypical witch. She is never found without her clunky hobnailed boots, black cloak, tall pointed hat and terrifying stare. She has done things that could be considered evil, and done them without the slightest hesitation or regret. She meddles continually in everyone else's affairs, blithely telling others off for exactly the same act as she does so. Her nose is easily put out of joint, and she is quick to take offence at any slight or lack of the respect that her status demands. In fact, she is everything a wicked witch

should be – except that her sense of justice is as deep as the rocks of the mountains she lives in, and she keeps the little malice she possesses very firmly locked away.

◊ *At least Granny would have approved of these witches' hats.*

Name: Granny Weatherwax
Age: Old
Description: Underneath her black robes, tall black hat and huge, heavy boots, Granny Weatherwax is still a handsome elderly woman – not that she'd ever acknowledge the fact.
Dominant abilities: Magic, flying, headology
Traits: Iron will, strong sense of justice, supreme confidence, utter relentlessness
Nature: Virtuous
Power: Very strong
Type: Classic
Domain: Headology, spells
Goal: To make sure that the proper order of things is not disrupted
Key equipment: Her hat
Creator: Terry Pratchett

Hermione Granger

ᚾᛗᚠᚷᚱᛏᛂᚾᛗᛩᚾᚳᚻᚠᚱᛏᛂᚹᚱᚷᛪᛩᚾᛩᛗᚾᛒᚻᛖᚻᛗᚾᛩᚾᚹᚹᛗᛏᛂᛁᚳᛏᛗᛒᚠᛗᛗᛒᛂᛩᚹᛩᚾᛗᚠᚱᛏ

One of Harry Potter's best friends at Hogwarts School of Witchcraft and Wizardry, Hermione Granger is an intelligent, determined and courageous young woman. Created by record-breaking author J. K. Rowling, Hermione has matured over the course of the Harry Potter books, growing from an insecure, bossy child into a brilliant, empathic young woman. She is a gifted witch, frequently coming top of her school year in tests, and capable of mastering the most complicated spells. Whether she has the raw power to back up her technical genius has yet to be seen.

Biography

The only daughter of very non-magical parents, Hermione Jane Granger was very surprised to learn that she was a witch. Her parents, dentists in Oxfordshire, were equally taken aback. Being an intelligent, responsible girl with a studious nature, she threw herself into whole-heartedly learning everything she could about her new world. It was only when she first got on the train to Hogwarts School that she discovered she had already learnt far more than most of her fellow students, including the ones from magical families.

Hermione first hid her nervousness and shyness behind a bossy, imperious exterior. It did not make her popular, and neither did her habit of demonstrating her knowledge at every chance. Any time a teacher asked a question, you could be sure that Hermione's hand would fly up. She was very concerned with rules and not getting into trouble. In fact, in many students' eyes, she was a real teacher's pet. She became one of Harry Potter's friends when she, Harry and a friend of his called Ron Weasley fought and vanquished a dangerous mountain troll. The boys' casual attitude to rules has slowly rubbed off on her, and as the years have gone by, she has relaxed a little. She is still forceful and will always be top of her classes, but she is now much less bossy. She has also shown herself to be extremely empathic and understanding, with a very big heart. As well as assisting struggling students and helping her friends understand the feelings of the people around them, she is developing a strong sense of social justice. She is a keen believer in the rights of magical creatures, and has already campaigned on behalf of certain species.

Hermione has had an extremely adventurous time at Hogwarts School – to the point that it's a miracle that she's been able to learn as much as she has. After helping Harry to overcome a range of spells set by the school teachers in the first year, she was turned to stone by a basilisk in her second year and missed several weeks of class entirely. She made up the work anyway, and then in the third year obtained a special time-travelling device so that she could repeat some hours every day and take every lesson available. That was too much even for her, however, and she dropped enough subjects in the fourth year to make sure that her timetable was possible in reality. She started a fledgling romance that year with a student from a foreign school, but it looks as if her true affections will eventually bring her and her friend Ron together. No stranger to peril, she quite literally put her life on the line in her fifth year by helping Harry contend with a group containing many of the most evil adult witches and wizards that the magical world had known. There is no doubt that further mortal dangers await her.

World

What if vulgar magic were real? Undoubtedly, the government would know about it. There would be a special department set up to deal with it, and to minimize the contact between magical and non-magical people, so as to help prevent friction and further disasters like the witch trials. In the Harry Potter books, magic exists alongside boring everyday life, regulated and overseen by the Ministry of Magic. Wizards and witches are

forbidden to let normal people – "muggles" – see anything odd happen. Only the Prime Minister is let in on the secret.

Unsurprisingly, not all the magical folks are happy with the arrangement. Dark wizards and witches are a known part of magical society. They keep themselves hidden, but they believe that full-blood magical people should rule all of society, and that the muggles should be theirs to play with as they see fit. Their leader, Harry Potter's greatest enemy, is Lord Voldemort, a dark wizard whose power is equalled only by the headmaster of Hogwarts School, Albus Dumbledore.

◊ *Emma Watson plays Hermione Granger in the Harry Potter films.*

◊ *Left: The adventure begins as the train takes new pupils to Hogwarts.*

A flying Ford Anglia? Well, anything can happen in a world like this.

At the start of the books, Voldemort is barely more than a shade, having been blasted nearly to extinction at the height of his evil influence when a curse he aimed at Harry mysteriously rebounded. Harry is a critical part of Voldemort's plans to return first to full life and then to regain power, and the books chronicle the efforts of Harry, Hermione and Ron to thwart Voldemort's plots. Without Hermione's help, Harry would surely have been killed by now, and Voldemort's eventual victory would be almost certain.

Magic

As its full name suggests, Hogwarts School teaches a blend of witchcraft and wizardry to its students. Girls are called witches, and boys wizards, regardless of the various powers and abilities that they excel at. Hermione is very good at transformation, potions, herb-lore and at beating curses, but she is hopeless at riding a broomstick or making predictions. Her spellcraft, however, – a blend of witchcraft and wizardry – is excellent. Hermione has so far demonstrated prodigious levels of talent in almost all of her lessons, and has repeatedly been tipped as the foremost witch of her generation.

Name: Hermione Granger
Age: Teenage
Description: Bushy brown hair, prominent front teeth and a bossy manner hide the fact that Hermione is a very pretty girl when she can be bothered "with all that fuss".
Dominant abilities: Magic, intelligence
Traits: Highly skilled, brave, kind, understanding, hard-working and ambitious
Nature: Good
Power: Strong
Type: Classic/Wizard hybrid
Domain: Transformation
Goal: To help Harry Potter beat Voldemort
Key equipment: Wand, pet cat (Crookshanks)
Creator: J. K. Rowling

Samantha Stephens (Elizabeth Montgomery) enjoying a rare peaceful moment with her formidable mother, Endora.

Samantha Stephens

One of the best-loved sitcoms to come out of the 60s, *Bewitched* was the story of a pretty young witch determined to have a happy, normal life with her all-too-mortal husband. It ran to eight seasons, spanning the jump from black and white to colour, and has been on air continually ever since. Despite its cute and fluffy exterior, the show had surprising depths, backed up by a very strong ensemble cast centring on the show's star, Elizabeth Montgomery, who brought Samantha to life so enduringly.

Biography

Samantha's life before her marriage to Darrin (in the first episode) has always been something of a mystery. Although always happy to reminisce or to gossip about her huge witch family, she was no keener to go into details about her past than her conservative husband was to hear about it. The clues are there though, strewn through the series as a set of throw-away comments and memories.

Samantha isn't mortal – at least, not as we define it. In *Bewitched*, the witches do not age at anything like the same rate as the rest of us. All through the series, Samantha and her formidable mother, Endora, casually mention past events and people that they have known. The witches are able to travel in time, which muddies the water somewhat. Interestingly however, one of the show's unbreakable rules was that a witch would lose her powers if she travelled to a time before her own birth. Continuity lapses aside, episode no. 119 saw Samantha travel to Old Plymouth in 1620, and no. 229 had her in the court of King Henry VIII in 1570. She retained her powers in Plymouth, but not with King Henry, so she must have been born some time around the turn of the sixteenth century.

She grew up totally immersed in witch culture, with important figures in history and legend often popping around. She may have met Sir Walter Raleigh when her mother brought him home in 1600, but she was certainly in Salem during the witch trials of 1690. She describes herself as a child at the time, from which it can be assumed that as an immortal – or, at least, having a very long lifespan – it took her a century or more to become an adult.

A moment
of tension in the
Stephens household
as Samantha faces
down Darrin.

Samantha's lifespan is another mysterious question. Her mother, Endora, makes flippant references to having known Atilla the Hun, the emperors Claudius and Julius Caesar, Diogenes, and even Helen of Troy – which would put her birth before 1180 BC. She is said to admit only to being one thousand, but comments that she has changed her mind many times in three thousand years. On the other hand, Samantha's sweet but dotty aunt Clara was thought to be losing her powers because of her extended age, and there are hints that she is one thousand years old herself. Add in Endora's dubious claims of being a child bride when Samantha was born, and the matter becomes thoroughly confused.

What is certain is that despite being an extremely powerful witch, particularly in the realm of transformation, Samantha met Darrin, fell head over heels in love, and decided – to the horror of much of her family, especially her mother – to settle down as a home-maker and raise children in a happy, normal family environment. The show tells the story of Sam and Darrin's efforts to do just that, despite Endora's best efforts to wreck the marriage, and a constant stream of chaos courtesy of the rest of Samantha's eccentric family.

World

Bewitched was highly unusual at the time of its broadcast in that its central character was a very strong, determined, resolute woman who wouldn't brook any interference in her life. This was a long way from the usual television portrayal of submissive housewives at the time. However, in an interesting reversal of the women's liberation stereotype, Samantha chooses to make a life for herself as a mother and home-maker. She is prepared to battle the forces of hell itself, if necessary, for the right to do so. Her husband, Darrin, is typical small-town conservative, and just as fearless and resolute in defending the life that the pair of them have chosen. Sam, at least, is familiar with the creatures of the witch's world; Darrin frequently finds himself having to face down warlocks and monsters to try to retain a sense of normality in his life. Any chances of living a normal life are doomed from the start, of course. Even without Endora as the living embodiment of all bad-humoured mother-in-law jokes, the constant stream of other family members causes repeated chaos. When Samantha and Darrin's first child, Tabitha, is born, she immediately manifests powers of her own.

In many ways, Darrin's struggle to cling on to normality was a reflection of the way the ordered family world of the fifties was giving way to the psychedelia of the sixties and the uncertainty beyond. As in the Harry Potter books, the witches' world was kept totally separate from everyday normality. This gave the show perfect scope to highlight its dominant theme, the insanity of racism and bigotry against mixed marriages, while also leaving room to poke fun at consumerism, vanity, materialism and mass hysteria, amongst other social issues.

Magic

As befits the show's comedic theme, occult elements of the situation were downplayed in favour of character development and humour. Samantha's particular speciality was transformation – for instance, she was able to turn a derelict, cobweb-filled hut into a luxury cabin, complete with all the fixtures and fittings, literally with no more than a twitch of her nose. Other miraculous feats were accomplished with as much ease. On the occasions that she needed to use spells, they often sounded like childish nonsense, a careful ploy to help ensure that there was nothing sinister about her character.

In addition to transformations and summoning assorted individuals from across history, mythology and her family tree, Sam was also able to travel in time, fly on her broomstick, travel to different witchy dimensions, and create things out of thin air. The other adult witches had a similar range of powers – though Endora, who spent her entire time trying to make Darrin miserable and embarrassed, seems to have had no real power over luck or future events. By contrast, baby Tabitha was said to be at a stage where she was using "wishcraft" – if she wanted something, she created it or otherwise made it happen.

Name: Samantha Stephens

Age: 450, going on mature twenty-something

Description: A beautiful girl-next-door with tidy blonde hair, a sweet smile, respectable yet attractive clothing, an unfailingly pleasant demeanour and a cute twitchy nose – Sam was the perfect image of everything a young sixties wife was supposed to be.

Dominant abilities: Magic

Traits: Determined, loving home-maker and wife

Nature: Good

Power: Fairly strong

Type: Classic

Domain: Transformation

Goal: To enjoy married life and raise her children happily

Key equipment: None

Creators: Sol Saks and William Asher

Nancy Downs

ᚾᛗᚠᚷᛈᛏᛁᚾᛗᚩᚾᛈᛁᛈᛈᛏᛁᚠᚠᚷᚩᚾᚩᛗᚾᚷᛗᚠᚷᛗᚾᚩᚾᛈᛈᛈᛗᛏᛁᛁᛁᛗᚾᚷᛗᚾᚷᛁᛗᚠᚩᚾᛗᚠᚷᛏ

A hit movie about a group of outcast teenage witches, *The Craft* was released in 1996. Predictably, it drew all sorts of condemnation from Christian and Wiccan groups – the former because it portrayed witchcraft too accurately and sympathetically, the latter because it portrayed witchcraft too inaccurately and unsympathetically. The truth, of course, was that it was a great Hollywood romp, with all that that implies. The heroine of the film is a young "natural witch", Sarah, who moves to a new school and falls in with a group of fellow magically minded outcasts. It is the leader of the group though, troubled trailer-trash Nancy, who steals the show and makes the film such fun – played magnificently by Fairuza Balk.

Biography

Nancy Downs is a troubled teenager. She lives in a squalid, run-down trailer with her alcoholic mother and a physically abusive stepfather. She has a very bad reputation at the Catholic high school she attends, St Benedict's Academy in Los Angeles. Angry, self-loathing and reckless, Nancy's only companions are a bookish, badly scarred burns victim named Bonnie and a coloured girl called Rochelle, ostracized in the largely white, privileged atmosphere of the school. Determined to make the most of their outsider status, the three girls dabble in witchcraft, dress head to toe in black, and go overboard with heavy make-up, silver jewellery and petty crime. Nancy, with the least to lose, habitually pushes herself further towards the edge than her more timid friends. But without a fourth participant, their witchcraft goes nowhere.

When Sarah, still recovering from the death of her mother, is moved to the school, she too is quickly targeted as an outsider. Bonnie spots her levitating a pencil for fun in a boring French lesson, and the three decide to recruit her. On a trip to the local magic shop – a staple of the genre familiar to anyone who has watched Buffy – the girls are followed by a creepy, snake-wielding hobo. Just as they are starting to get scared, he is killed by an out-of-control car. All four admit that they were trying to get rid of him psychically. Linked by the bond of shared presumptive guilt, the girls start practising some proper magic.

After a few of their minor spells are successful, Nancy organises a ritual for the group which each can use to attain her heart's desire by calling on her personally favoured deity. The four meet on a beach at dawn and perform their ritual. Deformed Bonnie wants beauty; tormented Rochelle wants revenge on her main attacker; shy Sarah wants to toy with a cruel, handsome boy's affections. Nancy, however, is more ambitious, and demands that her deity fill her with all its powers – and make her rich into the bargain.

The spells work quickly. In Nancy's case, she is at home when her stepfather draws back his hand to strike her mother. She pulls a ferocious face at him and he drops down dead of a coronary; subsequently, an unexpected life insurance policy provides a six-figure lump sum for Nancy and her mother. Dizzy with success, Nancy discovers that she can use the power of her deity at will. The other girls are equally successful, with morally dubious results. By now, Nancy can walk on water and air, change her appearance, summon insects and snakes, and throw people around by telekinesis, but the power is driving her mad with megalomania. Meanwhile, Sarah's boy has become violently obsessed with her, and Sarah is getting cold feet about the whole thing. Nancy changes her appearance to Sarah's and seduces the boy, then throws him out of a window to his death when the real Sarah finds them.

Sarah flees, vowing to stop Nancy. Coming back to the side of "good", she receives help from the woman in the magic shop, but finds herself at home and isolated that night. Predictably, Nancy and the other two fly in to the attack, besieging Sarah with hideous illusions, telekinetic assaults, threats to murder her father, and all sorts of general inducements to try a successful repeat of a prior suicide attempt. At the last minute, Sarah assumes the same power than Nancy took for herself and turns it against the now-mad witch. Nancy's power is broken, Bonnie and Rochelle are driven away, and Sarah emerges healed, whole and bursting with power. The film ends with poor Nancy strapped down in an insane asylum, ranting from the depths of delusion.

◊ *Nancy Downs (Fairuza Balk) is a troubled modern witch with attitude.*

unfailingly punished — such wilful sin as Nancy indulges in is inevitably going to lead to disaster.

Magic

The producers of *The Craft* employed a long-standing Wiccan priestess as a consultant on the film, with the proviso that they were trying to make a film rather than a documentary. Her influence is largely responsible for the realistic feel of the rituals. The concept of the law of threefold return — that which you do to others bounces back to you three times over, so make sure it's nice — and the correspondence of the four girls to the four classical elements of Greek philosophy are touches which resonate strongly with modern pagans and Wiccans. However, the magic in the film is frequently spectacularly vulgar, and makes little use of spells, charms or even the evil eye. Nancy spends most of the time just drawing on the power of her chosen spirit — named, improbably enough, after the eponymous dead French girl from *Manon des Sources*.

⬥ *The four girls perform their ritual on the beach.*

World

The Craft is set firmly in the sort of high school that Hollywood teen-focused films are invariably set in. All the students are utterly loathsome without provocation, adults are ignorant and unavailable, and the teens are left to muddle through their own angst as best they can. The four witches are all stuck in the painful position of being outsiders, banding together for self-defence and survival against a hostile crowd. Witchcraft, in this situation, is mainly a tool and a metaphor for the fear that the majority feel towards outsiders — and a way of justifying that fear. The girls all act badly with their new-found power, and while only Nancy takes it to the darkest extremes of gleeful murder, none of them is innocent of wrongdoing. Even Bonnie, whose wish is understandably self-focused rather than malicious, uses her new-found beauty as a weapon against the world. In the moralistic world of Hollywood — where even minor sins such as disobedience, flaunting sexuality, independence and worldly indulgence are

Name: Nancy Downs
Age: 17
Description: Gorgeous-but-psycho goth-style girl hyped up on a 50/50 blend of Prozac and crack cocaine
Dominant abilities: Curses, flying, transformations
Traits: Megalomaniac, vindictive, low self-esteem
Nature: Bad
Power: Strong
Type: Classic/Wiccan fusion
Domain: Illusion
Goal: To get her own back
Key equipment: None
Creators: Peter Filardi and Andrew Fleming

Glinda the Good

ᚻᛗᚠᚷᚱᛏᛁᚾᛗᚻᚾᛏᛁᚠᛖᚱᛏᛁᚠᛈᚱᚷᚷᚾᚦᛗᚾᚻᚷᚠᚻᛗᚾᚻᚾᛈᚠᛈᛗᛏᛁᛖᛗᚻᚹᚠᛗᛗᚻᛁᛗᛈᚦᚾᛗᚠᚷᛈᛏ

When L. Frank Baum published *The Wonderful Wizard of Oz* in 1900, he had little idea of the monster he was creating. In the introduction to the second book, *The Marvellous Land of Oz*, he told readers that §he had written the book reluctantly, and only in response to receiving well over a thousand letters demanding a sequel. Echoing Sir Arthur Conan-Doyle's doomed attempt to kill off Sherlock Holmes, at the end of his fifth book, Baum tried to cut Oz off, making it inaccessible and thus unavailable for further stories. The outrage was so huge that he had to recant, and he ended up writing eight more books. The Oz books are overflowing with magic and mystery, but one of the most popular and enduring characters (after Dorothy herself) is Glinda, Good Witch of the South.

◊ *The Wicked Witch of the West is an intimidating character.*

Biography

The main bulk of the Land of Oz is divided into four quadrants, with a glittering Emerald City at its heart. The land to the south of the Emerald City is called the Quadling Country. In the very southernmost part of the Quadling Country, in a splendid palace, lives Glinda the Good, the Royal Witch and Sorceress of Oz.

Glinda is the guardian and protector of the land of Oz, and has a truly dazzling array of magic powers at her disposal which she uses exclusively for the benefit of the people of Oz. Everyone in the land loves and respects Glinda, from the lowliest creature up to Ozma herself, the dainty little queen. Even the famous Wizard respects her and pays tribute to her, because she was the one to teach him magic, and she is still the master of all sorts of spells. Glinda is famous for always being kind and helpful and willing to listen to everyone's troubles no matter how busy she might be.

All the inhabitants of Oz are immortal, but no one can even begin to guess Glinda's age. However, she is extremely beautiful, regal and dignified. Her hair is like red gold and is said to be softer than the finest silk; her eyes are the blue of summer skies, always smiling and open. She has peach-blush cheeks and a sweet rosebud mouth. She is tall and

elegant, wearing rich gowns that trail behind her, but she does not bother with jewellery – there is no stone that could compete with her flawless perfection

The most beautiful girls from all over Oz compete for the honour of being selected as one of Glinda's fifty attendants. She gathers them from all over the whole land of Oz, including the Quadlings, the Gillikins, the Munchkins, the Winkies and the inhabitants of Ozma's Emerald City. They help maintain Glinda's palace and all of the marvels inside it. The heart of Glinda's palace is her room of magic. This is the place where she stores all her magical potions and equipment, and it is a storehouse of wonder. For example, when she sends the Scarecrow off on a delicate mission, she gives him a magical rope. He has to cross a mountain range, but the rope is still able to help: when he takes it out of his pocket and throws it up into the air, it unwinds itself for hundreds upon hundreds of feet, eventually tying itself to a spar of rock at the very top of the mountain. Once it is fastened and the Scarecrow is gripping it tightly, it contracts again, raising him up to the top of the peak – and then lowers him down the other side smoothly, making the hazardous journey extremely easy.

However, by far the most powerful of all Glinda's magic objects is her Great Book of Records. This magical tome records all the events that have happened, all over the world, just as they occur. Glinda reads this book every day and in this way manages to keep abreast of everything that is happening, both in Oz and in the lands outside it. It also allows her to see when the people of Oz are in danger, so that she can help them. Her duties restrict her to helping the people of Oz, but she is always interested in the goings-on in the rest of the world.

When she travels, Glinda uses a floating bubble to transport her around Oz. It follows the brick roads where it can – it is the red brick road that leads to Quadling Country – and may draw some of its power from them. There have been some rumours that Glinda is a fairy, but it seems very unlikely. What is known for sure is that Glinda rescued the Quadlings from a wicked witch called Singra who established the land. Her protection of the land of Oz seems to have started then, spreading to the rest of it as the other wicked witches were destroyed.

Although the film differs in some respects, Glinda is helpful and constructive towards Dorothy from the first time they meet – at the end of *The Wonderful Wizard of Oz*. Glinda explains to Dorothy how to use the Silver Shoes to return home to Kansas in return for the Golden Cap. She then uses the cap to command the winged monkeys to take the Scarecrow to Emerald City, the Tin Man to Winkie Country and the Cowardly Lion to the Dark Forest, so that the three of them can take up their rightful positions as rulers of those places. Finally, she gives the cap to the King of the Monkeys, so that no one can ever enslave his people again. When Dorothy returns in later Oz books, she and Glinda are firm friends.

World

The land of Oz is a rich tapestry of magical and fantastical elements of all sorts. It is vivid, almost hallucinogenic in its intensity; consequently, it has frequently been seen as an allegorical representation of all sorts of things. The most common claim, always denied vigorously by Baum and his family, and now largely discredited, is that Oz is a metaphor for the populist rural American struggle to get the banking Gold Standard system replaced with a dual Gold/Silver standard – a move that would have been very beneficial for the impoverished farmers of the US heartland. A vivid and convincing case can be made for the parallels, of course; unfortunately, it just seems not to have been what Baum had in mind.

Other allegories are just as convincing. Some have argued that Baum, known to have been a member of the semi-occult organisation the Theosophical Society, painted Oz as a form of Theosophist utopia, representing a magical and mystical journey. According to this line of argument, Dorothy is the actual power – the Wizard – because she is the one who makes things happen. Another suggestion is that the real power is her dog Toto, as a metaphor for the jackal-headed Egyptian god, Anubis, because it's Toto's fault that Dorothy ends up in Oz in the first place. Oz has been seen as a pattern for psychological self-help, as a Jungian guide-map of archetypes, as a complicated Buddhist

Zen koan (teaching metaphor), as Freemasonic symbolism, and even as a variant of the Tree of Life of the Hebrew Kabbalah – partly because the Hebrew name for the Tree of Life is the Otz Chiim, and Otz can also be written as Oz.

When all is said and done, this diversity of interpretation really proves one thing – that Baum succeeded in creating a vivid, engaging and varied world with the power to capture the imagination and with the balanced completeness to be turned to fit just about any system you like. Oz is no more a Freemason's temple than it is a financial parable. It is a cunning and well-crafted literary construction, a thrilling canvas for the stories he told.

Magic

Glinda is a consummate magician. She knows a dazzling array of spells to help with all sorts of situations, but she also owns charms, magical items and other trinkets that can produce magical effects of all sorts. Her powers are immense, the greatest of anyone in Oz, but she has to restrict herself just to that country – and seemingly, before Dorothy's arrival from Kansas, just to the South. Surely, if she had been permitted to venture across Oz in defence of its people before Dorothy's arrival, she would have been able quickly and easily to free the land from the wicked witches of the East and West. She remains the archetypal figure of good authority in the Oz landscape – more queenly, somehow, than the young Queen Ozma herself.

Name: Glinda the Good
Age: Immortal
Description: Beautiful, elegant and timelessly regal
Dominant abilities: Magic
Traits: Kind, patient, loving, wise, well-informed
Nature: Good
Power: Very strong
Type: Classic/Wizard fusion
Domain: Spellcraft
Goal: To protect Oz
Key equipment: The Great Book of Records
Creator: L. Frank Baum

3
"Double, Double, Toil and Trouble"

"Double, Double, Toil and Trouble"
Witches in Legend and Myth

itches are a vital element in the landscape of part of our cultural heritage – the myths, legends and folk-tales that have come down to us through the generations. In the days before mass media, these stories were our guides and teachers, the salutary lessons that showed us which sorts of behaviour would bring success and which would bring disaster. The witches from many of these tales are examples that can teach us a lot, even today.

Baba Yaga

ᚾᛗᚠᚱᛏᛁᚾᛗᛞᚾᛁᛋᛖᛖᚱᛏᛁᛈᚠᚠᚷᛞᚾᛗᛗᛗᛂᛖᚱᛗᛞᚾᛖᚱᛖᛗᛏᛁᛏᛖᛗᚦᛖᛗᛂᛁᛖᛞᚾᛗᛖᚷᚱᛏ

Baba Yaga is one of the most ghoulishly imaginative witches envisioned anywhere. A prominent recurring feature of folk tales from Russia and the entire Slavic region, Baba Yaga is most certainly not good – she loves eating children, for example – but neither is she always entirely evil. There are many instances of her providing invaluable assistance to people who deserve it. Often described as *Kostyanaya Noga*, which means bony-legged, she is skeletally thin and perpetually hungry. Her hut, which may be a creature in its own right, is supported by scrawny chicken legs, and can walk around, complete with its fence of human bones. When Baba Yaga travels, she flies through the air hunched up in a large mortar (a stone spice-grinding bowl), using its pestle (the grinding stone) as an oar, and trailing her broom behind her to sweep away her wake.

Legend

Baba Yaga's name declares her identity as well as any of the legends which feature her. We often translate the Russian word *Baba* as an old woman, following on from the better-known term *Babushka*, which means "granny". However, the proper meaning of *Baba* is subtler. Any woman who had lost her virginity could be a *Baba*. The term is offensive and indicates a whining, scheming nag of a woman – the sort of person who would have been called a "fishwife" in medieval times, spiteful, jealous and restrictive. The word *Yaga* (or *Jaga* in some areas) is more versatile. It has meanings that range from the direct, such as "witch" or "evil woman", through to more esoteric associations, such as "a snake" or "a horror". Most interestingly, however, the term extends to the meaning "wrath". As a directed emotion rather than just a source of fear, wrath is the first hint that perhaps there is some purpose to Baba Yaga's existence.

In tales, Baba Yaga appears as a terrifying witch who lives in the heart of the deep forests. Her home is often difficult to find, unless some sort of magical fairy-tale item is used to show the way – a magic feather, for example – or unless the seeker has been

sent to the witch in order to come to harm. She lives in a tall, tottering wooden hut that stands on living chicken legs. The hut is always turned away from the traveller, showing him or her its back, and the intrepid visitor has to command it to turn around:

> *"Izboushka, Izboushka! Turn thy back to the forest and thy front to me!"*

The hut will then rise up slowly and painfully on its chicken legs and turn around with a continual chorus of painful screams, loud snaps and pops and other noises that reveal the hut's terrible old age and Baba Yaga's cruelty in allowing it to continue to suffer. It is interesting that there are frequent hints

◈ *Baba Yaga flying around in a tall, thin pestle as depicted by Ivan Bilibine.*

that the hut is an evil being in its own right. Its ability to move around on its legs notwithstanding, it clearly understands and responds to human language. It has the freedom to decide whether or not to let someone in, and how long to make them wait. Most important, though, in some tales its windows are described as eyes that it can see with, and its doorway is said to be a mouth – perhaps one that it can speak with?

The hut is surrounded by a rickety fence made of human bones. The bones are topped with human skulls, and their eyes glow in the dark, making the fence appear to be ringed with lights. The fence has a bone gate hung on human leg-bones instead of gateposts. Skeletal hands take the place of hinges, and feet are used to bolt the gate shut. Its keyhole is a mouth full of sharp teeth that can bite. Further protection is provided by a hungry dog and a cunning black cat, and a birch tree that can scratch out eyes. Three spectral pairs of strong, menacing hands, her "soul friends", help Baba Yaga around the hut. Other servants at Baba Yaga's disposal include three horsemen – one white, one red and one black – who represent (or perhaps even are) the dawn, the day and the dark of midnight.

Baba Yaga herself is usually described as an ugly, bony old hag with iron teeth and long, lank grey hair that's not been washed or cut for centuries. Her back is so bent and twisted with her great age that sometimes her head is almost brushing the floor. Her nose is very long, and equally bent. In some stories it reaches round to touch her pointy chin; in others, it is so long that it actually brushes the ceiling of her hut when she sleeps. It is studded with ugly, hairy warts, as the rest of her face is. She is as thin as a skin-wrapped skeleton, with sunken eyes that glitter with malice, and her reeking clothes are little more than ancient rags.

Often, the witch waits for victims to come to her, but sometimes she goes out hunting for fresh meat. Although she can order her house to walk to a new location on its chicken-legs, Baba Yaga prefers to hunt from the air. She flies around with her mortar and pestle, as mentioned before. A host of shrieking and wailing spirits accompany her on her flight. As she passes, wild, icy winds blow, and

the trees all around are blown about, creaking and groaning, leaves whipping around in the air. It means that her approach is easy to spot, but she travels so quickly that running away doesn't usually help. Victims she snatches are taken back to her clay oven for baking.

When visitors approach her hut, Baba Yaga usually relies on senses other than sight or hearing to detect the newcomer and tell something about them. A typical greeting might be something like:

> *"Ugh, ugh! Russian blood! Never met by me before, now I smell it at my door. Who comes here? Where from? Where to?"*

If she intends to feast on her visitor, Baba Yaga will invite the traveller in, give him or her a hot bath to clean themselves, and provide a hearty Russian meal. Only then will she reveal her intentions. Guests are offered a seat on a giant spatula than can be manoeuvred into Baba Yaga's big clay oven where she bakes all her victims. Even there, they have a chance to escape their destiny if they are wise; where they sit on the spatula determines whether they will fit into the oven or not.

More commonly, the visitor is given tasks to do – difficult, even seemingly impossible in some cases, but always within the ingenuity of the person if they stretch themselves and their resources, and behave properly. If the tasks are completed successfully, the witch will not eat the guest. There are other rules too, which the visitor is not told about, and breaking any of those will allow the witch to dine on her guest. Asking questions about things within the hut can be fatal, for example. In general, a wise, meek, hard-working and minimally prepared guest can find the way to survive and escape – rewarded for his or her work, even.

In some stories, Baba Yaga already knows about the trials that her visitor is undergoing, and is predisposed to help. In these cases, she can provide all sorts of magic tricks and items that the visitor will most certainly need during the quest, and she can also give good advice. She is most likely to behave like this if the person has been wronged, knows what has to be done to set things right and is

just passing by. Bravery, determination and righteousness, it seems, are ways to reach the witch's good side.

Interpretation

Baba Yaga is a complex figure, much more than just a stereotyped wicked witch. There are indications in several tales that even when she appears to be at her most evil, plotting to eat her victims, she is in fact administering a test of worthiness – or even just keeping up appearances so that she doesn't seem to be a push-over.

An example is the tale of Vasilisa the Beautiful, where the young heroine is ordered by her evil and jealous stepmother to visit Baba Yaga on a false errand. The stepmother blows out the candles one night and hides the matches. She then tells Vasilisa that she must get a light so that the house's candles can be relit, and only Baba Yaga can help. Really, everyone knows, Vasilisa is supposed to be eaten by the witch. She obeys, however, and goes to the witch's hut. Baba Yaga knows of the stepmother and puts Vasilisa to work on near-impossible chores. She also threatens to eat the girl at every possible turn. Vasilisa survives only because she is helped by a magic doll that her mother left to her. Eventually, Baba Yaga learns that Vasilisa is being helped by a blessing from her mother, and throws her out in disgust – *"You'd better be off then. I don't like people with blessings around here"* – but she also gives her one of the fence-skulls for the light she was sent for.

When Vasilisa returns home, she discovers that the errand her stepmother gave her has become genuine: ever since she has been away, no light will kindle in the house, and even burning spills, candles and lanterns brought into the house snuff out as

◊ *Edouard Zier again, with Baba Yaga riding in a Western-style pestle. Note that she seems to have left her broom behind on this occasion.*

soon as they are brought over the doorstep. The skull from the fence has burning eyes, and when Vasilisa goes home, the eyes are not extinguished; instead, they get brighter and brighter and burn the evil stepmother and her two equally evil daughters to ashes.

The implication, although it is never stated, is that Baba Yaga has taken a far more active and sympathetic role in the situation than it appears. The stepmother's house has been cursed into darkness from the moment Vasilisa is sent on her errand; Baba Yaga admits knowing the stepmother. The impossible chores are within the range of Vasilisa's magic doll; would Baba Yaga really have missed the presence of something so powerful when she can detect a Russian soul as a person comes near, or was she just ignoring it? Finally, at the start she only promises to give Vasilisa a light as asked, but instead she gives the girl the means of her liberation and salvation from her murderous in-laws.

Of course, in some myths Baba Yaga remains unequivocally menacing. In "The tale of the Two Orphans", a pair of children are sent to Baba Yaga to die by a similarly spiteful stepmother while their father is away. They stop off at their own grandmother's on the way, and are given biscuits, meat, a phial of oil, a ribbon and instructions to be kind and generous to all. Baba Yaga sets them impossible tasks and a warning of being eaten, and it is only by using their grandmother's supplies to win over all Baba Yaga's guardians – biscuits for the geese and the dog, meat for the black cat, oil for the bone gate's hinges and the ribbon to decorate the birch tree – that they are able to escape from the witch's house. It takes two more items, given to them by the black cat itself, to foil the witch's pursuit and get back to their home, where their father hears of his new wife's evil and throws her out.

Throughout the story, there is no suggestion that Baba Yaga wants anything other than baked child for dinner. This sort of tale is counterbalanced by stories where Baba Yaga features briefly, just to give help. In both "Fenist the Bright Falcon" and "Ivan and the Frog Princess", Baba Yaga appears and freely offers the seeker advice and even help in the form of enchanted objects.

Magic

Baba Yaga seems mostly to express her magical powers through objects. She has a little chant that she is said to recite when she is flying in her mortar, but that is mostly encouragement to the bowl. A lot of the time, her power seems to be innate, or to be a product of the things she keeps around her. She is sometimes said to be the guardian of the Waters of Life and Death. These miraculous liquids hold the key to resurrection. Sprinkle a corpse with the Water of Death and it will be healed of all wounds, repaired for its onward journey. If you then sprinkle it with the Water of Life, the person is revived and, being repaired, does not immediately die again.

Baba Yaga's oven is another symbol of rebirth, linking to the womb and to ideas of renewal and replenishment. The act of baking itself can be seen as symbolic of creating new life from old. This imagery is highlighted by Baba Yaga's habit of cleaning and feeding guests before eating them – it is clear that she is preparing them for their journey, either to death (if they sit wrongly on the spatula) or to renewal.

Rather than being a symbol of evil and death, perhaps Baba Yaga is more profitably seen as being akin to a force of nature – savage, untamed, voracious, but full of power and knowledge, occasionally helpful. Specifically, she is the wisdom of the harsh trial that brings about rebirth and renewed power; only the lazy, hopeless and foolish really need to fear being eaten.

Name: Baba Yaga
Age: Very old, possibly immortal
Description: Ugly, hunch-backed, warty hag with iron teeth and filthy grey hair
Dominant abilities: Magic, flying, wisdom
Traits: Cruel, impatient, hungry, follows rules
Nature: Neutral tending to evil
Power: Strong
Type: Classic
Domain: Charms and other magical objects
Goal: To feed on humans
Key equipment: Hut, pestle and mortar
Culture: Slavic/Russian

Caridwen

ᚾᛖᛘᚠᚱᛏᛁᚾᛗᛟᚾᚲᛁᛖᛖᛏᛁᚠᚠᚷᛟᚾᛟᛗᚾᚺᛗᚠᚺᛗᚾᛟᚾᛖᚠᛖᛗᛋᛁᚲᛁᛗᚺᛖᛗᛗᚺᛁᛗᛖᛟᚾᛗᚠᚱᛏ

The most famous of all the Welsh witches, and
sometimes linked to the Irish goddess Brighid,
Caridwen is best remembered for her children –
including the greatest bard ever to walk the Earth,
Taliesin. Cerridwen and Keridwen are alternative
ways of spelling her name. Her story is told in the
Mabinogion.

Legend

According to the legends, Caridwen lived in the
middle of Lake Tegid in Penllyn, in Wales, at the
time of King Arthur and the Knights of the Round
Table. Her home was a lovely mansion of stone
and marble, and it sat upon a rocky outcrop at the
centre of the lake. Her husband, Tegid Voel, was of
noble descent, and may even have been part giant.
Together, Caridwen and Tegid Voel had three
children, Morvran, Creirwy and Avagddu.

Morvran, the eldest, was a healthy son, and
although he passes largely out of legend, he does
crop up in accounts of Arthur's court, offering
advice on a way to make life more pleasant for the
people of the realm. The next child, Creirwy, was
a girl – the most beautiful maiden in all the world.
Such beauty carries its own adventures with it, but
Caridwen was not worried for the girl, knowing
that her loveliness would win her acceptance and
champions aplenty. It was the last child who worried
Caridwen. Avagddu was the complete opposite of
his sister, dark where she was fair, moody where
she was happy, and ugly where she was lovely – the
ugliest man in all the world, in fact.

Caridwen was very aware of how important it
is to be good-looking in order to be successful, and
feared that despite Avagddu's learning and decency,
he would be cast out of the courts for being so
plain. The only answer was to make sure that his
merits were so loftily impressive that none would
ever be able to deny him his importance. She spent
long years researching in her magic tomes, the
books of the arts of the Fferyllt, evaluating options.
Eventually, she decided to brew a potion called
Greal, that gave Inspiration and Knowledge, in her

cauldron. In that way, even in the highest courts,
Avagddu's knowledge of the mysteries of the world
and the future would win him respect and honour.

Once her preparations were complete, she knew
that she would have to keep her cauldron boiling
for exactly a year and a day without pause. She got
a blind man, called Morda, to keep the fire burning
fiercely, and she stole a child named Gwion Bach,
the son of Gwreang of Llanfair in Caerinion, to
keep stirring the cauldron so that the potion would
not burn. She herself had the task of gathering
each charm-bearing herb and ingredient that she
would need every day. Each item had to be collected
at precisely the right moment, when the correct
astrological forces were in operation, so it was full-
time work ascertaining what she could gather at

◈ *Caridwen
had the power to
change herself into
any living shape,
including that of a
hawk.*

which moment, locating it, and then collecting it when the stars were right.

One day, very near the end of the year, Caridwen was out gathering plants and reciting incantations. As Gwion was stirring the potion, it just so chanced that three drops of the Greal brew spat out of the cauldron and caught him on the finger. Having been boiled for so long, the liquid was incredibly hot and Gwion instinctively sucked his burned finger to cool it down. Unfortunately, those three drops were the very ones that bore the charm of Inspiration and Knowledge. In the instant that Gwion placed them into his mouth, he became enlightened and saw everything that was to come. The cauldron split in two, because all of the liquid within it was poisonous save for the three drops, and the now-useless potion drained away into the river nearby, where it went on to poison all the horses of King Gwyddno Garanhir of the Lost Land.

Gwion, meanwhile, was seized with terrible fear, because he knew how great Caridwen's powers were, and he could see that her fury would be without measure. He burst his chains with a thought and immediately ran away, heading for his own home.

When Caridwen returned, she saw that all her work for the whole year had been wasted, and flew into a mighty rage. She grabbed a nearby chunk of wood, and smashed poor, blind Morda round the head with it so hard that one of his useless eyes popped out onto his cheek. He protested, as best he was able, that he was innocent of any wrongdoing. Caridwen was calmed enough to realize what must have happened, and accepted his word, but she set out to chase Gwion.

Caridwen followed Gwion's trail at a terrible speed, so that in a short time he saw her coming after him. Using his new powers, he changed himself into the shape of a hare and fled away at top speed. Caridwen saw the change, however, and transformed herself into a greyhound to follow. Soon she was catching up again, and as he approached a deep river, Gwion switched into the form of a sleek trout, and sped off underwater. Caridwen saw the change again, and dived in after him, transforming herself into an otter to continue the chase. They darted down the river, through weed and round

rock, and still Caridwen gained. As she got close, Gwion desperately flicked himself up into a leap and, as he burst the water, turned himself into a bird and flapped off. As soon as she saw what he had done, she too broke the water, and transformed into a hawk. Her keen eyes quickly spotted him, and she powered towards him. Twist and turn as he might, Gwion could not shake her. Deep in mortal fear, as she was about to dive and rend him, he spotted a big pile of wheat grains winnowed out on the floor of a barn. He darted into the pile and transformed himself into a grain of wheat. Caridwen, undaunted, changed herself into a tall-crested black hen, and scratched her way through the wheat, looking for him. Eventually she spotted the grain that was Gwion, and gobbled him up.

But that was not the end of it. She found that she had become pregnant, and nine months later she gave birth to a beautiful golden-haired boy. Her intention had been to kill the child and reclaim the potion, but when she saw him, she was unable to do the act because of his beauty. Instead, she wrapped him in a bag of leather and, on April 29th, she cast him into the sea and God's mercy. He was eventually found, and named Taliesin, which means "golden brow", and became the first and greatest of bards with his gift of Inspiration and Knowledge, but that is another story.

Interpretation

Caridwen is widely acknowledged as the first of the great Welsh witches, the spiritual mother of witchcraft and also of the Bardic tradition. Some traditions identify her with the Irish goddess Brighid, the patron of learning, poetry and healing – Christianized as St Brigit. In the original legends, however, Caridwen is no more than a mortal witch, albeit a very skilled and powerful one. Although her intentions are driven by maternal concern, her methods are clearly somewhat unpleasant, and her temper tantrum shows the violence inherent in her nature. Like Baba Yaga, though, in the end her story is about transformation. Gwion is killed, but the seed of his potential is reborn in the golden child Taliesin. Gwion can be seen as partly being Taliesin's father, and as partly becoming Taliesin himself.

Magic

Clearly, Caridwen's powers of transformation are without equal. She could assume any shape she wanted with no more than a flicker of thought. Her knowledge of herb lore, astrology, spellcraft and general wisdom gives her the power to prepare and brew the potion Greal. She is sometimes thought to fly on the back of a huge crow when she travels – it may have been the method she used when she snatched Gwion. Her sight is long enough that she can see the ruined potion from where she is gathering herbs at the North Pole itself, so she must have had a strong clairvoyant streak too. Some commentators have claimed that Caridwen is actually a corn goddess, on the strength of Gwion's final transformation and one possible interpretation of her name to mean "White Grain", but the name could also simply mean "White One", and other commentators have claimed her as a representation of the moon goddess. Either may be a bit farfetched, in honesty: sometimes, being a witch and the mother of the greatest of bards is enough.

Name: Caridwen
Age: Middle-aged
Description: Dark-haired, stocky woman with very white skin, red cheeks and black eyes
Dominant abilities: Spells, potions, herbology
Traits: Violent, demanding, hard-working, maternal
Nature: Neutral
Power: Very strong
Type: Classic
Domain: Transformation
Goal: To gift her ugly son with wisdom
Key equipment: Cauldron
Culture: Celtic/Welsh

The Gingerbread Witch

ᚾᛗᚠᚼᚱᛁᚾᛗᛰᚾᛁᛚᚠᚱᛁᛇᚠᚱᚷᛰᚾᛰᛗᚾᚼᛗᚠᚼᛗᚾᛰᚾᚠᚠᛗᛏᛁᛁᚱᛗᚼᚠᛗᛗᚼᛰᛁᛗᚠᚾᛗᚠᚼᚱᛁ

The story of Hansel and Gretel is familiar to most of us in the Western world. The striking imagery of the gingerbread house and the evil witch inside using it to lure hungry children to their doom has proved a powerful attraction for tellers of cautionary tales or years. It is one of the best-known of all the Brothers Grimm's collected German folk tales and, interestingly, probably the one that gets toned down the most. Unlike some of the legends we've looked at here, the anonymous witch of the story is an archetypical evil crone, horrible just for its own sake – which perhaps is part of the story's enduring power.

Legend

The gingerbread witch finds Hansel and Gretel eating her house.

A poor woodcutter and his family lived on the edge of a dark forest. The times were very hard, and the family never had enough to eat. The woodcutter's wife scolded and scolded, but there was nothing he could do. One year the winter was warm and there wasn't as much demand for wood as usual, and the family's plight became even more desperate.

One night, the woodcutter's daughter, Gretel, overheard her parents talking. "We must get rid of the children, so that we have enough food for ourselves," her mother said. The woodcutter protested strongly, but his wife was determined. "If we do not, we will die, and then the children will die anyway." Eventually, she persuaded him to leave the children in the woods.

Terrified, Gretel ran to her brother, Hansel, and told him what their mother was planning. Hansel though for a minute, then ran out into the garden and collected two large pocketfuls of white stones. The next morning, the woodcutter called the children to accompany him while he worked in the forest. They went along with him nervously, carrying some bread for lunch, and every so often, Hansel dropped a stone out of his pocket to mark the way. After some time, they came to a clearing.

The woodcutter told his children to wait there while he went to cut wood, saying sadly that he would be back soon. The children waited and waited, but as they had feared, he did not come back. When it started getting dark, the children knew they had been abandoned.

They spent the night out in the forest, alone and scared, but they survived unharmed. The next morning, Hansel found the first of the stones he had dropped, and the children followed the trail. Eventually, after some hours, they came back to the house. Their father was overjoyed to see them, but their mother could not hide her anger. She told them off for wandering away from where they had been left, and told them how scared both parents had been, so that Hansel and Gretel were uncertain. However, fearing that they might be taken away again, Hansel went to get more stones from the garden that night. To his surprise, he discovered that he and Gretel had been locked in.

The next morning, as he had feared, they were sent with their father again. This time, without any stones to mark the trail, Hansel dropped crumbs of his bread and, when it ran out, crumbs of Gretel's bread too. In that way, he managed to keep the trail marked. When their father left, even sadder than the time before, Hansel wasted no time starting on the trail back. But he had found no more than the first crumb when he saw the birds and squirrels running off left and right with his bread. The trail was gone.

Hansel and Gretel started walking anyway, trying to guess the way back, but it was not long before they were hopelessly lost. Just as darkness fell, they spotted a light through the forest. They ran towards it, and came into a clearing where they discovered the most amazing house. It looked strange and colourful, and smelled sweet and tasty. They went close, and discovered that the whole house was made up of gingerbread and cakes and sweets of all sorts. Starving after a day of no food, they began to nibble on the walls. Hansel took a big piece of gingerbread off one corner of the house, and Gretel had a big piece from a window, which proved to be a sheet of spun sugar, as clear as glass. They were just filling their mouths and bellies when the front door opened, and an ugly old

woman came out, calling out to know who was there eating her home.

The children were scared, but the old woman soothed them and told them kindly to come inside. Then she gave them both a big meal of all sorts of cakes and pastries and delicious foods, and put them to bed in big comfortable beds with marshmallow pillows and candyfloss blankets, and they went to sleep feeling better than they had done for many days.

When they woke up, however, they quickly discovered that things were very wrong. While they had slept, the witch – for so she was – had locked Hansel in a thick iron cage, and had put a tight iron band around Gretel's leg, chaining her to a stake in the middle of the hut. When the witch saw that the children were awake, she wasted no time in telling them what was in store. Gretel would do all the work, cleaning the house and cooking the meals and darning the witch's socks, while Hansel would stay

in the cage and eat lots of food until he was nice and fat. Then, the witch would roast him and eat him, and Gretel would take his place in the cage.

And so it happened. Every day, Gretel slaved for the witch, cooking and cleaning and feeding Hansel. Every evening, the witch would make Hansel stick a finger out and pinch it, to see if he was fat enough to eat yet. On the third night, though, Gretel passed a small chicken bone to Hansel, so that he could stick that out of the cage and the witch, who could not see very well, would think that he was still skinny.

In this way, the children passed several weeks, with Hansel getting fatter and fatter, but hiding the fact from the witch. They could not find a way to escape, though. If Gretel moved at night, the noise of her chains woke the witch, who would beat her savagely. Meanwhile, the cage was far too cleverly made and thick for a little boy like Hansel to escape from it.

Eventually, the witch got so hungry that she

decided it was time to eat Hansel, no matter how thin his finger was. She forced Gretel to stoke the oven up high, and then told her to check the temperature, to see if it was ready to cook a little boy. Gretel, thinking fast, told the witch that she didn't know how to test the temperature. The witch beat her, and then, complaining all the time, opened the oven door to see for herself. As soon as she did, Gretel got behind her and pushed her in, and then locked the door. The witch screamed and screamed, but in a matter of moments, she burned to ashes. When the oven cooled, Gretel got the witch's keys out, and released herself and Hansel. They searched the house for food to take, and made a big pile, but in a locked room they found a chest, and in the chest, they found the witch's jewels. They gathered them up, and put them with the food, and left the evil house.

They were very deep in the forest, so it took them several days to find their way, but they had plenty of food, and the creatures of the forest stayed away from them. Eventually they happened upon a trail and followed it back to the edge of the forest. There, in a clearing, they found their father, who wept for joy to see them, and apologized to them again and again. Then he told them that he had felt so guilty at what he had done, that he had banished their cruel, selfish mother forever, and spent weeks searching for them. They showed him the witch's jewels, and then the three of them went home together and lived long and happy lives, and were never hungry again.

Interpretation

In the legend, the gingerbread witch is a figure of malicious hunger. The house is undoubtedly a magical construction, and presumably protected by spells that stop the forest creatures eating it away overnight. Other spells may serve to bring lost children to it; Hansel and Gretel are far from the first children that the witch has captured. She catches them easily because their hunger and sadness make them vulnerable; the lesson perhaps is that no matter how bad things are, if something seems too good to be true it probably is. The children's will to survive keeps them alive once the witch has caught

them – patience, virtue and determination being the cardinal values. The children's mother is almost as heartless as the witch, so it is fitting that she too should get her come-uppance. In some versions of the legend it is said explicitly that she has died since forcing her husband to abandon the children. Throughout, the witch serves almost exclusively as a source of menace and evil – her main qualification for witchdom seemingly being that she eats children.

Magic

The witch is a sadistic taskmaster, but the magic that she demonstrates is mostly implicit in her house and its sweet furnishings. If it wasn't for the fact that we are told repeatedly she's a witch – and the impossibility of the house – then she could almost be a psychotic pastry chef.

Name: Unknown; sometimes humorously nicknamed "Ginger"
Age: Very old
Description: Ancient, nearly blind crone with usual complement of warts, humps and stringy grey hair
Dominant abilities: Baking
Traits: Malicious, cannibalistic, sadistic
Nature: Evil
Power: Fairly weak
Type: Classic
Domain: Sweets and pastries
Goal: Eating children
Key equipment: Gingerbread house
Culture: Germanic

The Stygian Witches

ᚾᛗᚠᚷᛒᛏᛂᚾᛗᚢᚾᛏᛚᛒᛒᛏᛂᛒᛒᚷᚦᚾᚦᛗᚾᚻᛗᚠᚻᛗᚾᚦᚾᛒᛒᛗᛏᛂᛚᚠᛗᛗᚻᛂᛗᚠᚾᚾᛗᚠᚷᛏ

The Stygian Witches were a peculiar group of three Greek crone-sisters, the Graeae, who shared between them just one eye and one tooth. They were brought back to prominence in our culture by their portrayal in the classic 1981 epic Greek fantasy film, *Clash of the Titans*. In this famous Ray Harryhausen movie, they were played by three veteran British actresses, Flora Robson, Anna Manaham and Freda Jackson.

Legend

As is so often the case in Greek mythology, there are a number of different and contrary accounts of the Stygian witches. Some things are certain, though. They were the daughters of Phorcus and Ceta, and may have been born as triplets. They were the sisters of the Gorgons (the famous Medusa and her two obscure sisters, Euryale and Sthenno), and also their assigned guardians. They were grey-haired from the moment of birth – Graeae means "Grey Woman" – and shared between them just a single eye and a single tooth. They were able to pass these body parts around between them, so that each could take her turn seeing and eating. However unlikely it may sound, the Graeae are described as originally being beautiful – "fair-faced and swan-like" – although by the time they feature in any legends, they have become old and hideous.

The witches were named Deino, Pemphredo and Enyo. Their names give some indication of their perceived nature – respectively, they mean Dread, Alarm and Horror. They lived in a dark cavern near the entrance to Tartarus, close to the island where the Gorgons were banished. Enyo, in particular, lived up to her name; she often appears drenched in blood, and was said to lay waste to entire cities. There are also suggestions that she may have been related to Ares, god of war, either as his mother, sister or daughter, although that is more of a comment on her nature than her genealogy. All three were said to be extremely wise in knowledge, monster-lore and witchcraft.

In the best-known myth about the Stygian Witches, King Polydectes sent the hero Perseus on a mission to obtain Medusa's head – even in death, the gorgon would still have the power to turn people who saw her to stone. Perseus was aware that he would be aided in his task by a group of nymphs, but didn't know where to find them, or where to look for Medusa. He did know how to find the Graeae, however, so he went to visit them, and as they were passing their eye between them, he snatched it from them and demanded that they tell him everything he needed to know, or he wouldn't give it back. The desperate Graeae obeyed and answered all his questions. Despite their assistance, Perseus broke his promise to return the eye, and later threw it into Lake Triton.

Interpretation

The Graeae are thought to have been the focus of a group of swan cults across ancient Greece. Strange as it may sound to us now, swans are not just symbolic of beauty, but they were also thought to represent cunning, prophecies (particularly of death), access to other realms, and a range of other, darker things. The Stygian Witches were probably worshipped as the avatars of that set of symbolism – particularly being born grey-haired and with just one eye, and yet also described as swan-like beauties. The missing eyes would have implied sight into other realms, and the grey hair was a symbol of their wisdom and magic power. Peculiar modern suggestions that the Stygian Witches actually represented nothing more

◊ *The Stygian Witches were the focus of a mysterious swan-cult in ancient Greece.*

than the white froth on top of waves seem to be based on linguistic similarities between their name and the colour grey.

Magic

Although the Stygian Witches don't get much of a chance to showcase their abilities in the main body of Greek myth, they were known to be learned and powerful witches with all sorts of abilities at their disposal. They had powers of clairvoyance and prophecy, were wise on many subjects, and possessed enough magic power to be able to destroy cities if they so chose. Later stories imply that the witches managed to regain their eye somehow, for they were not left permanently crippled by Perseus's meanness.

Name: The Graeae: Deino, Pemphredo and Enyo
Age: Ancient
Description: Three ugly, cannibalistic old crone sisters squabbling over the use of their single eye and single tooth
Dominant abilities: Magic, wisdom, clairvoyance, prophecy
Traits: Petty, argumentative
Nature: Neutral
Power: Very strong
Type: Classic
Domain: Wisdom
Goal: To guard the Gorgons
Key equipment: Eye, tooth
Culture: Greek

The Witch of Endor

ᚾᛗᚠᚷᛏᛃᚾᛗᚢᚾᛏᚠᚱᛏᛃᚠᚠᚷᚢᚾᚮᛗᚾᚼᛗᚠᚼᚾᚮᚾᚠᚠᛗᛏᛃᛃᚠᛗᚼᛗᚼᛃᛗᚮᚾᛗᚠᚷᚢᛏ

In one of the strangest episodes recorded in the Bible, King Saul of Israel goes against the word of God, the laws of the land and even his own witch-hunting history to visit the Witch of Endor. At his request, she summons up the ghost of the prophet Samuel, so that Saul can interrogate him about the battles that are due to be fought the next day. It is seen as particularly strange for two core reasons. First, Saul himself had personally been responsible for launching an inquisition-style hunt that scourged all the witches and occult practitioners from the land. It is peculiar to think that such hatred and zeal might spontaneously reverse itself. Secondly, the Bible plainly states that the witch calls up Samuel himself, which ought to be impossible if the prophet is safely in heaven. Originally written around 1000 BC, the tale – found in I Samuel 28 – has caused problems ever since.

Legend

Israel was under the imminent threat of a Philistine invasion. King Saul sought advice from God through many different channels – dreams, visions, prayers and even prophets – but God did not answer. Becoming fearful, Saul called together his servants and asked them to find him a woman with a divining spirit who had survived his earlier purges. The servants revealed that there was a woman who had escaped the purges – the Witch of Endor.

Fearing punishment from his own laws, Saul then took off his clothes and put on a disguise and, taking two men with him, he went to visit the witch in Endor, between Mount Tabor and the Hill of Moreh. When they arrived, Saul asked her to use her familiar spirit to call up a ghost he could question. The witch was reluctant, pointing out that Saul had made such actions punishable by death. Still in disguise, Saul swore that no harm would come to her, and she hesistantly agreed. Saul then told her to raise the prophet Samuel.

Conjured up by the Witch of Endor, Samuel predicts Saul's death.

As soon as Samuel appeared – to the witch's apparent surprise – she recognized Saul for who he was, and challenged him for lying to her. Saul again reassured her that he would not take action against her. Then he made his case to Samuel, explaining that God would not answer, and begging for advice. Samuel reacted furiously, demanding to know how Saul had the temerity to question him when God himself had turned away from the king. Samuel then went on to explain that God had become Saul's enemy because of Saul's failure to act with sufficient wrath at the battle of Amalek. Israel was to be given to David for Saul's transgression, and the king and his children, along with much of the army, would join Samuel in death before the next day was over.

Samuel then vanished and Saul collapsed, horrified. The witch then reminded him that she had only done as he had ordered, and forced him to have something to eat, to regain some strength. The next day, despite Saul's best efforts, Samuel's prediction came true, and Saul and his sons were killed.

Interpretation

Obviously, the most problematic element of the story for Christians and Jews is that the witch is able to conjure up the ghost of one of God's prophets, who should be in heaven beyond the reach of her powers. The standard reaction to the tale is to discount the word of the Bible as inaccurate for once and to say that the witch was only conjuring up her own familiar spirit, which by default had to be one of Satan's demons, and which then pretended to be Samuel. But not only does that leave the problem that the word of the Bible appears to be untrue, there is also the issue of the witch being shocked to see Samuel. It seems more elegant to suggest that rather than allow the witch to summon her familiar, God himself sent Samuel's spirit to her to let Saul know what he had done and how he was to be punished for it. That also leaves the witch in the slightly better position of not having broken Saul's edict.

Magic

The standard dogma is that the witch – like all witches in Christian legend – is a satanic dupe, and any powers she possesses are given to her by Satan

via her familiar spirit. Obviously she was known for being able to talk to the dead and other spirits, but we don't know much about any other powers she may or may not have had.

Another depiction of the fateful moment when Saul learns of his impending doom.

Name: The Witch of Endor
Age: Middle-aged
Description: Simply "a woman"
Dominant abilities: Talking to spirits
Traits: Careful, helpful, concerned
Nature: Neutral
Power: Unknown
Type: Satanic dupe
Domain: Communing with spirits
Goal: To live in peace, presumably
Key equipment: Familiar
Culture: Middle-Eastern

4
"Posters of the Sea and Land"

"Posters of the Sea and Land"
Real-life Witches

History is rich in tales of witchcraft. Whether you believe in magic or not, there's no doubt that a lot of people have done so, all through the ages. While the powers associated with real witches are a lot less flamboyant than the fictional equivalents, they have the potential to be every bit as devastating. Witches today, of course, would never misuse their powers for evil – well, not the ones who openly admit their powers, anyway.

Old Mother Shipton

ᚾᛗᚠᚪᛏᛁᚾᛗᚩᚾᛁᛚᛈᛈᛏᛁᛇᚱᚪᚷᚾᚷᛗᚾᚼᛗᚷᛗᚾᚩᚾᛖᛈᛗᛏᛁᛚᛖᚼᛗᚾᚼᛁᛗᛖᚩᚾᛗᚹᚪᛏᛁ

Mother Shipton is England's most famous prophetess. She lived more than five hundred years ago in the town of Knaresborough, North Yorkshire. As she grew older, her prophetic visions and other powers became known and feared throughout England – so much so that she was even visited by representatives of some of the most powerful people of the time.

Biography

England was on the brink of a period of great change in the summer of 1488 when a fifteen-year-old orphan named Agatha Sontheil gave birth to an illegitimate daughter. Agatha was thought locally – with a certain lack of charity – to be a prostitute. Local rumour had it that she had been seduced by a charming stranger who had found her daydreaming on a sunny riverbank, and who then kept her in relative financial comfort, continuing his visits regularly. Agatha became pregnant, and was hauled up in front of the local magistrate for prostitution. She faced her pious accuser down, pointing out that the Justice couldn't say she was doing wrong when two of his own serving girls were pregnant with his children. Her case was dismissed in uproar.

Agatha went into labour in a dank cave on the banks of the River Nidd at Knaresborough. Close to the cave was a magic well that was known to turn objects left in it to stone within just a few weeks or months. It was an oppressively hot July night, and the women of the town knew that Agatha's secret lover was said to be strangely pale, white even, and cold to the touch – the girl herself admitted as much. Still, one of the women did come out to help her give birth. She would later tell the town gossips that there was a great stench of sulphur and a huge peal of thunder as the child was born – a strangely large and oddly shaped thing. As it came into the world, it jeered and laughed at the storm, and the thunder ceased.

Despite persistent local antagonism, Agatha continued to be financially supported by her unknown lover, and even managed to get the Abbot of Beverley Monastery to baptize her daughter,

Ursula. Knaresborough folk muttered that the baby was the daughter of the devil, but the baptism went ahead anyway. A couple of years later, Ursula was left in the care of a foster mother and Agatha went to Nottingham, where she took holy orders, to spend the rest of her life as a nun.

Right from the start, rumours surrounded Ursula. Certainly ill-favoured, and quite probably physically deformed in some way, it was said she had the power to avenge cruel remarks and taunts. The word "witch" was frequently aimed at her, even as a child – probably aggravated by the fact that she was clearly intelligent and mischievous. One of the earliest tales about her recounts how her foster mother came home from an errand to find her front door open. Fearing thieves, she called her neighbour to help her. The women went into the house, but heard a terrible shrieking and wailing, and said that an invisible force barred the kitchen completely.

They fled the house in terror and a passing priest calmed the women, then led the way back in to investigate. When they got to the kitchen, they found Ursula's cradle empty and the toddler sitting naked on an iron bar in the chimney, which was normally used to hold pots. The girl smiled happily at the group, obviously enjoying herself immensely.

Through her childhood years, rumours continued, fuelled perhaps by curiosity regarding the source of Ursula's continued financial health – nothing spectacular, but enough to keep her comfortable. When she was a young woman, cruel whispers started up again when a carpenter called Toby Shipton started to pay court to Ursula. Women muttered jealously that she must have used a love potion, but Ursula Sontheil and Toby Shipton were married in 1512. Ursula was 24. The marriage would not produce any children, but the couple were said to be "very comfortable".

Less than a month later, one of Mother Shipton's neighbours came to her asking for help in finding a set of stolen new clothes – an expensive loss. Ursula told her neighbour not to worry, and that she would make sure the clothes were returned the following market day. All the woman had to do was wait by Knaresborough Cross at midday. A few days later the market came around, and the neighbour did as directed. Within moments, a woman came through the crowd towards her, dancing and singing loudly, *"I stole my neighbour's smock and petticoat, I'm a thief and here I show it."* The woman handed over the clothes, and ran off, humiliated and terrified.

Not long after, a young local nobleman came to ask Mother Shipton how long he had to wait for his father to die. The young man needed money to pay debts, and hoped to inherit his father's wealth soon to escape trouble. Ursula sent him away without comment. Shortly after, he fell ill; then his father came to Mother Shipton to ask if she could help the son. She replied shortly:

> *"Those who gape out for others' death,*
> *Their own, unlooked for,*
> *steals their breath.*
> *Earth he did seek; ere long, he shall have*
> *Of earth his fill — within his grave."*

The father left, sad and confused. The son soon died, and one of his servants told the father of the son's visit to Mother Shipton. The story spread quickly, confirming her powers as a prophetess — and perhaps as an instrument of hard justice, too.

Mother Shipton's status as a seer was cemented by the prophecies she made that seemingly came true shortly afterwards. One prophecy said that water would flow over the Ouse river, and that there would be a windmill on a tower, and an elm tree by every door. Shortly afterwards, York was given a revolutionary system of piping. Water was drawn out of the River Ouse and across the bridge in pipes, pumped by a new windmill on a tower, and carried to many doorsteps. The pipes themselves were made of hollowed saplings and the tree used was elm, the only wood that doesn't rot in water.

She foretold a series of local events, including the collapse of York's Trinity Church tower, the murder of the Mayor of York by muggers in the Minster Yard, and the hard times coming to Beverley Monastery. It was a period of warfare, religious divisiveness and national uncertainty, and times were hard, so it is no surprise that word of Mother Shipton's wisdom and power spread across the country. It wasn't long before people were visiting her from all over England. We don't know what she had to say to most of them, but fortunately she made plenty of open predictions about national events to come, both inside and out of her own lifetime.

For instance, she predicted Henry VIII's successful "Battle of the Spurs" against the French, his dissolution of the monasteries (and the suffering it would cause the commoners), and the ascent (and eventual dishonour) of Cardinal Wolsey:

> *"Now shall the Mitred Peacock first begin to plume, whose Train shall make a great show in the World, for a time; but shall afterwards vanish away, and his great Honour come to nothing."*

Like most people in the country, she seems to have disliked Wolsey who was, it must be said, responsible for a great deal of suffering. She predicted that the ambitious Cardinal would see York, but never actually reach it. Incensed, he sent a pack of noble lords to silence Mother Shipton — the Duke of Suffolk, the Earl of Northumberland, and one Lord D'Arcy of Yorkshire. They were to warn her that Wolsey was on his way to York, and would have her burned when he arrived. She calmly took the kerchief off her head and the staff she carried, and threw them on the fire, where they did not burn. Then she retrieved them, and said, "If these had burned, I might have too." Then she warned Suffolk that he would one day be cast as low as she herself was, and somberly informed D'Arcy and Northumberland that they would be dead on the pavements of York.

Not long after, Wolsey journeyed to York. His last stop before the town was at Cawood Castle, some ten miles south, where the Primates of Northern England resided. That evening, he climbed the castle tower with some companions, looked over to the city, and said with satisfaction, "Someone has said that I would never see York." A companion corrected him, "No, she said that you might see it, but never reach it." Furious, he swore to have Mother Shipton burned as soon as he got to the city, in the very near future. Then Wolsey turned, and found that the speaker was his friend the Earl of Northumberland – there to arrest him and take him south on charges of treason. Wolsey was already ill and he died on the journey south; it wasn't long before Northumberland and Darcy themselves were dead on the streets of York as predicted, and Suffolk ruined and disgraced.

Henry VIII died soon after suppressing the fledgling rebellion, with the Church's power broken. Several years of royal tumult followed, and then Queen Elizabeth I took the throne, in 1558. Old Mother Shipton did not live to see much of her rule; she died – as she had predicted – in 1561. She was buried in unconsecrated ground somewhere outside York. She left behind her a body of prophecy, recorded haphazardly by different people at different times. Those prophecies accurately included the Commoners Rebellion, the death of the innocent pawn Lady Jane Grey, and the devastation of Queen Mary's rule, when the Catholic Church persecuted the Protestants so barbarically – with men, women and even children being burned alive – that England has rejected Catholicism as its national religion ever since.

Later predictions accurately foretold much of England's history, from royal troubles to the London plague and the fire of 1665/6. She even seemingly predicted modern transport, communication and education:

"Carriages without horses shall go
... and accidents fill the world with woe ...
Around the world thoughts shall fly
In the twinkling of an eye ...
Through hills men shall ride
And no horse or ass be by their side;
Under water men shall walk,
Shall ride, shall sleep, shall talk;
In the air men shall be seen,
In white, in black and in green.
Iron in the water shall float
As easy as a wooden boat;
All England's sons that plough the land
Shall be seen, book in hand;
Learning shall so ebb and flow,
The poor shall most wisdom know."

Perhaps it is worrying that part of her corpus of prophecies remains unfulfilled. While a couplet that says the world will end in 1991 has been proven an Edwardian fake addition, the unfulfilled prophecy is of less certain origin – it is quite possible that it is Mother Shipton's. In a long verse, the prophecy talks about the fall of mankind being presaged by a comet or an asteroid which blazes in the skies for seven days, and during this period mankind will become frenzied animals, killing and raping. After this period, she prophesies that the "lands will fall" and "oceans rise", destroying all but a fraction of humanity. The survivors will then go on to usher in a golden age of understanding – but that's scant comfort for the rest of us.

Name: Old Mother Shipton
Years: 1488 – 1561
Description: An ill-favoured woman, disfigured
Dominant abilities: Prophecy
Traits: Stern, but helpful unless provoked
Nature: Neutral
Power: Strong
Type: Wise Woman
Domain: Prophecy
Key equipment: None
Region: England

A portrait of the enigmatic Count de St Germain, painted in 1777.

Count de St Germain

ᚾᛗᚠᚷᚱᛏᛃᛜᛗᛜᚢᚾᛏᛚᚠᚱᛏᛃᛈᚠᚷᛜᚠᛜᛗᚾᚻᛗᚠᛃᛜᚾᛜᚢᚾᛈᚠᛗᛏᛃᛚᚷᛗᚻᚠᛗᛗᚻᛃᛃᛗᚠᛜᚾᛗᚠᚷᚱᛏ

Witch, alchemist, ascended master, consummate adventurer, notorious con-man… There are almost as many different theories regarding the Count de St Germain as there are commentators on his extraordinary life. Despite being one of the most influential members of eighteenth-century society in Europe, he remains shrouded in utter mystery. One

thing is absolutely certain, though – during the entire period of 74 years that he is known for sure to have been active, he maintained the appearance of a fit, handsome man of 45.

Biography

Despite being one of the most influential characters in modern history, the Count de St Germain is also one of the most enigmatic. Karl, Prince of Hesse described him as one of the *"greatest philosophers who ever lived – the friend of humanity, whose heart was concerned only with the happiness of others"*. Despite a horde of such

Museum, whilst other works were given to Tchaikovsky and Prince Ferdinand, amongst others.

St Germain had more talents than musical ones, however. His paintings were said to be reminiscent of Raphael and quite extraordinary in quality, particularly for his ability to render perfectly the shine of a gemstone on canvas; he was sought after as an art critic and as a verifier of paintings. His memory was so great that he could glance at a paper and then repeat it word for word days later, and he could write poetry with one hand whilst simultaneously drafting political missives with the other. His chief peculiarity was never eating or drinking with others, but instead subsisting on a form of oat gruel he prepared himself and drinking little other than a tea he made from dried herbs.

But his feats were greater than mere skill and quickness of mind can allow for. St Germain was regularly said to be able to answer questions before they were spoken, and to know the content of letters before opening them. Casanova recorded that he visited St Germain in his laboratory and handed the Count a silver coin which was returned, moments later – now made of solid gold. St Germain also claimed to know how to melt small diamonds into larger single stones, and astonished the French Ambassador to Holland by smashing a huge diamond to pieces with a hammer – the twin of a stone he had just sold to a dealer for a princely sum. On another occasion, he amazed King Louis XV by melting a flaw out of one of his larger diamonds, increasing the value of the stone by a huge amount.

St Germain claimed to have lived in ancient Chaldea, and to possess secrets of the Egyptian masters. He commonly spoke about times long past as if he himself had been there to witness them, right down to exact details. One evening, while telling a story to some guests about an event that had happened many hundreds of years earlier, he nodded over to his butler and asked the man if he had left out anything important. The butler chided him gently: *"Monsieur le Comte forgets that I have been with him only five hundred years. I could not, therefore, have been present at that occurrence. It must have been my predecessor."*

Louis XV was a good friend of the Count's and made frequent use of his diplomatic skills.

accolades from nobility right across Europe, nothing whatsoever is known of St Germain's early life – not even when or where it started.

The Count de St Germain is remembered as a man of medium height, approximately 45 years old, with a slim figure, graceful bearing, a radiant smile and astonishingly lovely eyes. He was amazingly skilled in just about every field that it was possible to be skilled in. He spoke French, German, English, Italian, Spanish, Portuguese, Russian, Danish, Swedish, Arabic and Chinese fluently, without any trace of an accent. He played most musical instruments – Frederick the Great commended his skill on the harpsichord, but his favourite was the violin. Paganini himself is known to have declared St Germain his equal with the instrument. Two works that the Count composed are in the British

If the Count's origin, birth, nationality and age remain matters of mystery, his presence in Europe through the seventeenth and early eighteenth centuries is a matter of record. He first surfaced in Venice in 1710, where he met many people, including Rameau and the Countess de Georgy. The Countess met him again fifty years later, at a party thrown by Madame Pompadour, and asked him if his father had been in Venice in that year. The Count demurred. *"No, Madame, but I myself was living in Venice at the end of the last century and the beginning of this. I had the honour of paying you court in 1710, and you were kind enough to admire a little music of my composition."* The Countess, shocked, declared that had indeed been the case, which meant that St Germain must then be at least a century old. St Germain just smiled.

All through the eighteenth century, St Germain left little ripples of amazement across the lives of the nobility of Europe. Every time, the descriptions of his appearance, talents and age remained the same. In 1723, the Countess de Genlis saw a portrait of St Germain's mother, but did not recognize the style of her clothes, and could not get the secretive count to comment. From 1737 to 1742, records show that he lived with the Shah of Persia and spent his time in alchemical research. When he returned, he spent a year in Versailles with Louis XV, and then got involved in the Jacobite Revolution in England. Once that was settled, he headed to Potsdam to spend time with Frederick the Great. He met Voltaire while he was there, and greatly impressed the man; Voltaire wrote to Frederick that in his opinion, *"the Count de St Germain is a man who was never born, who will never die, and who knows everything"*.

In 1755 St Germain accompanied General Clive to India. A couple of years later, he was back in France, where Louis XV gave him a suite and a laboratory in his royal chateau at Chambord, in Touraine. In 1760, Louis sent St Germain to Holland and England on a very delicate diplomatic mission, and it is thanks to his efforts that the historical Family Compact was signed between England and France; this led directly to the Treaty of Paris, and the end of the colonial wars. In 1761, St Germain was in St Petersburg in Russia, helping to win the throne for Catherine the Great. He left the country as a full Imperial General of the Russian armies, and shortly afterwards was placed in Tunis with the Russian fleet, still in uniform, using the title of Graf Saltikoff. Other honours and titles he claimed or was awarded during his adventures included being named Marquis de Montferrat, Comte Bellamarre, Chevalier Schoening, Chevalier Weldon, Graf Tzarogy and Prinz Ragoczy.

After Louis XV died in 1774, St Germain spent several years in Austria and Germany, apparently introducing Theosophical notions into the occult and mystic organisations of the day – including the Rosicrucian Society in Vienna, the Knights Templar, the Fratres Lucis, and the Knights and Brothers of Asia. He was a delegate to the Freemasons' Wilhelmsbad Conference in 1782. The Count de St Germain officially died on February 27, 1784, during chemical experiments in Eckernförde, near Schleswig in Denmark. There was no body, but his good friend, Karl, Prince of Hesse attested to his death, and his death certificate can be found in the Eckernförde Church Register.

If he did indeed die in Schleswig, it doesn't seem to have slowed him down much. St Germain is recorded as attending the great Masonic Paris Convention of 1785. He is then said to have had a very important interview with the Empress of Russia in 1786. After that, he went back to France in a last-ditch – and unsuccessful – effort to help stave off the revolution. The Countess d'Adhémar was one of

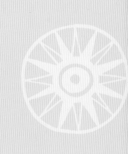

Madame Helena Blavatsky, founder of the Theosophical Movement and supposed Ascended Master in her own right, was famously photographed with St Germain more than a century after his official death.

Queen Marie-Antoinette's ladies-in-waiting, and she kept extensive diaries of the period. St Germain features several times. In 1788, he visited the Countess d'Adhémar, warned her that a conspiracy to overthrow the monarchy was underfoot, and asked her to take him to see the queen. The countess reported the visit and discovered that the queen had received warnings herself. A meeting was arranged, and St Germain asked the queen to set up a meeting with the king – and to encourage him not to mention it to his minister, Maurepas. But the king ignored the warning and called Maurepas for advice. The minister immediately went to see the Countess d'Adhémar. St Germain appeared in the middle of their conversation and informed Maurepas that his petty jealousy was about to destroy the French monarchy, because he didn't have enough time to devote to saving it.

On July 14, 1789, having apparently given up his efforts, St Germain wrote to Queen Marie-Antoinette, warning that her friend the Duchesse de Polignac – who was visiting her – and all of that line and their friends were doomed to death. On October 5, Countess d'Adhémar got a letter saying that the sun had set on the French monarchy, and it was too late; his hands were tied "by one stronger than myself". He prophesied the death of Marie-Antoinette, the ruin of the royal family and the rise of Napoleon. He himself would be going to Sweden to investigate King Gustavius III and to try to head off "a great crime". He added that the Countess d'Adhémar would have sight of him five more times, but not to look forward to the sixth.

In 1790, St Germain admitted his immediate plans to an Austrian friend, Franz Graeffer:

> *"Tomorrow night I am off. I am much needed in Constantinople, then in England, there to prepare two new inventions which you will have in the next century — trains and steamboats. Toward the end of this century I shall disappear out of Europe, and betake myself to the region of the Himalayas. I will rest; I must rest."*

The Countess d'Adhémar recorded five further occasions on which she saw the Count – fleeting visitations in 1799, 1802, 1804, 1813 and 1820. It is presumed that he also appeared to her on the day of her death, in 1822. A mysterious Englishman named Major Fraser appeared in Parisian society at the same time, with many of the same characteristics as the Count de St Germain, and of a similar age and breadth of skill. A Frenchman who had known St Germain, Albert Vandam, wrote in his memoirs about the striking similarity between Fraser and St Germain. Was this the same Major Fraser who, in 1820, published an account of his journeys in the Himalayas, in which he said he had reached Gangotri, the source of the most sacred branch of the River Ganges, and bathed in the spring of the Jumna River? No one knows, because Major Fraser vanished as suddenly as St Germain himself had done. There are further rumours that he also appeared to Lord Lytton in 1860, and there is a famous photograph from 1885 that purports to show the Count de St Germain standing next to Madame Helena Blavatsky, the founder of the Theosophical movement. As late as 1897, the French singer Emma Calve dedicated an autographed portrait of herself to St Germain. Some rumours suggest that he took the part of Russian healer and mystic Rasputin, and then survived to slip off to America, where presumably he was behind the Kennedy assassination. If so, little has been heard from him since.

Name: The Count de St Germain
Years: 1710–1784
Description: A slim, graceful, handsome man of 45, with striking eyes
Dominant abilities: Ageless, psychic powers, highly talented
Traits: Witty, generous, kind
Nature: Good
Power: Very strong
Type: Wise Man/Ascended Master
Domain: Alchemy, prophecy
Key equipment: None
Region: Europe

Gerald Gardner

ᚾᛖᚠᚷᛈᛏᛁᚾᛗᛟᚾᛁᛚᛈᛈᛏᛁᛈᛈᚷᛂᚾᚦᛗᚾᛂᛗᛖᛂᛗᚾᛟᚾᛈᛈᛗᛏᛁᛚᚠᛗᛂᛖᛗᛂᛁᛗᚠᛟᚾᛗᚠᛈᛏ

The undisputed father of Wicca, Gerald Gardner
was the force behind the modern revival of
witchcraft as a religious and magical force. No one
will ever know for sure whether he was passing on
an ancient, hidden English mystery tradition that
he had been initiated into, or whether he created
the whole thing from first principles and a powerful
knowledge of earlier occult systems. The argument
about the truthfulness of his account of initiation
into a surviving witch cult has been raging for 50
years – but in some senses it couldn't matter less,
because his work has been the foundation for the
explosion in modern witchcraft.

Biography

Gerald Brousseau Gardner was born near Liverpool
in England on June 13, 1884, the middle son of
three. His father worked in the family business,
trading timber, and served locally as a justice of
the peace. The family was descended from Scottish
ancestors, and included several members with
witchcraft links, including one Grissell Gairdner,
burned as a witch in 1610. Gardner's grandmother
was rumoured to be a witch or at least to have
some powers in that direction, and several of his
relatives claimed psychic powers of sorts. On the
more respectable side, the lineage included former
Liverpool mayors, and a Vice-Admiral of the Navy
who had been ennobled as a peer in the House of
Commons.

Gardner suffered from very severe asthma when
young, and was brought up largely apart from
his brothers and the rest of his family. During the
winters, his nurse, Josephine McCombie, took him
travelling in Europe to get him out of the polluted
air of Liverpool. Gerald spent a lot of time alone,
and filled the gap by reading voraciously. His
particular interests were history and archaeology.
Eventually, Josephine married a Ceylonese resident,

◇ *Gerald*
Gardner, the
father (and
possible creator) of
the modern Wiccan
movement.

and Gerald, now grown into a young man and quite distant from his family, elected to go with her to what is now Sri Lanka, and later to Borneo and Malaysia. He worked on a tea plantation for a while, eventually landing work with the British Government inspecting rubber plantations and opium fields, a job which earned him a considerable amount of money. Whilst in the Far East, he learnt a lot about the local spiritual beliefs, and became an expert on the history and design of Malaysian Kris Knives – his text *The Kris and other Malay Weapons* remains the standard book on the subject.

He married an English woman in 1927, and after he retired from the government in 1936, he moved back to England. He still did a lot of travelling around Europe and Asia Minor, and often claimed to have seen Cyprus in dreams before ever visiting there – a feat which he explained as past life memories.

Back in England, Gardner lived in the New Forest area, famous for its witchcraft history. He became involved with a quasi-masonic society, and then, within that group, was contacted by another, even more secret society, which claimed to be the inheritors of a witchcraft tradition reaching back into England's medieval history and before. In 1939, Gardner was initiated into the group by their high priestess, a woman with the unlikely name of Old Dorothy Clutterbuck. The coven trained Gardner in witchcraft and magic, and Gardner quickly established himself in the occult community. He even met with notorious magician Aleister Crowley in 1946, and was signed up as an honorary member of Crowley's occult order, the Ordo Templi Orientis.

Witchcraft was still illegal in England, so in 1949 Gardner wrote a novel espousing and detailing it, but set in the past and making sure it appeared fictional. This was moderately successful. When the anti-witchcraft laws were repealed in 1951, Gardner was quick to break ties with his coven and travel to the Isle of Man, where he purchased a newly renamed Museum of Magic and Witchcraft from an old friend. He established himself as resident witch, set up a new coven, of which he was the chief, and started work on recording the teachings he had learnt in the New Forest. He had a lot of assistance

in this from his chief initiate, Doreen Valiente.

In the meantime, Gardner published a non-fiction book called *Witchcraft Today*, supporting his claims of a hidden witch tradition that had initiated him. The book, published in 1954, was an immediate success. He and Valiente finished organizing their ritual knowledge in 1957 – a blend of the highly fragmented teachings of the New Forest coven with Gardner's own knowledge of Freemasonry, ritual magic and esotericism – and this "Book of Shadows" became the foundation of all modern Wicca today. Despite the title, the Gardner Book of Shadows was never printed or released; the material was for dissemination by coven training only, and it remains so. (The internet material going under the same name is faked.) By training others, who then set up their own covens and so on, Gardner's material formed the basis for the Wicca explosion. His final published book was *The Meaning of Witchcraft*, another non-fiction exploration.

The published books and the museum drew a lot of attention, and Gardner found himself hailed as "Britain's Chief Witch", but this did not stop him being recognized by the queen for his civil service work in the Far East in 1960. Gardner died in 1964, just a few years after his wife. His museum was broken up and sold by his chief beneficiary, but enough had already been done. Although he had pessimistic expectations for the future of the craft, his teachings continue to dominate Wicca today – a far livelier and more dynamic religion that he would ever have dared hope.

Name: Gerald Gardner
Years: 1884–1964
Description: A thin, wild-haired man with intense eyes and a mischievous smile
Dominant abilities: Unknown
Traits: Keen naturist
Nature: Neutral
Power: Said to be quite weak
Type: Wicca
Domain: Research, publication
Key equipment: None
Region: England and worldwide

Hypatia of Alexandria

ᚾᛗᚠᚩᚱᛏᛃᚾᛗᚩᚾᛞᛚᚠᚱᛏᛃᚠᚠᚷᚩᚾᚩᛗᚾᚻᛗᚠᚻᛗᚾᚩᚾᛈᚠᛗᛏᛃᛚᚱᛗᚻᚠᛗᛗᚻᚻᛁᛗᛈᚩᚾᛗᚠᚩᚱᛏ

One of the first known victims of Christian witch-hunting, Hypatia was murdered by a mob in Alexandria in AD 415 at the urgings of Cyril, Patriarch of the city. John, Bishop of Nikiu, described her as "an abominable messenger of hell", saying that "she was devoted at all times to magic, astrolabes and instruments of music, and she beguiled many people through (her) Satanic wiles. And the governor of the city honoured her exceedingly; for she had beguiled him through her magic. And he ceased attending church as had been his custom."

Biography

Hypatia, daughter of Theon of Alexandria, was born in AD 355. Theon, a leading mathematician and astronomer based at the Great Library, had boasted to friends that when his son was born, he would educate him into the perfect human being. He was not the least bit discouraged to discover that his new child was female. Theon educated Hypatia in art, literature, philosophy, mathematics, rhetoric, science, rowing, riding, mountaineering and swimming. The child spent a lot of time in the Museum of the University of Alexandria, immersed in rationality and knowledge. Her religious training was similarly straightforward and to the point. Theon told her, *"All formal dogmatic religions are fallacious and must never be accepted by self-respecting persons as final. Reserve your right to think, for even to think wrongly is better than not to think at all."*

The murder of Hypatia. Note that this old engraving's unsubtle attempts to shift the blame racially are totally spurious. A native Alexandrian, Hypatia was probably Arabic in appearance, and her actual attackers were almost certainly locals too.

When she surpassed her father's knowledge, Hypatia journeyed to Athens, where she continued studying, and then travelled across Europe. When she finally returned from her travels, she was given a position teaching geometry, algebra and astronomy at the University.

During the course of her career, Hypatia wrote scores of books – both original mathematical and scientific research, and commentaries on older philosophical and mathematical works. She also collaborated with her father on many more works. She was said to be strikingly beautiful and received many offers of marriage, but she always declined them, saying that her research was more important.

She invented several important devices, including some that are still in use today, such as the astrolabe (a navigational tool for sailors), the hydroscope (which measures the specific gravity of a liquid), and the planesphere, a chart of the stars' motion across the sky. She taught extra lessons from home, and dedicated herself entirely to spreading knowledge.

Unfortunately, being a mathematician and philosopher was becoming a dangerous business. In 364, the Council of Laodicea had forbidden priests from practising maths: *"They, who are of the priesthood, or of the clergy, shall not be magicians, enchanters, mathematicians, or astrologers."* Not long after, Emperor Constantius made it illegal to

presence. His successor was his extremist nephew, Cyril. One of Hypatia's students, Synesius, had been one of Theophilus's closer friends, which may have helped protect her, but Synesius did not long survive Theophilus. Cyril wanted to purge Alexandria of scientific thinkers, philosophers, mathematicians, pagans and Jews, and sectarian tension rocketed in the city. The Roman Prefect of the city, Orestes, was also a friend of Hypatia, and Cyril came to believe that her influence was stopping him from extending his power over Orestes. Cyril began a smear campaign against her, spreading tales that she was a satanic witch, a divinatrix and black magician.

In 415, during Lent, Cyril sent a group of his military zealots, known as parabolans, to eradicate the dangerous witch. Hypatia – a brilliant 60-year-old philosopher and mathematician, praised throughout the city for her compassion, wisdom and elegant beauty – was dragged from her carriage and into a nearby church, stripped naked, and had the skin ripped from her body with sharp-edged shells. She was then torn limb from limb, and her tattered corpse was carried triumphantly to Cinaron, and there burned. There was no investigation into the murder; no arrests or charges. Not long after, the Great Library and University themselves were destroyed, and the greatest collection of knowledge and wisdom in the ancient world was burned, ushering in more than a thousand years of ignorance and superstition. After his death, Cyril was canonized as a saint.

"consult" mathematicians and soothsayers. The Archbishop of Alexandria, Theophilus, considered paganism and science to be enemies of Christianity, and even burned down a pagan teaching institution and lesser library, the Temple of Serapis, in 389. Part of the problem was the Ptolemaic system, an astronomical discovery which made it possible to track the movements of the planets and even predict eclipses – but prediction, even of something as mechanical as the movement of the stars, was seen as foretelling the future and therefore going against God.

In 412, Theophilus died. Whilst he had disliked Hypatia as a pagan and scientist, he had tolerated her

Name: Hypatia, daughter of Theon
Years: AD 355–415
Description: A beautiful, elegant woman
Dominant abilities: Mathematics, philosophy, teaching
Traits: Genius
Nature: Good
Power: None
Type: None
Domain: Science
Key equipment: None
Region: Alexandria – then technically part of Greece, but now in Egypt

Silver Ravenwolf has been interested in Wiccan matters since a very early age. At the age of five, she recalls being seated beneath a willow tree in a neighbour's yard and wishing that God were female – or that he should be balanced by having a wife. Seeing married parents, married grandparents, friends' parents, even remembering teachings about Jesus and his parents, it seemed odd to the child that God should be alone, without someone to love. At seven, she saw a group of five angels standing at her bedroom door.

At 13, she experienced her first exposure to Tarot cards, thanks to a generous older cousin, and also created a special puppet to use for wishing; she used him as a means towards various childish goals – like ice cream! When she was 15, fundamentalist neighbours saw Silver with a school-assigned book called *The Witch and the Priest* and accused her of being a witch herself: the fuss was laughed at back home, but it set her mind whirling. Her mother's death from leukaemia when Silver was only 17 was a major religious test – one that organized religion failed resoundingly. Silver's mother called on representatives of all sorts of denominations to pray for her, but repeatedly, all the family saw from the priests was greed, missionary zeal and personal disinterest. Silver turned her back on traditional religion and found some of the answers she was looking for in Wicca.

Silver's first steps into the public pagan community were through a newsletter in the early 1980s called *Witch Press*. By concentrating on non-discriminatory, progressive views and dedicating herself towards helping newcomers obtain support, she gained the recognition of her peers. Worldwide notice came in 1990 when her first major book, *To*

Silver Ravenwolf's books aim to make Wicca more accessible and less religious, which has caused some controversy.

Silver Ravenwolf

ᚾᛗᚠᚷᚱᛏᛃᚾᛗᚩᚾᛁᛚᚠᚱᛏᛋᛖᚠᚠᚷᚩᚾᚩᛗᚾᚻᚷᛗᚠᚻᚷᚾᚩᚾᚠᚠᛗᛏᛃᛚᚠᛗᚻᚠᛗᛗᚻᛃᛗᚠᚩᚾᛗᚠᚷᚱᛏ

The most successful Wiccan author at the turn of the twenty-first century, Silver Ravenwolf has written some 18 highly successful books on witchcraft and is the head of a network of 36 covens across the USA and Canada, the Black Forest Witches, specifically for training Wiccan clergy. Silver was born in 1956, and has found great success integrating her experiences with her four initiated teenage children into her teachings. She is famed for her accessible, easy-to-read style, and her best-selling work to date, *Teen Witch*, is aimed directly at younger practitioners.

Ride a Silver Broomstick, was published. Since then, her writing has taken her all over North America and placed her in front of audiences of thousands; she grants hundreds of interviews a year.

In addition to her interests in traditional Wicca, Silver also maintains a lively interest in a native Pennsylvanian healer tradition known as "Pow-Wow". It has nothing to do with Native American lore, but instead stems from the original German settlers of Pennsylvania, the misleadingly named Pennsylvania Dutch (Dutch, in this instance, being a corruption of *Deutsch*, the German word for, well, "German"). Silver studied Pow-Wow intensively under the famous Pow-Wow healer Preston Zerbe. Pow-Wow forms an integral part of Silver's Wiccan training, and third-degree members of her Black Forest clan are also counted as certified Pow-Wow Artists.

Silver spends the bulk of her time engaged in writing and related publicity work, giving talks and seminars, and maintaining an interest in e-commerce. With her husband, Mick, she also maintains the Black Forest lodges. Her magical interests encompass Wicca, using magic to help the police in detecting dangerous criminals, hypnotherapy, astrology, divination, Pow-Wow, Tarot and Hoodoo. Her witchcraft lineage is considered Euro-Wiccan.

Silver isn't entirely free of controversy – few public figures are, after all. Specifically, she has attracted some criticism from the Wiccan community at large for de-emphasizing some of the more religious and worship-focused aspects of Wicca. Given her childhood experiences, it is no surprise that she is inclined to look beyond religious ritual for its own sake. Balanced against the critics is her huge legion of fans, young and otherwise, who feel that she is making the powers of witchcraft available and accessible in a manner that has never been offered before.

◈ *Tarot cards are an indispensible part of most Wiccans' magical tool sets.*

Name: Silver Ravenwolf
Years: Born 1956
Description: Pleasant, trim woman now in her forties
Dominant abilities: Witchcraft, writing
Traits: Teacher, healer
Nature: Good
Power: Unknown
Type: Wiccan
Domain: Books
Key equipment: Unknown
Region: Pennsylvania, USA

Tamsin Blight

The White Witch of Helston, Tamsin Blight, was without doubt the most famous of the Cornish "Pellors", cunning-men and women who followed the folk arts. She lived during the first half of the nineteenth century, and was said to be able to heal illnesses, remove curses and spells, provide protection and charms and, if provoked, to be able to dish out spells and curses just as readily.

Biography

Thomasine Blight was born in 1798 in Redruth, west Cornwall. She gained a reputation as a healer and witch during her late teens, and was already well known for her skills before she began formally practising business as a cunning-woman around 1830. Her customers included anxious farmers who needed her help with healing cures for sick cattle, young women who were concerned about their chances of making a good marriage, and people of all sorts who needed healing.

She moved to Helston, and in 1835 she married a man named James Thomas, himself a significant local cunning-man in his own right. The pair formed a most incredible double-act and became famed for their amazing cures. It was said that even when she was on her deathbed, sick people were still carried to her on stretchers and laid beside her and would rise up and walk down the stairs in perfect health. The couple lived together happily for fifteen years, and then an indiscretion of James' got him into trouble, and he had to leave Cornwall.

Newspapers at the time made much of the scandal – James was said to have been "in the habit of receiving money annually for keeping witchcraft from vessels sailing out of Hayle". His method of ensuring safety was novel, to say the least; he had to engage in sex with several young men from the vessel. It was a common remedy of his to prevent curses from taking hold; he was also said to have induced two other young men, a mason and a miner, to have sex with him in order to protect them from a curse that was waiting for them. There was a host of similar tales.

It was the end of the marriage, unsurprisingly. Tamsin Blight wasted no time distancing herself from her husband, and he was forced to flee Cornwall entirely. She made it known publicly that she had always been the true Pellor, the one with the powers, and that he had been tapping into her strengths. The

Tamsin's Blight's home of Helston is famous today for its Floral Dance in celebration of spring.

couple remained estranged, and Tamsin died just a few years later, in 1856, at the age of 58.

The Pellor tradition that she claimed to be tapping into was a very real and devoted current of witch-like thought and teaching. It was a way of seeing, of understanding the familiar and simple in new terms. Its powers were concerned with balance, both in the natural world and in the human world. Pellors were said to have close contact with the Fairies' realms and to be able to speak to the assorted spirits and energies involved. No one knows how much of the Pellor's craft survived into the twentieth century, but there are still people around today who claim to be Pellors in the traditional sense.

Name: Tamsin Blight, aka Tammy Blee, The White Witch of Helston
Years: 1798–1856
Description: Stern-faced country woman
Dominant abilities: Healing, removing curses
Traits: Wise
Nature: Good
Power: Strong
Type: Wise Woman
Domain: Healing
Key equipment: Unknown
Region: Cornwall, England

5
"In a Sieve
I'll thither Sail"

"In a Sieve
I'll thither Sail"

Equipment, Ingredients and Magical Objects

Witches are known for using a dazzling array of different things in the course of their craft. Some of the objects are almost part of the uniform – signatures of witch-hood, at least in the tales, like pointy hats and long black cloaks. Others are far more specialized. "Eye of Newt" may be one of the most famous potion ingredients, but it's difficult to say how often any given witch would actually need some.

Outfits

Clothing is a critical part of being a witch, or at least of being recognized as one. Without the right outfit, it's impossible to be taken seriously – and that's true right across all areas of life, not just in witchcraft. Classic witches have the most famous and obviously recognizable clothing style, of course. The most important elements are a tall conical **black hat**, with a wide rim – possibly originally taken from the Welsh national costume – and a long **black cloak**. Both are traditionally viewed as being a bit tattered; it is assumed that the witch has had her hat and cloak for years. Underneath the cloak, most witches wore rough, homespun blouses and skirts in dark grey or brown colours – cheap, peasant clothing in keeping with their generally impoverished status. The classic witch was generally thought to spend her entire time out and about on her business, so she was presumed to stay in her usual outfit through the day.

Other types of witch had less rigorous dress codes. Wise women and cunning-men generally made sure they appeared as prospering but unexceptional folk of the town or village that they lived in. In other words, their dress would be that of the area for the time, presented reasonably smartly. Who, after all, would want to employ a wise-woman who looked as if she couldn't even make her own life successful and comparatively easy? Consequently, wise women are normally thought of as appearing "matronly".

Satanic dupes and warlocks were thought to be making an effort to blend in with society, so they generally dressed just like everyone else around them – during the day, anyway. At night, particularly when attending sabbats, satanic dupes were expected to dress head-to-toe in **black hooded robes**, perhaps even also donning frightening **animal masks** for extra protection. These robes would then be thrown off for the inevitable orgy that followed the main rites, but masks were kept on. The rest of the time, though, they looked like everyone else. Involuntary witches took this even further. Having no idea themselves that they were anything unusual, they always seemed to be dressed as perfectly normal members of society.

Wiccans, finally, tend to dress in a variety of modern styles according to their age, experience and maturity. Any generalization is little better than a stereotype of course, but there are certain clichés associated with the craft today. It is common for new Wiccans, particularly teenagers, to dress head to toe in black, punctuated perhaps with silver jewellery, body piercings, tattoos and/or heavy make-up. As Wiccans get older, the black may remain, but moderates into plain black trousers/jeans and black tops/T-shirts with maybe a pendant or a couple of rings for decoration. Alternatively, some Wiccans plump for long, flowing dresses in vivid colours such as greens and purples, typically worn with long, flowing hair. There is no "uniform", however, and nowadays anyone could be a witch, from the banker in the Italian power-suit to the skateboarder in trousers baggy enough to fit six friends, or the little old dear in the cashmere sweater.

◊ *If identification were needed, the hat, cloak and broomstick all say "witch".*

Broomsticks

As much a part of the classic witch's uniform as the pointed hat, **broomsticks** – specifically besoms – are indelibly associated with witchcraft in the public imagination. A besom is a broom consisting of a faggot of twigs bundled around a five to six foot pole and tied together with string. It was a rough tool, but one that every medieval woman would have made daily use of. However, it wasn't until the sixteenth or seventeenth centuries that the broom became closely identified with witches; before then, witches were thought to fly on all sorts of things, including bare sticks, shovels, pitchforks and even assorted animals.

There is no certain reason for the association, but it may go back to ancient fertility rites when Celtic people used to climb onto brooms, poles and forks and ride them like hobby-horses through the fields, leaping up high as they did so to encourage the crops to imitate them. During much of the eighteenth century, it was even believed that witches flew their brooms with the twigs pointing ahead, with a candle stuck in amongst the twigs to provide some light. Some authors have suggested that broomsticks might have been a good way of internally administering hallucinogenic "flying potions", but there is little evidence to back up this rather odd phallic notion.

Interestingly, legend does say that new, inexperienced witches were prone to losing their concentration and falling off their brooms. On nights that were particularly associated with witches' festivals – such as Hallowe'en on October 31 and Beltane/Walpurgis on April 30 – villagers would often lay spikes, hooks and scythes on the ground, so that any witch falling off her broom would be killed. Church bells were also thought to be able to force broomsticks to the ground, so the bells would often be rung during the night on those festivals.

Magical tools

There weren't many tools that all witches needed for their spells and other magical business. Most of the time, ingredients for spells and curses were gathered according to the needs of the charm. However, one of the items that every witch possessed was the athame, or ritual dagger. These knives were double-edged, often with curved or even wavy blades, with a black hilt. Both blade and hilt were sometimes carved with magical symbols of various sorts. The very best **athames** were magnetic, forged from meteoric iron.

Legend had it that each new witch was given an athame by the witch who trained her on the night of her initiation into full witchcraft. The knife was used to cut and chop ingredients and herbs, carve magic circles and other symbols into the ground, and to dominate and control spirits and demons of all kinds. If sacrifice was required, the athame would be used to make the blood-letting cut.

The other vital tool was a **scrying-stone**. This was used for divination and prophecy, and for accessing the clairvoyant ability of looking into distant places – sometimes even distant times. The most common forms of scrying stones were mirrors, polished semi-precious stones, balls of crystal and dark bowls filled with water or scrying potions. By gazing into the reflections and letting her mind – and vision – wander, the witch could find out answers to any questions, peek into the future, or even put the evil eye on people out of normal sight.

When they weren't being used, scrying-stones had to be kept wrapped in black velvet, and ideally placed in a closed box. They could never be touched by sunlight without losing their powers. Candle-light was acceptable, though, and many witches were thought to use a candle close to the stone to provide a pinpoint of light within the stone on which to focus. Others apparently preferred dim ambient light. Either way, by gazing into the depths of the stone, the witch's sight would cloud over and she would see pictures emerging in the depths. If she was seeking answers to a problem, the images could be symbolic – hints and omens. On other occasions, she might see real locations and events as they happened.

Flammable substances

ᚾᛗᚠᚷᛒᛏᛁᚾᛗᚬᚾᚱᛚᚦᚱᛏᛃᚠᚱᚷᚬᚾᚬᛗᚾᚻᛗᚠᚻᛗᚾᚬᚾᚠᚠᛗᛏᛃᚱᚠᛗᚻᚠᛗᛗᚻᛃᛗᚠᚬᚾᛗᚠᚷᛒᛏ

◇ *Witches'
bonfires often had
to be built from
specific types of
wood, or needed
special herbs
thrown over them.*

Fire was a very important part of many witches'
spells and celebrations. In medieval lore, witches'
sabbats almost always took place around large
bonfires, partly for warmth and partly to provide
some flames for the devil. Often, such **bonfires** were
supposed to contain specific ingredients to help call
up dark forces – certain trees were favoured over
others for their wood, and then herbs, incenses and
other substances might be added too. If the devil was
supposed to manifest through the fire, then sulphur

was frequently required as an addition. In some
celebrations, witches were supposed to take turns
leaping through and over the flames, which would
generously withhold from burning them. On other
occasions, sabbat fires could become supernaturally
deadly, imbued with the power to burn through
almost anything.

When working indoors, open fires were
seemingly less important. **Cauldrons** obviously had
to be hung over or placed in cooking fires, but there
is little evidence that these fires were anything other
than perfectly normal. The magic, in other words,

takes place inside the cauldron, rather than outside it. When flame was required for casting a spell, it usually seems to have been in the form of a candle. Witchcraft traditionally makes great use of **candles** – for help in scrying, as shown earlier, but also to illuminate during spell-casting, to mark out the boundaries of magic circles, and as a component of the spellcraft itself. Different types of spell are still said to require candles of different colours.

In addition to that, there is a whole range of traditional "special" candles for use in different specific spells and charms. They include Adam and Eve Candles in the shape of a couple making love and Likeness Candles supposed to represent – and embody – a specific target individual, as a voodoo doll does. The best known of all, however, was the **Hand of Glory**, made from the rendered fat of a murderer and mounted in the severed hand of a hung corpse. It was said that the Hand of Glory would keep the occupants of a house asleep whilst it was lit no matter what, leaving the wielder free to carry out whatever mischief she wanted.

On top of that, all sorts of herbs and **incenses** were regularly burned as part of spellcraft and charm making. These could range from the simple to the highly exotic – incenses could be crafted from all sorts of unlikely unguents. According to anti-witch literature of the medieval period, one of the favoured ingredients used in incense- making was the fat of unbaptized babies – also supposedly popular for use in flying potions.

Books on magic

Traditionally, literate witches recorded their spells and magical remedies as taught to them. This record was used for personal reference; if the witch trained an apprentice, the training and teaching would all be oral. These volumes were not supposed to be passed on at death even, and some were thought to be magically protected. This sort of work was known as a **Book of Shadows.** Some witches recorded their activities in there as well, turning the volume into a sort of magical diary. This is standard practice in Wicca today; candidates prepare their

◆ *An ornately bound Wiccan Book of Shadows.*

BURY ME IN A NAMELESS GRAVE
I CAME FROM GOD THE WORLD TO SAVE
I BROUGT THEM WISDOME FROM ABOVE
WORSHIP LIBERTY AND LOVE

THEY SLEW ME FOR I DID DISPARAGE
THEREFORE RELIGION LAW AND MARRIAGE
SO BE MY GRAVE WITHOUT A NAME
THAT EARTH MAY SUCK IN MY SHAME

✦ *This Book of Shadows was used in the Rites of Thoth up to 1950.*

own Book of Shadows that records teachings, spells, training exercises, odd coincidences, and anything else relevant. In general, most Books of Shadows are bound in black leather. A more direct type of magical instruction manual was known as a **grimoire**. These were books of magic spells, mostly designed to help the reader raise up demons, dead spirits or other apparitions. They were often cited as evidence for satanic dupe witchcraft, although there is little evidence that anyone got very far using any of them. Some have survived to the modern day; they tend to be impenetrably written, dense tomes packed with cryptic instructions and poorly rendered seals and diagrams.

Early superstition said that they had to be written in red ink, and bound in either black leather or human skin. Selling them would cancel out their powers, so they had to be passed on freely; not that this last restriction stopped any of the many publishers who printed and sold copies. Some of the most famous grimoires include The Greater and Lesser Key of Solomon the King, the Grimoire of Armadel, The Grimoire of Honorius, the Grimoirum Verum, and The Grand Grimoire of the Red Dragon. Many of them are available in shops today, albeit almost always in appallingly bad translations.

The majority of the grimoires focused on necromancy and theurgy – raising the dead and magically channelling the power of God – rather than witchcraft. As such, they would only really have been of interest to satanic dupe witches, and even then probably only to wannabies. After all, why bother trying to use a grimoire to call up a demon if you're already meeting with one on a monthly basis? As such, any witch who could read would be more likely to have books on herb lore, or tables of astrological and astronomical charts, than to waste shelf-space with such obvious black-magic focused tomes.

The witch's garden

ᚾᛗᛖᚷᚱᛏᛃᚾᛗᚦᚾᚱᛚ ᚠᛖᚱᛏᛃᚠᚠᚷᚦᚾᚦᛗᚾᚻᛗᚠᚻᚹᚾᚾᚦᚾᛖᚠᚱᛗᛏᛃᛚᚱᛗᚻᚠᛗᛗᚻᛃᛗᚠᚦᚾᛗᛖᚷᚱᛏ

Traditionally, witches lived somewhat out of the way of the main body of a town or village. This gave them greater freedom to practise their arts without being observed, but wasn't necessarily suspicious – many farmers and other cottage dwellers would have lived in relative isolation. Consequently, witches were comparatively free to cultivate useful **magical herbs** and other spell ingredients. Poisonous, supernatural and/or rare herbs would be mixed in with less unusual plants; indeed, most people seeing a witch's garden would not have known what they were looking at.

Comparatively innocent plants that could be turned to assorted magical uses would have included apple, corn, fennel, foxglove, hawthorn, lavender, lettuce, mistletoe, oak, oat, pear, poplar, poppy, rowan, saffron, speedwell, St John's wort, walnut and yarrow. They all had various purposes in the witch's spell repertoire. For example, oats were rumoured to be used by witches to feed severed organs that they had temporarily captured from unfortunate victims, while lettuce stalks could be crushed to give an opium-like substance.

Other plants were less commonly found in working gardens, and many of them were highly toxic. Hellebore, also known as Christmas rose, is strongly toxic, and was a common ingredient in formulations used by early herbalists – even Greek sages such as Theophrastus, known as the father of botany, spoke highly of it. Ergot, the winter form of a fungus that grows on corn, was also toxic, and prone to inducing visions. It includes chemicals that are similar in derivation to that of LSD, but ergot poisoning could also lead to gangrene. Henbane, another poison, was used in many flying ointments, and was also rumoured to have aphrodisiac powers if one inhaled the scent of burning seeds. For several centuries, it was even routinely added to pilsner lagers.

◇ *Herbs were dried for future use in potions and spells.*

Thornapple was related to nightshade, and could induce violent derangements. Hemp was prized for its narcotic value, while hemlock was thought to be able to induce impotence and prophetic trances. One of the most famous of all the magical poison plants was monkshood – also called wolfsbane, aconite and soldier's cap. It was added to meat to be used as wolf poison in the Middle Ages, which is where the name "wolfsbane" comes from, but it was also supposed to be used to help contact the dead and induce prophetic trance. It was a very dangerous poison if eaten, or even if the sap got into a cut.

Mandrake, lovage and sweet flag were all used in the preparation of many flying potions, along with toxins like monkshood, henbane and ergot. Mandrake, whose root is reminiscent of a bipedal form, was thought to be highly magical and extremely dangerous to remove from the ground. Many people believed that a mandrake root would shriek when removed from the soil, with sufficient force to kill anyone nearby stone dead. Once prepared, though, it was a powerful ingredient. Heather was also very useful for flying, but not as a potion ingredient – its twigs were favoured for brooms that were supposed to take to the air.

With its resemblance to a deformed human shape, mandrake root was seen as a very powerful substance, but its shriek when uprooted could kill a grown man stone dead.

Plenty of plants were magical in their own right, in theory. Elder trees offered a home for spirits that might be passing, and could be used in making contact with the other side. Purple orchis was useful for love charms. Vervain gave the strength of iron to those who imbibed of it, and could be used to increase a man's sexual stamina, but it had to be gathered during the dog days of Sirius each year, from spots where the sun did not strike. Hazel was vital for dowsing, and the tree was a favourite with fairies. A ring of woodbine garlands could be used for healing, if the patient was passed through it nine times.

Most of the various magical herbs and plants had special requirements for harvesting. Even many of the ones that didn't would be available only during a comparatively short period of the year. For that reason, witches invariably kept large stocks of different properly harvested herbs. A witch's kitchen (or home in general) could therefore often be identified by the sheer variety of preserved plants.

Sky-cladding

This is the lack of equipment rather than an item in its own right. Modern legend frequently associates witch rituals with **nudity** – going "sky-clad", as it is poetically known – particularly if the spell is being cast outdoors, or as part of a general sabbat which was expected to end in an orgy. However, for all practical purposes, nudity in witchcraft is an innovation that was introduced by Gerald Gardner, who was himself an extremely keen nudist (and, some have said, voyeur), and insisted that his coven always worked naked. This was formalized by his priestess, Doreen Valiente, as part of the "Charge of the Goddess", a sort of Wiccan creed, with the line "and as a sign that ye be really free, ye shall be naked in your rites".

Before Gardner's invention, the only real association between nudity and Western witchcraft was in Church propaganda, which frequently depicted witches' sabbats as repugnant **orgies** in which rings of aged, sagging men and women fornicated with grotesque demons around huge flaming bonfires. Propaganda aside, there is little hint that any medieval witch practised her spells nude – frankly, the weather in medieval Europe would have made that a risky proposition for much of the year. Gardner himself admitted that it was his experience of Indonesian witches practising naked that led him to insist on it as the will of the Goddess. It goes without saying that Indonesia's climate is far better suited to prancing around naked at night than is the case in England or Germany.

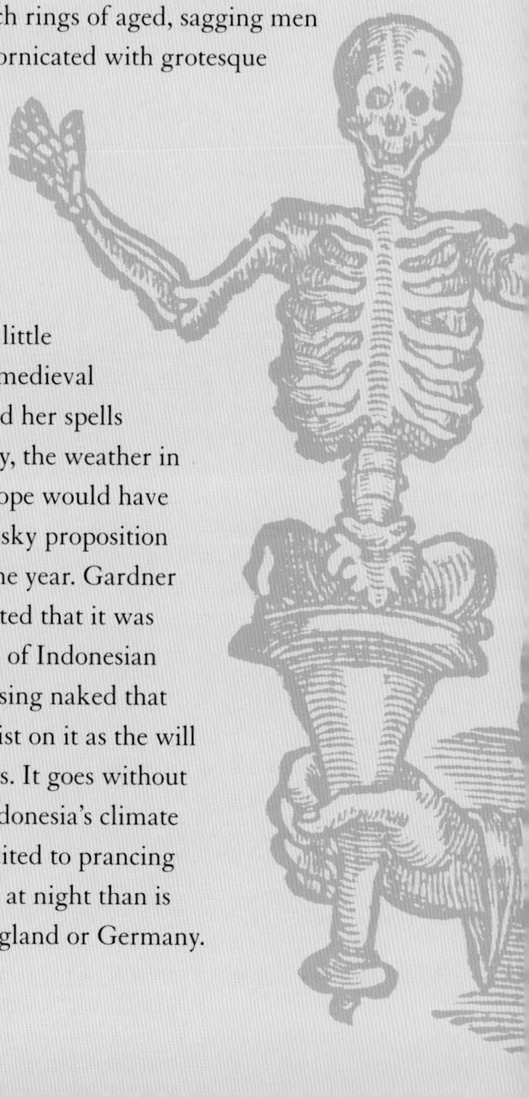

Mondragolla mascholo

cipera fiolli
se adio piaxera p̄ la
soa mixericordia et
sapie che se alla dona
vien dada el mascholo
el cōcipera fiolo maſ
chollo e seli vien dada
la femena el cōcipe
ra fia femena Esse

alla dona vien t
dada el mascholo
ella femena iſieme el
cōcipera fioli ch̄ non se
ra ne femena ne homo
Ma hauera como omo
e como femena :····

Questa erba se i genera
desperma de homo et na
se i terenì chaldi et vmidi

Wards against evil

Brass bells protect cattle from evil spells.

Whilst witches were purported to have a huge range of spells and tokens and other charms by which they could cause harm, the general populace was hardly powerless to resist their evil. There were all sorts of substances and objects that could be used to fend off witches and diffuse their powers – so many, in fact, that it's a wonder any witch ever managed to cause any harm at all.

Gemstones were thought to be particularly powerful against witchcraft. The extra expense of obtaining a rare stone was thought to add to its efficiency as a ward. Amber and coral were effective in warding off uses of the evil eye, while ruby, sardonyx and cat's-eye were thought to protect against general malicious witchcraft. Stones were worn in rings or, even better, used as part of an amulet that also contained helpful magical signs and symbols. A cheaper option, if you were concerned that a witch might try to enter your house, was to scatter **small stones** on the floor, just inside your door. A witch would be compelled – by obsessive-compulsive tendencies, perhaps – to count each one before proceeding, and if it took too long, daybreak would come and drive her off. Rice and even salt were used for the same purpose, with the extra advantage of being even harder to count. A stone with a natural hole through it – a **hagstone** – was a good ward to protect sleepers. In a bedroom, it would protect against night terrors; in a stable, it would keep horses from being hag-ridden to exhaustion.

Metal was useful, too. Brass was thought to repel evil spirits and witches. **Brass bells** were specially made to keep witches from livestock, and were hung round cattle's necks to keep them safe from

blighting. A **silver penny**, nailed to the bottom of a drinking trough, would make sure that the animals who drank from that trough were completely safe from all witchcraft attacks. Iron was a strong charm against demons, sorcerers and fairies. **Iron knives** and **crosses** were particularly popular; a witch was unable to cross cold-forged iron, and burying a cold iron knife under your doorstep, point down, made sure that no witch would ever be able to enter your house. In some places, whole villages were protected this way with knives ringing the area. Babies could be protected by hanging an open pair of iron **scissors** over their cradle. In Wales, where there was concern about young men being fooled into marriage by fairy maidens, it was said that the touch of cold iron would drive these sirens off.

There were plenty of resources around the kitchen, too. A special type of **beer**, if brewed in eggshells, could be used for driving off all sorts of evil spirits. It could protect against witch-sent nightmares, fend off fairies and dwarves who might want to replace your

An iron knife dating from the ninth or tenth century – perhaps once used as protection against witchcraft?

child with a changeling, and even drive away the hounds of the Wild Hunt, should one come near. Just plain **water** was a good defence, though. Witches, like vampires, were unable to cross running water, so a stream was always a powerful barrier. Church-prepared **holy water** was even better, of course. It was standard practice to sprinkle it at doors and windows, and on cattle, crops and children, to keep off witches, evil magic, bad spirits and all sorts of other nasties. Some churches sent out regular supplies of holy water to the surrounding community to ensure everyone was kept safe. **Salt** could help a home-owner to recognize a witch – they were supposedly unable to eat any salted foods.

Another powerful ally in the war against witchcraft was the humble chicken. **Roosters** were a major symbol of rebirth, light and the powers of good. Crowing roosters were enough to break up sabbats and to dispel enchantments. Witches hated them. Roosters could not keep witches away during the hours of darkness, however. On the other hand, it was possible to cancel a witch's spell by stealing a **hen** – from the witch, ideally – and sticking iron pins into its heart. The hen's sacrifice would drain the witch's power away.

Other items that witches couldn't pass included, ironically enough, a **broomstick**, if it was placed inside the threshold of a house. It could also be used as a charm against blight, if buried in a field.

Horseshoes had similar power. Iron horseshoes, nailed over doors, windows or chimneys, prevented evil from entering in. One could even be fixed to the

◊ *A symbol of light and goodness, roosters were hated by witches.*

◈ *The rowan tree was a powerful antidote to witchcraft.*

bed, to ward off nightmares. Once they were put in place, horseshoes had to be kept where they were, so they were usually nailed up very securely. If the cup of the shoe was pointing up, it would be good for attracting luck and good fortune, but no use for warding off evil; to keep witches out, the cup had to be pointing downwards. Another effective charm was a **wolf's head** nailed to the door – it would keep witches (and probably everyone else) away.

There was even a wide range of plants that could be useful in warding off witchcraft. The greatest of remedies was the fruit, leaves and even wood of the **rowan** tree. Crosses of rowan wood could be placed over a child's crib to keep it safe. They had to be renewed every May Day. Twigs of rowan tied to a horse's or cow's halter line would keep witches off the animal. Branches, placed cross-wise in a cowshed or stable, would keep evil away during the night entirely. In churchyards, rowan trees kept the dead in their place, preventing them from rising unwontedly. Rowanberry necklaces had the power to

cure those afflicted with magical disease. If there was no rowan around, **ash** trees were an acceptable substitute. It was even preferred in Cornwall, where ash twigs were tied around cow horns to rob witches of their power. **Hazel** was good against fairies. At midsummer livestock would be burned lightly with hazelwood brands to keep fairies away. Double **hazelnuts** – two nuts in one shell – were thought to be a strong weapon against fairies and witches, and to drive them away if flung at them.

Garlic, of course, is famous for fending off vampires, but garlic festoons were also good for repulsing witches and their spells. **Holly** was equally strong; sprigs of holly with berries attached provided a barrier that evil could not pass. The plant known as **houseleek** was also a powerful protector. All across Europe, people planted it on the roofs of their cottages to keep away witches and also to help prevent fires. **Misletoe** served a similar function, barring not just witches but also bad luck, fires and illness.

◈ *Left: Upward-facing horseshoes attract good fortune.*

6
"When Shall We Three Meet Again?"

"When Shall We Three Meet Again?"
Famous Covens from Fact and Fiction

⬙ A notorious coven — the three witches from "Macbeth", portrayed here by Henry Fuseli.

It has long been assumed that witches work better in groups. A coven of witches is a group of three or more who co-operate with each other, including meeting up from time to time to work on spells together. Some covens were presumed to live together under one roof, while others had members distributed throughout a widespread area – even, in a few notable cases, the whole world. Covens could be an invaluable source of support, fellowship and learning, or they could be little more than an excuse for satanic dupes to get involved in orgies.

The Berwick Witches

ᚻᚾᛁᚷᚱᛏᛁᚾᛗᚩᚻᚾᛁᚠᚱᛏᛁᚠᚱᚷᚩᚻᚩᛗᚾᚻᛗᚠᛣᚻᚩᚾᚩᚾᚠᚱᛗᛏᛁᚠᛁᚱᛗᚻᚠᛗᛗᚻᛁᛗᚩᚻᚾᛗᚷᚱᛏ

In 1590, North Berwick was a small village on the coast of Scotland, a short distance east of Edinburgh. A quiet, unassuming place, it was to become the centre of a series of trials that horrified all of Britain. From the first hints of witchcraft and foul play, detailed investigations undertaken by the King of Scotland himself gradually uncovered a vast plot to use satanic powers to take over the whole country. The leader of this heinous coven, Agnes Sampson, became the first person to be executed in Scotland for witchcraft, and several of her group followed her.

The story says that in the late autumn of 1590, a large coven of perhaps as many as 200 witches – both men and women – came together in an empty church near to North Berwick. Their goal was to conjure up a murderous storm, and use it to kill the King of Scotland. The spell called for the sacrifice of a black cat – one that had been specially prepared. First the cat was christened with the name of a recently dead local sailor, in a mocking send-up of Christian ceremony. It was then passed through the flame of a large fire repeatedly, burning and torturing it as it absorbed certain herbs and incenses from the material that was being burnt.

The dead man's corpse had been stolen from the local cemetery, and the witches hacked off the hands, feet and genitals of the man. The hands were tied to the semi-conscious cat's forward paws, left to left, right to right. The feet were tied to its rear paws, again left to left. Finally, the penis and testicles were threaded through and tied to the cat's belly. When the preparations were complete, one of the witches carried the prepared cat to the pier at Leith village and cast it into the sea with a final invocation.

No sooner had the cat sunk under the water than the skies turned as black as pitch and a howling wind erupted. Within moments, a terrible storm was in full force. A ship that was sailing in to Leith from Kinghorn was caught up by the towering waves and

The ruined church of North Berwick.

dashed against rocks, killing many sailors, but the witches kept the storm going. Their object wasn't just mayhem and death, it was the specific murder of King James of Scotland, on his way back to the country from Denmark with his new wife. The witches kept the storm rolling and directed it throughout the night, targeting the man-of-war carrying the royal couple. To their horror and dread, however, it managed to ride through the storm, avoiding destruction.

The first hints of the story emerged accidentally, during an investigation into suspected witchcraft in the Edinburgh area. Geillis Duncan, a young woman who worked as a servant in the city, had become known for her skills in nursing the sick back to health. This attracted attention. Geillis worked for a deputy bailiff named David Smeaton. He observed that she used to sneak out of the house some nights. Her destination on these occasions was a friend's house, an older woman. Geillis and her friend were in the habit of taking in any person who was injured, ill or otherwise in distress. They then proceeded to heal these poor unfortunates as best they could. They patched up all manner of people effectively and quickly, and started developing a good reputation as healers.

Naturally, this gave Bailiff Smeaton grounds for great suspicion. How could such things be done naturally and lawfully? He could not imagine it, and so was certain that his maid was performing her healing through "extraordinary and unlawful means". To help investigate his suspicions, Smeaton had Geillis questioned. The girl was tortured for several days, first by means of a form of early thumbscrew called "pilliwinkes" that were progressively tightened, forcing nail-heads and studded screws through the flesh and bone of the fingers, and then by binding her head with rope and winching it so tight that it ripped through skin and flesh. However, she held out until the questioners claimed to have found a witch-mark – a numb spot which did not respond to being jabbed with a needle – located on her neck. Finally, she confessed to having had the help of the devil in healing the sick.

Under further questioning, Geillis named a selection of fellow witches, including Agnes Sampson, Agnes Thomson, Dr James Fian, Barbara Napier and Euphemia McCalyan. Agnes Sampson – a "grave and matronly gentlewoman" – was revealed as the eldest and most senior of the witches, and was called in. Agnes initially refused to confess to any

North Berwick's strikingly lovely landscape.

◇ A late-sixteenth-century print illustrating the story of the Berwick witches.

wrongdoing, so her interrogators shaved every hair from her body and searched for a devil's mark of some sort, as had been found on Geillis Duncan. Once they had spotted a likely mark, they proceeded to torture the woman in a similar manner to Geillis, with a binding-rope around her head and neck. When that did not yield results, they forced an iron "bridle" into her mouth. This gouged into her tongue, lips and cheeks, and prevented her from sleeping. She broke within a few days, and started confessing, and King James was there to listen to her confessions.

Agnes Sampson proved a fairly creative confessor. She started modestly, as Geillis had – they had used magic spells to cure diseases, she had a satanic familiar in the form of a dog called Elva, and so on. Agnes's tales quickly became more colourful, however. She readily implicated the others named by Geillis, and brought yet more people into the list. Eventually, the network would spread to 70 or so people who were implicated in

the plot, including a local nobleman, the Earl of Bothwell. According to Agnes, large groups of witches held regular conventions together at the North Berwick church, of up to 90 women and six men. They lit the place up with black candles, got drunk on wine, and worshipped Satan with chants. Geillis Duncan provided musical entertainment on a Jew's harp.

On the occasion of October 31, 1590, the devil had come to the congregation, and they had worshipped him by performing the obscene kiss on his backside. The devil then instructed them on how to use the magic of images to turn spells against the king, and gave them the instructions on how to prepare the magical cat sacrifice to raise a storm. They were ordered to destroy James and his bride, Anne. When Agnes Thomson asked the devil why he was so determined that James should be killed, the dark one answered that James was his greatest enemy in all the world, and that he hated and feared him. Agnes Sampson then explained the ritual with the cat and the attempt to sink James's ship. The king, recalling that his voyage home had been rough, immediately concluded that the matter was true, and that he was in mortal danger. Agnes was burned at the stake shortly afterwards, and Geillis followed her very quickly.

One of the people mentioned by Geillis was Dr James Fian, the master of Saltpans School. Like the others, he initially refused to confess to any wrongdoing, but after a period of some days during which he was questioned by the torturers, he recanted and was prepared to give details and name names. Fian admitted that he served as clerk of the coven. His job was to bear witness to recording the names of the witches at each coven gathering, and in addition he had to take their oaths of service to the devil. He would also write down and record any specific matter that the devil ordered him to record.

Fian then gave an example of his magic by telling the inquisitors about a love spell that he had attempted to cast on a young local gentlewoman who had caught his eye. Having spotted the girl, he went to her brother, whom he taught, and persuaded the lad to get him some of his sister's hair from her head while she was asleep. The brother – ignorant of the reason – agreed, and tried to do just that. Unfortunately, the girl woke up and yelled for their mother. When the mother questioned her son and forced the story out of him, she became suspicious of the reason for the request. She directed the lad to get some hairs from one of the family's cows to give to the schoolmaster. The lad obeyed, and Fian, none the wiser, cast his spell. He was both surprised and dismayed to be followed around by the cow for some days.

Fian was tortured further, but did not confess to anything else despite the king's best attempts. It is recorded that Fian's legs were totally destroyed by the torture process known as the "boots". This cruel device was basically a pair of spiked wedges which ran the entire length from knee to ankle, roped around each leg. The torturer would ask a question and then hammer the "boot" tighter. Typically, questioning continued until the wedges were so close together that the legs were reduced to useless marrow-soaked shards. Death frequently followed.

It is known that Fian's corpse was burned in late January 1591. A fourth member of the conspiracy, Agnes Thomson, was also burned at the stake.

King James, feeling vindicated by his uncovering of such heinous plots against him – and justly proud of his status as the devil's main enemy on Earth – went on to write a scholarly treatise, "Demonology", based on what he had learnt. When Elizabeth I died in 1603, James became King of England as well. In his opinion, the English witchcraft laws were weak and lenient, and he did his best to strengthen them, to help bring justice and the rule of God across the kingdom. Not coincidentally, James I holds the record for hanging more witches than any other English monarch.

It was finally ascertained that nine individuals had been the ringleaders of the North Berwick coven. These were Agnes Sampson, her daughter (whose name is unrecorded), Agnes Thomson, Barbara Napier, Donald Robson, Geillis Duncan, Euphemia McCalyan, James Fian and Margaret Thomsoun. Almost 60 other individuals were named as lesser members. Agnes Sampson, Agnes Thomson, James Fian and Geillis Duncan were executed as witches. The rest may simply have been imprisoned, or even released after their "questioning".

Name: The North Berwick Coven
Key members: Geillis Duncan, James Fian, Euphemia McCalyan, Barbara Napier, Donald Robson, Agnes Sampson, Miss Sampson, Agnes Thomson and Margaret Thomsoun
Date: 1590
Description: An extended coven of classic witches/satanic dupes uncovered when a small-minded junior bailiff found it unimaginable that his maid might be able to help tend the sick without an ulterior motive
Known for: Trying to kill King James and his wife
Nature: Evil, apparently
Power: Strong
Type: Classic/Satanic dupes
Region: North Berwick, Scotland

Jaguar Moon

ᚾᛗᚠᛝᚱᛏᛃᚾᛗᚢᚾᛌᚠᛈᚱᛏᛃᛈᚱᚠᚲᚾᚦᛗᚾᚼᛗᚠᚼᚲᚾᚦᚾᛈᚠᛗᛏᛃᛚᚦᛗᚺᛖᚠᛗᚼᛃᛝᛗᚠᚦ

A Wiccan coven on the cutting edge of magical and physical technology, JaguarMoon has been in existence for five years. Dedicated to helping solitary witches and novices grow in the craft, the coven exists only on-line, where members can access from all over the world if needs be. It also offers an almost unique chance to examine the workings and purposes of a modern Wiccan coven from the inside without actually having to join first.

As a teaching coven, JaguarMoon structures its work to offer students a strong grounding in – and understanding of – every aspect of basic Wicca. Students are then encouraged to draw their own conclusions. By keeping the teaching within a coven structure, and having both teachers and mentors on hand, it means that students have the opportunity to participate in a genuinely functional coven without the need for a binding commitment.

The High Priestess of JaguarMoon, Lady Maat, has been interested in witchcraft since childhood. Her first exposure to modern paganism was enough to hook her, and at thirteen she dedicated herself to following the Wiccan craft. After years of experience with a wide range of covens, magical groups and solitary workings, she became involved in the 1997 formation of a new, experimental cybercoven called ShadowMoon under a High Priestess named Lady Mystara and her acting High Priest, White Pine.

ShadowMoon proved to be a successful basis for coven operation, and Maat found herself rounding out her knowledge of magickal topics while also getting to know a group of like-minded people. One of her first friends in ShadowMoon was a fellow entrant named Hyssop. The ShadowMoon coven borrowed heavily from traditional Gardnerian Wicca, with Lady Mystara

An anonymous coven of modern witches cast a reconciliatory spell to mark the 300th anniversary of the Salem witch trial.

adding in all sorts of information and teachings from her personal experience. After the introductory instruction period, Maat was initiated into ShadowMoon formally and started helping Mystara to make a coherent tradition out of the ShadowMoon material. This eventually led Maat to create a complex lesson plan from the voluminous amounts of material that Mystara wanted to impart to the coven. Hyssop's husband, Ash, also joined the coven and became another good friend of Maat's.

The coven got into trouble when White Pine left the group – and Wicca in general – for personal reasons. The extra workload was too much for Lady Mystara to cope with and, despite assistance from Maat and others, she became ill. Mystara had a vision of founding a tradition of hundreds of cybercovens worldwide, and she started pushing ShadowMoon's initiates to progress as quickly as possible, so that they could go out and start forming the next wave. Not everyone was comfortable with the new direction. Coven work quickly turned into little more than priesthood training, and the tone of the teachings became increasingly traditional Gardnerian. Hyssop, who had little interest in running her own coven, left the group; her husband, Ash, followed.

Maat decided to stay with ShadowMoon up to the third degree initiation, so becoming a High Priestess in her own right, and then planned to leave to form her own group – partly in line with Mystara's vision, and partly because she too was less comfortable with the direction ShadowMoon had taken. One night,

⬥ *Witch burning in the sixteenth century.*

Maat had a powerful dream in which Grandmother Jaguar – Totem guardian of the South, and of rebirth and growth – came to her and told her that the new coven would be called JaguarMoon. Independently, Hyssop, Ash and another of Maat's friends, Estrella, all contacted her during the following week to offer their services if she should ever choose to start a coven of her own.

Lady Maat was raised to the third degree in May 2000, and hived off from ShadowMoon as planned. On May 8th, she met Ash, Hyssop and Estrella in cyberspace, and together they dedicated the new coven. Right from the start, Lady Maat was determined to take a different path from that of ShadowMoon. Her goal was to provide structure without stifling rules, and to embrace a philosophy that supported the coven's members as people instead of trying to separate them from the world. Combined with a focus on teaching those who wanted to learn, the coven offered a space where students could experience and learn from the group structure without having to take any formal oaths. Critically, the coven decided not to push ShadowMoon's goal of creating its own tradition; if that happened, it would be accepted, but the emphasis would be on learning, not on being trained.

JaguarMoon has gone from strength to strength. As a teaching coven, it follows the path of American Eclectic Wicca – a broad path that bases philosophy and ritual chiefly on the modern Wiccan thinking of American authors such as Starhawk and Scott Cunningham. Most of its adherents accept that Wicca was created by Gerald Gardner, but also feel that his work was historically rooted. Pragmatically, the path's ethos could be summed up as "Use what works; discard what doesn't." The coven is structured loosely as a wheel, with Lady Maat at the centre as High Priestess, linked to all the coven members and students. They in turn are linked to their mentors, and loosely to one another.

JaguarMoon believes strongly in providing a firm structure in the traditional Wiccan sense of initiation, oath, magickal tradition and lineage and so on, but applied in such a manner as to avoid restriction and hierarchy wherever possible. Keeping an eye on the future and the possibility for opening its own branch in the traditions, the coven prefers to record material and results and track possibilities for evolution and improvement. Chaos has its place, but growth is more likely when there is form and direction. JaguarMoon is in its fifth year, a proven test of stability for any magickal group, virtual or real. Membership numbers for the core coven have stayed fairly consistent – around 100 students have been trained by the group. At the same time, the coven has also been progressing its internal members, recently raising another of its number to the third degree.

Concentrating as it does on teaching and training, JaguarMoon believes in offering its students a broad range of magickal information. In the coven's tradition and belief system, teaching is a sacred devotion to the God and Goddess, as well as being a good way to develop, and to help others do the same. It does not believe that Wicca is the "One True Path" and encourages all seekers to make up their own minds. Having completed the year's training course, students are left with a strong grounding in basic Wicca. The class – called "The Art of Ritual" – includes material on almost every aspect of modern witchcraft. This includes the history of Wicca, the structure of covens, the witch's Rede and ethical issues, healing, visualisation, meditation, herb-lore, basic ritual, working with divine beings, and much more besides.

The goal, simply, is to help solitary witches and novices develop their own concepts and practices and learn how to separate true knowledge from mumbo-jumbo. The course has no grades or exams. Learning is at the student's discretion, but takes an average of five to seven months. The only fee is a nominal contribution towards bandwitch cost – $20 a year – but the coven has a policy of never turning down an applicant for financial reasons.

Contrary to some people's expectations, Lady Maat finds that interacting through the medium of cyberspace is no barrier to effective group magick. In Wicca, group spellcraft is all about making an energy connection with one another. Cyberspace may be a notional idea, but the truth remains that via the use of a computer as a tool, there is a direct energy link between your keyboard and the screen of any person you are communicating with. It is a simple fact of physics – the information you send is encoded as energy and transmitted to the recipients.

The results, Maat says, speak for themselves.

Cybermagick and technopaganism are still fledgling fields, but they are a powerful research interest at JaguarMoon. Drawing on her cybermagick experiences with ShadowMoon and JaguarMoon, Lady Maat published a groundbreaking book in 2002, *The Virtual Pagan*, under her day-to-day name of Lisa McSherry. This work was a cut-down version of a longer, more detailed ebook, CyberCoven.Org, which is available on the web at the site of the same name. An advanced work, "CyberCraft.Org: Creating Magickal Groups", is now ready for print, and Lady Maat is working on a book of spells to accompany *The Virtual Pagan*.

For further information, JaguarMoon can be found at http://www.jaguarmoon.org

Name: JaguarMoon
Key members: Lady Maat, Lady Mouse, Hyssop
Date: 2000+
Description: A teaching coven following the American Eclectic Wiccan tradition, dedicated to providing teaching and support to all parties interested in seriously developing in Wicca
Known for: Stable, welcoming atmosphere
Nature: Good
Power: Unknown
Type: Wicca
Region: Cyberspace

The Charmed Ones

ᚾᛗᚠᚲᚱᛏᛁᚾᛗᛟᚾᛁᛁᚠᚠᛏᛩᚠᚠᚲᛩᚾᛩᛗᚾᛩᛗᚠᛩᚹᚾᛩᚾᛈᛈᛗᛏᛁᛁᛏᛗᛩᚠᛗᛗᛩᛩᛗᚠᛩ

A popular and long-running television series,
Charmed tells the story of three bickering sisters
who discover that they are witches destined to
save the world from the forces of evil. The three
Halliwell sisters uncover their talent after inheriting
a sprawling San Francisco manor house from their
grandmother. After taking over the house, the
youngest of the three, Phoebe, discovers an ancient
green leather book hidden in the dust at the bottom
of a trunk in the attic. On closer examination, the
sisters see that it is titled "The Book of Shadows".

Inside the front cover, an ancient woodcarving
depicts three witches gathered in a circle, casting
spells. A scriptwork incantation faces it: "Hear now
the words of the witches, the secrets we hid in the
night. The oldest of spells are invoked here. The
great gift of magic is sought. In this night and in
this hour I call upon the ancient power. Bring your
powers to we sisters three. We want the power. Give
us the power." By reading the words aloud, Phoebe
unlocks the power hidden in the three sisters,
changing their lives forever.

The sisters quickly discover that the Book
of Shadows is a lot more that just an old book.
It predicts the arrival of a coven of three ultra-
powerful good witches, the descendants of a long

line of white witches. The protectors of the innocent, the Charmed Ones are warned to beware of evil warlocks, Dark-lighters and other beings who will try to kill them and absorb their powers. Prue, Piper and Phoebe quickly realize that they are the Charmed Ones of the book, and they find that they are going to have to put aside their differences and work together – while keeping the family secret hidden – if they are going to survive.

It turns out that the girls – glamorous twenty-somethings doing their best to maintain their "normal" lives – come from a line of witches dating all the way back to the Salem witch trials. Their ancestor, Melinda Warren, was burned at the stake, but prophesied that her line would continue, and

each generation of the Warren witches would be stronger than the one before. Every woman in their family since then has had magical powers. The three Charmed Ones are different, though; they have the cumulative boost of the "Power of Three", which greatly enhances their magic if all three of them get involved in casting the spell.

In addition to their spellcraft, each of the three has magical gifts. Prue, who is the eldest and works in an auction house, can move objects just by concentrating on them. She later develops the ability to leave her body. Piper is the middle sister and manages first a restaurant and then a nightclub. She can stop time for a period, effectively freezing everyone else, and later also gains the power to cause

◇ *The sisters discover an ancient leather-bound book in the attic.*

explosions. Phoebe, the youngest, is a martial arts expert, a psychology student, and can see into the future sometimes. She later learns how to levitate herself, effectively gaining the ability to fly.

The Charmed Ones dedicate themselves to saving "innocents" – everyday people under threat from the forces of darkness. They are assisted by a range of angelic, kindly ghosts called White-Lighters. Their enemies include assorted demons, who were never human; warlocks, who were human but sold themselves to evil; and Dark-Lighters, the bad equivalent of the White-Lighters – spirits released from Hell to cause havoc and tempt mortals.

Piper eventually conceives a child with a White-Lighter, greatly increasing the intensity of the demonic attacks on the trio because the forces of evil know that the baby, Wyatt, is destined for even greater things than the Charmed Ones. Some time later, Prue is killed by a demon, and the two remaining sisters are joined by a previously unknown half-sister named Paige. The three share the same

mother, but Paige was also fathered by a White-Lighter and, after Prue's death, is drawn to the family. Paige works as a social worker and has the ability to teleport from place to place. She can also teleport objects directly to her from distant locations. Together, the new trio continue where the sisters left off, doing their best to vanquish the heart of all evil, the Source, so as to make the world safe for ever.

Name: The Charmed Ones
Key members: Prue, Piper, Phoebe and Paige Halliwell
Date: 1998–2005
Description: A hereditary coven of three beautiful, glamorous, wealthy, young starlet-witches working for the forces of good
Known for: Squabbling, helping people
Nature: Good
Power: Very strong
Type: Classic/Wicca
Region: San Francisco

The Salem Witch Coven

ᚾᛗᚷᛈᛏᛁᚾᛗᛟᚾᛏᛚᚠᛈᛏᛁᛈᛈᚷᛉᛟᛗᚾᛉᛗᚠᛉᛗᚾᛟᚾᛈᚠᛈᛗᛏᛁᛚᛏᛗᛉᛗᛗᛉᛁᛗᚠᛟ

The Reverend Samuel Parris was a figure of some political controversy in 1690s' Salem. Originally appointed by a group of would-be breakaway villagers, his contract included the title and deeds to the parsonage he was housed in – a most unusual and very generous benefit. His position thus caused a significant amount of tension. To add to his woes, his wife was an invalid, and his nine-year-old daughter, Betty, was also sickly. He was assisted around the house by his orphaned niece, 12-year-old Abigail, and by a Barbadian slave woman, Tituba, who used to tell the children and their friends spooky stories and lead them in fortune-telling experiments.

Following some distressing fortune-telling sessions, Abigail and Betty started to have odd fits. No medical cause could be established, and witchcraft was immediately suspected. The girls were questioned as to who could have possibly bewitched them. Although reluctant to talk at first,

they eventually capitulated – and in so doing, gradually uncovered a vast purported coven right through Salem society.

The first names the girls gave were those of the slave woman Tituba and two other women of the village, Sarah Osborne and Sarah Good. Osborne was old and had not been to church in over a year; Good was homeless and slightly mad, and begged from door to door, muttering as she did so. All three women were outsiders, and prime candidates. With accusations ready, magistrates became involved. Betty, Abigail and six other girls were present for the questionings, and all eight would regularly throw themselves around the floor screaming and wailing in the presence of the accused. The two Sarahs maintained innocence – American witch investigations did not use torture, thankfully – but the slave woman, Tituba, was quick to confess.

Her testimony was vivid. She described cats that talked, blood-red rats, and a tall man in black. She said that she had signed a book, and that the other accused – and others whose names she could not read – had also signed. The three were jailed, but Tituba's

◈ *The Salem Witch Museum.*

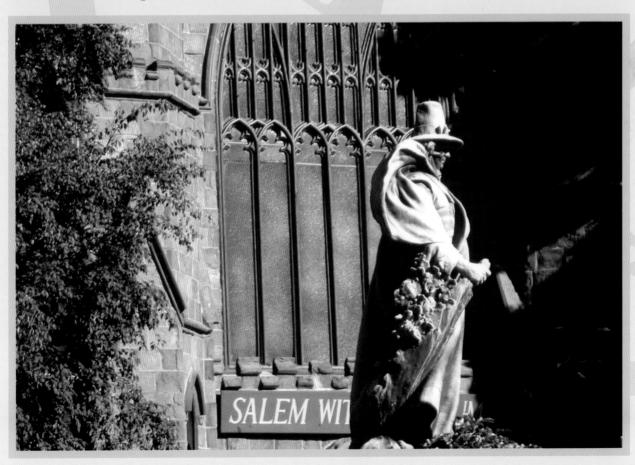

◊ *The Salem witch trial provoked stormy scenes in the courtroom.*

comments about other names struck home, and accusations continued. Another of the girls, Ann Putnam, accused a woman named Martha Corey. She attended church regularly, but was unpopular because of her opinionated, outspoken nature. The next accused, Rebecca Nurse, was kind, generous and well liked however, and her inclusion started to cast doubts on the child's testimony. A farmer and taverner named John Proctor was vocal in his doubt, saying that Ann and the other girls would cast all of Salem as devils, and what they needed was a sound beating; soon he and his wife Elizabeth were in jail. Ann then turned her testimony to the former minister of Salem, George Burroughs, and named him as the Black Man and leader of all Massachusetts' witches. Having been widowed three times, with rumours of abuse hanging

over him, he was a plausible candidate. By the middle of 1692, some 200 people were in jail, mostly on the evidence of Ann Putnam and the other girls.

A new court was formed to investigate the whole matter and verify that all 200 were part of the coven. The imprisoned witches were tried in small batches. The first trial was of a lone woman, Bridget Bishop. Builders claimed to have found dolls stuck through with pins whilst repairing her cellar, and she was swiftly hung. The second trial group included Sarah Good and Rebecca Nurse, with three other women. The children gave substantial "spectral evidence", and all except Rebecca Nurse were found guilty. As soon as the jurors announced her innocence, however, Ann and the other children started thrashing and screaming and rolling around on the floor. The judge asked the jury to reconsider, and in the face of the children's behaviour, they changed their minds. All five were duly hanged. Even on the gallows, Sarah Good was protesting her innocence.

Six deaths did little to calm the fever. More and more people started displaying "witch affliction" similar to that which the girls were manifesting, and naming people as their tormentors. People from all walks of life were accused. Another group were tried, found guilty and hanged, again mostly through spectral evidence, and then another and another. But doubts were creeping in. The former minister, George Burroughs, recited the Lord's Prayer flawlessly on the gibbet – a feat supposedly impossible for witches – before his execution. Another man, Giles Corey, refused to answer any questions at all, protesting against the stupidity of the whole thing. The court's legal remedy to his silence was to weight him with rocks until he answered. He stayed silent for two days, while the weight was increased. Finally, he was killed, never once having answered a question – a clear protest against the trials. Finally, Rebecca Nurse's sister, Mary Easty, wrote a moving petition just before her execution in which she did not plead for clemency, but said merely that she knew the magistrates would not harm an innocent willingly, and begged them to let God direct them to be absolutely certain of the guilt of those they hung after her.

Finally, the public appetite for blood started to lessen, and by October most people believed that at least some of the executed had been innocent. Shortly after, the remaining prisoners – still well over 150 people – were pardoned for release, on the grounds that the Governor would rather release ten witches than kill one innocent person. The total death toll was 19 hangings, one death of natural causes in prison (Sarah Osborne) and one death by crushing. Reverend Parris and his family left the village a few years later, having given back the title and deeds to the parsonage in return for a sum of back-pay. Some ten years later, in 1706, Ann Putnam gave a public apology to all the families affected by the trials, saying that she had been deceived by Satan. She died unmarried, and was buried with her parents in an unmarked grave.

One of the witch houses in Salem.

Name: The Salem Witches
Key members: Tituba, Sarah Osborne, Sarah Good, George Burroughs, Bridget Bishop
Date: 1690–1692
Description: A disparate coven hiding within Salem society and cursing people – especially one group of young girls – with occasional fits
Known for: The only witch executions on US soil
Nature: Evil
Power: Weak
Type: Satanic dupes
Region: Massachusetts

7
"Something Wicked This Way Comes!"

"Something Wicked This Way Comes!"
The Most Evil of Witches

Jadis, the evil White Witch, keeps Narnia on permanent ice.

Witches are a target of suspicion by default. Their powers and talents are unfamiliar to our everyday life, easily open to abuse. We have been told for centuries that they are evil, satanic, in league with the devil and so on. The powers that are most commonly associated with them are geared to cause harm. So it's little surprise that there's a certain assumption that witches are going to be bad. Some, however, are a lot worse than others. Over the course of this chapter, we'll have a look at some of the very worst of all witches – the most destructive, the most murderous, the most power-crazed of a notoriously bad type to begin with. Encouragingly, they are all the constructions of fiction and mythology: for once, the real witches of history were not able to be evil enough to get a look in.

The White Witch

ᚺᚹᛈᛁᚷᛏᛁᚺᛗᚩᚾᛁ ᛚᛂᚠᛏᛁᛈᚠᚷᚪᚩᚾᚩᛗᚾᚻᛗᚠᛐᚹᚾᚩᚾᛈᚠᛈᛗᛏᛁᛚᛐᛗᚻᚠᛗᛗᚻᛁᛗᚠᚩᚾᛗᚠᛌᚾᛐ

The White Witch is the tyrannical dictator of the magical land of Narnia – and the great villain of the book *The Lion, The Witch and the Wardrobe* by C. S. Lewis. Merciless, cruel, power-hungry and sadistic, she was universally feared. She controlled all sorts of evil creatures, and if anyone did anything to upset her, she would turn the offending person into a lifeless stone statue.

Biography

The White Witch was mired in deceit and foul play right from the start. Her very rule was based on theft; she used the basest of trickery to gain the position of ruling over Narnia. Once she had attained that position, however, certain ancient magic spells woven through the land sealed her right to rule. Under the terms of these spells, the fairness of her position was irrelevant. The same magic gave her literal ownership over anyone who willingly chose to follow her – such beings became her possessions entirely – and she was also given control of traitors, whether they chose to follow her or not. Amongst other benefits, owning a person gave the White Witch the right to kill that person at any moment she chose, for any reason whatsoever.

The White Witch made her home in a labyrinthine castle formed out of ice. Her powers were especially resonant with coldness and winter. To help enforce her rule, she had a sprawling army consisting of foul-tempered, murderous wolves, cruel black-haired dwarves, and a wide range of other evil creatures of all types. She also maintained a huge network of spies hidden amongst the bulk of the populace, making use of those people who had chosen to follow her, or who had come to her through treachery. Anyone who tried to defy her will or thwart her orders would invariably end up petrified into one of the many statues that ghoulishly filled her ice castle.

Originally, the White Witch came to Narnia from a different world. Jadis was the Empress of the gigantic city-world called Charn, and ruled over her race, the Jinn, descendants of Lilith. Tiring of Jadis's rule, her sister attempted to rebel and seize power. Despite Jadis's half-giant heritage, the two sisters were closely matched, and the struggle became desperately bitter. Rather than lose to her sister, Jadis uttered the Deplorable Word, which instantly destroyed every other living thing in the whole of Charn. After a time alone in the ruins of Charn, she found her way into the Wood Between Worlds, an endless forest filled with pools of water that served as portals to other realms. From there, she came to Narnia as it was being created by the Emperor-Over-Sea.

On her way through the Emperor's garden, she stole a special apple. Eating it made her immortal, and bleached every last drop of colour in her skin, leaving her as white as snow. Knowing that the Emperor's son, Aslan The Lion, had given dominion over Narnia to the "sons of Adam and the daughters of Eve", Jadis made her way over the sea to Narnia. By the time she arrived, no true human had been in the land for centuries. She claimed descent from Eve, and demanded authority as a servant of the Emperor-Over-Sea. In the absence of any real humans to tell the difference, she was taken at her word, and given power. As soon as the newly titled White Witch was in power, the ancient and mysterious laws of the Deep Magic protected her. She wasted no time in twisting the land into a barren, hopeless, eternal winter – "Always winter, but never Christmas" – and instituting a repressive regime. As the Emperor's executioner, she killed her victims on a stone altar.

A century passed. She had long been aware of a prophecy which stated that two male humans and two female humans would end her reign and reclaim their rightful thrones. Her spies were always hunting for any true human who might have stumbled into the enchanted land. When the four children who are the heroes of the book found their way into Narnia, the witch tempted one, Edmund, over to her side with enchanted Turkish delight. She then used her pawn to aid her attempts to kill the others. Edmund finally became aware of her evil, though, and repented. Aslan the Lion gave his life to free him from her grasp, and the White Witch thought she had finally won complete dominion.

The Deep Magic resurrected Aslan, however, and in that moment she was defeated.

Author C. S. Lewis readily acknowledged that *The Lion, The Witch and the Wardrobe* was a Christian allegory tale. Aside from the general thrust of the story, there are many clear parallels between the White Witch and the biblical figure of Satan. Her right to kill her followers, for example, is a simple reworking of Satan imposing spiritual death by taking sinners to Hell. Lewis's objective was to create a story that would help introduce children to Christianity's spiritual concepts, without making heavy weather of the actual dogma attached to it. As such, the White Witch is probably best thought of as a rather upper-echelon variant of a satanic dupe.

Name: Jadis, The White Witch

Age: Immortal

Description: Pale, almost albino woman with a thin face and sharp, cruel features

Dominant abilities: Magic, weather control

Traits: Dictatorial, short tempered

Nature: Evil

Power: Very strong

Type: Satanic dupe

Domain: Transformation, weather

Goal: To crush all joy out of Narnia

Key equipment: Wand

Creator: C. S. Lewis

Elly Kedward, the Blair Witch

ᚾᛗᚠᚷᚱᛏᛃᚾᛗᚦᚾᚷᛚᚠᚱᛏᛃᚠᚠᚷᚦᚾᚦᛗᚾᚺᛗᚠᚦᚺᚾᚾᚦᚾᚠᚠᚾᛏᛃᚺᛁᛏᛗᚺᚠᛗᛗᚺᛃᛗᚦᚾᚾᛗᚠᚷᚱᛏ

Unlike most witches, the legends surrounding Elly Kedward really begin with her death. In the 200 and more years since her passing, she has kept up a steady stream of murderous acts and other forms of malicious mayhem. Her most recent appearance ended in the murder of three students in the Black Hills above Burkittsville, Maryland, USA in 1994 — events that were depicted in the film *The Blair Witch Project*.

Biography

Elly Kedward emigrated to the USA from Ireland late in the 18th century, possibly to get away from the chaos of the Gordon Riots in 1780. In 1785, already advancing in years, she settled in the small town of Blair, in Maryland. She quickly found that her separatist beliefs marked her out in the strict Catholic atmosphere of the small town. The following year, as autumn wound to a close, she became the focus of a witch scare. Several of the town's children told investigators that the woman had lured them to her home individually, and then pricked their fingers with pins to get drops of their blood.

◊ *Heather Donahue was one of the Blair Witch's most recent victims.*

A trial followed quickly, and the puritan community found Kedward guilty of witchcraft. There seems to have been either some doubt or fear involved in the decision, however, for rather than burning the witch, the townsfolk decided to exile her from the village without food or blankets. As the first snows of winter were coming down, Elly Kedward was taken up into the wooded hills behind Blair and abandoned to die of exposure.

That should have been the end of it, but it proved to be only the beginning. Details are only sketchy, because the panic was so intense that no one stopped to chronicle events, but by the end of that winter, all of her accusers had mysteriously vanished. This included over half the children of the town, all her jurors, the party who banished her, and most of those who gave evidence against her. As soon as the snows were melted enough, the terrified survivors abandoned the town and fled. They declared the town of Blair anathema, and told everyone that it, and the Black Hills behind it, were cursed. As a follow-up, a small, sensationalized book was published in 1809 titled *The Blair Witch Cult*. It gave a highly coloured and fictionalized version of the events of the winter of 1786–7, and described many satanic rites that Elly Kedward is supposed to have performed. The contents were never authenticated; few copies were sold, and only one is known to have survived to the present day.

In 1824, railroad barons driving tracks through Maryland discovered the abandoned site of Blair. They were quick to make use of the location; it was swiftly repaired and resettled, and named Burkittsville, population 194. Today, Burkittsville is still in place in Frederick County, Maryland – approximately one hour by car from Washington DC.

Less than a year later, a group of townspeople were at the Tappy East Creek, near Burkittsville. Several children were playing in the water, including a little girl named Eileen Treacle. To the people's horror, she fell into the shallow water and was drowned. Several witnesses insisted that they saw a ghostly white hand rise up from the water, grab the little girl, and drag her under while she screamed and thrashed. The girl sank into the mud of the stream, and then everything was quiet again. Despite extensive frantic searching by the girl's parents and many other townspeople, no trace of her body was ever found – peculiar, given that the water she was playing in was only a foot or so deep. For the next thirteen days, the water of the creek was covered with a black, oily film and choked with many strange wooden stick figures floating in the filth.

Nothing much happened for the next 50 years, except that there were persistent rumours from farmers using the creek to water their cattle that the stream was polluted in some way. Every so often, a cow drinking from the creek would mysteriously sicken and die, or give birth to a calf with "unnatural" defects. After a time, the farmers started keeping their animals away from the creek entirely.

Then, in 1886, an eight-year-old child named Robin Weaver went missing from Burkittsville town. A search party of seven men immediately went out to look for the child. Two days later, the search party had not returned so a second, larger party was assembled. Robin Weaver returned while the second party was away, seemingly unaware that any time had passed. Meanwhile, some distance up the creek at a location known as Coffin Rock, the second search party found the first. The seven men were bound to each other in a circle on the coffin rock, hand to hand and foot to foot, facing out. Each man had been mutilated around the head and feet with strange, pagan symbols carved deep into the flesh, and then disembowelled. By the blood around the symbols and ropes, it was clear to see that all

seven had been alive whilst the atrocities were performed on them. The second party hurried back to town to fetch the Sheriff and witnesses. When the group returned to Coffin Rock some few hours later, there was no trace of any of the bodies. Even the bloodstains on the rock had been removed. Only the stench of death remained, thickening the air and revolting the group.

Another 50 years passed before Elly Kedward made her presence felt again, this time through the person of a local hermit. Rustin Parr was born in 1903. A quiet, pleasant young man, Rustin was orphaned at an early age, and lived with his aunt and uncle. He was said to have a deep and powerful love of nature, and no one was particularly surprised when he started building a house up in the hills in 1925, at the age of 22. The site of the house was four hours walk from town, and it took him the best part of five years to finish its construction. During that time, he worked at his uncle's shop diligently, building the house in his spare time. When he finished construction in 1930, he had a beautiful three-story cottage next to a pretty creek. He kept working at his uncle's shop for a few more years, but gradually he started spending less time in town and more time in the woods. When his aunt died in 1935, his uncle moved back to his native home of Baltimore, and Rustin's visits to town dried up almost completely. He lived peacefully up in the Black Hills, smoking his pipe and happily exploring the woods. His visits to town were biannual, to pick up supplies of items he couldn't get for himself.

In November of 1940, children started to disappear from Burkittsville. Eight were reported missing between then and May 1941. Finally, on May 25th, Rustin Parr came down to Burkittsville market and declared to all and sundry that he had finally finished. The police took custody of the 38-year-old man, and were horrified at the story he told them. Whilst walking through the woods, Parr claimed to have seen the ghost of an old woman in a long, dark, hooded cloak, but with unpleasantly furry legs. At first the ghost evaded him – he would call out or chase, only to find that she had disappeared. After a time the ghost stopped appearing visually, and lodged itself in his head as a set of eerie voices issuing commands and telling him things he didn't want to know. The voices spoke in odd languages sometimes, too. Identifying themselves as Elly Kedward, the voices gave Parr orders that he found he was unable to resist. At first he was made to do odd things such as go to sleep in the cellar for a week at a time, but it wasn't long before he was ordered to sneak down to Burkittsville and snatch the first two children that he saw.

All in all, Parr took eight children from the town, starting with Emily Hollands and ending with Kyle Brodie. He kept them in the cellar, and tortured them ritually for days at a time before killing them. Parr was told to maintain a rota, with one being treated, and one waiting, but found himself unable to perform while he was being watched. His answer was to make the victim-in-waiting stand in the corner of the cellar, facing the wall, so he didn't have to look at the child. After he had killed seven children, the witch appeared to him and told him that he was finished; all he had to do to finish up was to go into town and tell everyone, and then she would leave him alone for ever. Parr released the Brodie boy, weeping as he did so, and then went into town to obey his last orders.

The police hurried up to Parr's house. When they got there, they found the cottage looking weathered and dilapidated. Kyle Brodie was sitting on the front porch, dazed and clearly in shock. The child was unable to speak. In the cellar, police discovered seven graves holding the missing children. From the more recent corpses, it was clear that each one had been severely mutilated around the head and feet, with strange symbols hacked into the flesh. The children had then been fatally disembowelled.

Kyle Brodie, who had spent two months in the Parr house, never recovered. He never spoke another word, and spent the next thirty years in institutions until his early death. Rustin Parr was tried, convicted and hanged with almost unseemly haste, but not before a mob of furious townspeople had stormed out to the house and burned it down to the foundations.

In 1994, a high-school student named Heather Donahue, who had grown up with the legends, chose the Elly Kedward tale as the subject for her film coursework. She got a pair of other students to assist her, and set out to make a short documentary about the witch. The team interviewed several people in Burkittsville about the legend, and then went up into the Black Hills to get some footage at Coffin Rock and an old Indian burial ground. They were never seen again, despite a massive manhunt, but a year later their equipment and footage was found, inexplicably built into the crumbled foundations of the Rustin Parr house.

After several years of police review, the footage was deemed inconclusive – to the fury of the missing children's bereaved parents. They took it to a film company, who tidied it up and released it as a movie, *The Blair Witch Project*. The film clearly shows the three terrified students being hunted through the woods by a supernatural force that can only be Elly Kedward. The manifestations get more and more surreal and violent – including a grove filled with peculiar stick figures – until one of the three vanishes entirely overnight, leaving all of his kit behind. A package with a tooth and bloody chunk of lip is left in his place the following morning. Shortly afterwards, the remaining students are herded by shrieks and calls to a building that appears to be Rustin Parr's dilapidated house, the one that was burned down in 1942, and there they are killed.

Elly Kedward has not been seen since, but it would seem that she is due to claim seven more lives some time around the year 2040.

Name: Elly Kedward, the Blair Witch
Age: Sixties at her assumed death in 1786
Description: Elderly Irish woman; latterly, an old cloaked woman with the legs of a goat
Dominant abilities: Mind control
Traits: Murderous
Nature: Evil
Power: Strong
Type: Classic/Satanic
Domain: Emotional control
Goal: To get revenge for her (possibly unjust) banishment
Key equipment: None
Creators: Daniel Myrick and Eduardo Sánchez

Medea, the Witch of Colchis

ᚾᛗᚠᚷᛒᛏᛁᚾᛗᚢᚾᛏᛚᚠᛒᛏᛁᚠᚠᚷᚢᚾᚢᛗᚾᚻᛗᚠᚻᛗᚾᚢᚾᛈᛈᛗᛏᛁᛚᚠᛗᚻᚠᛗᛗᚻᚻᛁᛗᚢᚾᛗᚠᚷᛒᛏ

Greek mythology is full of bloodthirsty figures, but Medea is renowned as one of the most brutal and casually murderous of them all. Her actions were not unprovoked, however; her legend is rife with ill-treatment and misfortune, to the extent that she has been hailed from time to time as an extreme exemplar of women's liberation. She was the niece of the notorious witch Circe, and the granddaughter of the sun god Helios. Her father, Aeetes, was king of the land of Colchis, which he ruled from the city of Aea.

Biography

Medea's adventures began when the Gods picked her out as an instrument of nemesis. King Pelias of Iolcus had ordered the death of a woman who was seeking refuge in the supposedly sacrosanct Temple

Medea shows Jason their dead children, murdered by her own hand.

of Hera. This infuriated Hera, Zeus's wife, who decided to get revenge. When King Pelias sent the hero Jason and his Argonauts to steal the Golden Fleece for him from King Aeetes, Hera decided to use Medea against Pelias.

Accordingly, when Jason arrived in Colchis, Medea saw him and instantly fell head over heels in love with him. She offered to use her magic powers to help him win the Golden Fleece – her father's greatest treasure – and in return he promised to take her back to Greece and marry her. Medea duly helped Jason overcome all the Fleece's guards and wards, even using her magic to make the sleepless dragon that stood over it go to sleep. Jason and his Argonauts, with Medea and her youngest brother Aspyrtus, fled from Colchis with the fleece. King Aeetes set his fleet to chasing the Argonauts.

Medea, aware of the danger, hit upon a plan to slow her father down. She called her brother over, slashed his throat open, and then dismembered him limb from limb and threw the pieces overboard, enchanting them to float. Aeetes had to stop his pursuit so that he could gather up his son's corpse for a proper funeral, which gave the lovers a chance to open up a lead.

The Argonauts had to stop at Crete, and while they were there, Medea murdered the warder of the island, an invulnerable bronze man named Talos. It is said that she promised to make him immortal as well as invulnerable, but then used drugs and spells to drive him mad once his guard was down. Once he was insane, he was unable to stop her pulling a nail out his body, and all the divine blood gushed out of him, killing him.

Jason and Medea then made it to Corcyra, still pursued by Aeetes and the Colchians. The King of Corcyra, Alcinous, gave the fugitives a refuge. Aeetes demanded his daughter and the Fleece back. Alcinous replied that he would give them up only if Medea was still a virgin and had not slept with Jason; otherwise, he said, she belonged to Jason, and the Fleece with her. Anticipating her husband's actions, the Corcyran queen, Arete, married Jason to Medea, and the Colchians were forced to give up.

The Argonauts were free to return to mainland Greece at last. First the couple went to see Jason's father. Medea offered to make him young again, which she did by slitting his throat and filling his corpse up with a special potion which restored life and youth. Then they went to King Pelias, and Jason gave him the Fleece. Meanwhile, Medea persuaded King Pelias's daughters that she could do the same thing for the king as she had for Jason's father. The girls agreed and helped Medea to chop Pelias into mincemeat and boil him up. There was to be no resurrection, though; Medea then left, and Hera's revenge was complete. Pelias's son Acastus succeeded to the throne and expelled Jason and Medea from the city.

The couple settled in Corinth, and lived happily enough for ten years, but eventually Jason wearied of Medea, and decided to take a younger wife, one who was neither foreign nor a witch. He selected Glauce, daughter of King Creon of Corinth. Medea, furious and humiliated, pretended to accept Jason's decision. She secretly prepared a poisoned wedding gown for Glauce, and when it was ready, sent it as a present. On the day of the wedding, Glauce put it on, and the poison caused the flesh to catch fire on her bones. Creon tried to smother the flames to save her, but he too was burned to death, and the fire went on to devastate the entire castle.

Medea then returned to the house she shared with Jason, gathered up their sons and murdered them, stabbing them to death with a knife so as to increase Jason's pain. It is said that Jason, unable to endure the agony of losing both sons and his bride to be, killed himself.

Medea fled to Athens, and used her magic to make the king there, Aegeus, fall in love with her. King Aegeus protected her against the new king of Corinth, Creon's son, and even had a child with her. However, Aegeus did not know that he already had a son, the hero Theseus. Medea and Aegeus lived peacefully for some years, but when Theseus arrived, Medea became afraid that her son would not become king. She tried to persuade Aegeus to kill Theseus, and almost succeeded, but Aegeus recognised his son at the last instant. Medea and her son were banished; surprisingly, she seems not to have been able to kill King Aegeus in revenge.

Medea is seen here brewing the magic potion that restored Jason's father to his youth.

Weary, Medea returned home to Colchis, and found that her father, Aeetes, had been deposed by his brother Perses. Irritated by this change in events, she murdered her uncle, tracked her father down, and restored the kingdom to him. Her son, Medus, went on to found a country called Meda in the area of Ecbatana, and eventually died in a war against a neighbouring kingdom. Medea herself, however, is said to have moved on to a land called Aria, and used magic to force its inhabitants to rename themselves Medes in her honour – the people who would eventually be ruled by the biblical King Darius. There are no tales of Medea's death, and it is rumoured that she lives on, sowing mischief and killing all who get in her way.

Name: Medea, granddaughter of the sun god
Age: Possibly immortal
Description: A beautiful, seductive woman with long red hair and golden skin
Dominant abilities: Spells, mind control
Traits: Ambitious, murderous, ruthless, prone to terrifying anger
Nature: Evil
Power: Very strong
Type: Classic/Sorceress
Domain: Transformation, wisdom
Goal: To have things go her way
Key equipment: None
Creator: Greek mythology

Keziah Mason

ᚾᛗᚡᚷᚠᛏᛃᚾᛗᛟᚾᛡᛒᚠᚠᛏᛃᚠᚠᚷᛟᚾᛟᛗᚾᛉᛗᚠᛉᛗᚾᛟᚾᚠᚠᛗᛏᛃᛒᛡᛢᛗᛉᚠᛗᛗᛉᛃᛗᚠᛟᚾᛗᚡᚡᛏ

An eccentric resident of Arkham, Massachusetts, Keziah Mason spent her entire adult life living alone. She never courted, refused to go to church, threw stones at children who approached her home, and was suspected of lighting fires in the crops of farmers who irritated her.

Biography

Keziah Mason was born in 1605, and bad rumours followed her around right from the beginning. Unlike many such rumours, however, there is reason to believe that in her case, they were deserved. When she was finally brought to trial in 1692, there was strong circumstantial evidence that she had murdered several Arkham children over the years. Two had broken her windows with stones, and vanished after less than a fortnight. A third had spread insulting songs about the old woman, and was discovered in bed, stabbed to death, within days. A fourth drew offensive chalk pictures of her on nearby buildings, and vanished a few days later. He was discovered almost six months later, dismembered, with his arms, legs and body arranged in a the form of a pentagon and his head dumped in the centre.

That was the final straw. Mason was carted off to the local jail and accused of witchcraft in the summer of 1692. She confessed immediately – proudly, even. She declared that the Black Man of the Woods had given her a new name, Nahab, and taken her to sabbats as far away as China, Africa, England, Spain and Leng (a fictitious place which may be located somewhere around the borders of China and Tibet). At his urging, she had defiled churches, corrupted maidens, and spread tuberculosis to dozens of people. Most peculiarly of all, she said that he had taught her how to travel through time and space by the means of certain angles, drawn in chalk. Her partner was an uncanny familiar called Brown Jenkin, a rat-like creature with an evil, wizened human face that could speak in the tongues of men, after a fashion. She brushed off questions about the murdered children, seemingly being more interested in talking about her witchcraft.

 A protesting witch suspect is pushed towards a fiery doom.

Cute, fluffy evil – a snaggle-toothed comedy witch with her snaggle-toothed comedy cat.

Keziah Mason was tried, convicted and condemned to death, but somehow managed to escape from her cell the night before her execution. She left behind nothing more than some chalk lines, which appeared "wrong" and unsettled her jailors.

The crone was sighted in Arkham repeatedly over the next two hundred years, and blame for more than a dozen deaths was laid at her door. Eventually, in February 1928, a brilliant but fragile young mathematics student at Arkham University, Walter Gilman, began to have dreams about Keziah Mason and her familiar, Brown Jenkin. Gilman reported being terrorized by these night-time visions, but at the same time developed an almost superhuman knack for solving Riemannian spatial equations. He developed a slow fever, and started to exhibit a disturbing tendency to sleepwalk.

Gilman's dreams began to include a trans-dimensional component, in which he would discover himself floating in a hyperspatial abyss and travelling to other worlds. A small statue he inexplicably woke up clutching one morning caused quite an upset at the university because of its strange design and material. At the same time, the dream segments with Keziah and her familiar were also getting more vivid, and included ritual components.

When one of his dreams involved helping Keziah kidnap a two-year-old Polish girl, Gilman

was horrified to wake up and discover the child missing. The next night – Walpurgis Night, a notorious Witch's sabbat – he woke from dreams to find himself in an unfamiliar room, dressed for bed, with his feet caked in mud. Keziah Mason was with him, preparing to sacrifice the child. Gilman lashed out, crushing the witch's skull, only to discover that her familiar, Brown Jenkin, had already killed the child. The next night, Gilman himself was killed when the Brown Jenkin familiar burrowed up through his body and ate his heart while he lay sleeping.

Name: Keziah Mason
Age: 323
Description: An ugly, hunched crone with a vicious temper
Dominant abilities: Teleportation, mind control
Traits: Murderous
Nature: Evil
Power: Very strong
Type: Classic
Domain: Curses, transformation
Goal: To learn the blasphemous secrets of the outer abyss
Key equipment: A familiar called Brown Jenkin
Creator: H. P. Lovecraft

Bellatrix Lestrange

ᚾᛗᚠᚺᛏᛁᛊᚾᛗᚭᚾᛁᛏᛒᚠᛏᛁᚠᚠᚻᚭᚾᚭᛗᚾᚻᛗᚠᚻᚾᚭᚾᛒᚠᛗᛏᛁᛏᛁᛏᛗᚻᚠᚾᚻᚻᛁᛗᚠᚭᚾᛗᚠᚺᛏ

One of Lord Voldemort's most dedicated and sadistically evil lieutenants, Bellatrix Lestrange was incarcerated in Azkaban Prison when Voldemort lost his powers trying to kill Harry Potter. She bided her time in Azkaban, confident of her master's return, and escaped shortly after he managed to resurrect himself. She is now back by his side, and has sworn to help him in his avowed intention to kill Harry Potter.

Biography

Bellatrix Black was born in the 1950s. A child of the pureblood Black family, she was inclined towards the Dark Arts from her earliest years. Her sisters include Narcissa Malfoy and Andromeda Tonks; Sirius Black is their first cousin. She married Rodolphus Lestrange after graduating from Hogwarts School of Witchcraft and Wizardry, and she and her husband joined Lord Voldemort's elite army of Death Eaters in the 1970s. Together, they participated in a number of thoroughly despicable acts.

When Voldemort was defeated, Bellatrix – along with her husband, her brother-in-law Rastaban and a fourth friend, Barty Crouch Jr – embarked on a quest to track down what had happened to their leader. They kidnapped a pair of Aurors, elite anti-Dark Magic wizard police, and tortured them for information. Bellatrix was so savage that she drove both of them permanently insane. The four evil-doers were captured shortly afterwards and sentenced to life imprisonment in Azkaban for the crime.

Bellatrix escaped from Azkaban as part of the mass breakout of 1996, and rejoined Lord Voldemort, who was then newly re-arisen. She is now counted as one of his top lieutenants. In the Department of Mysteries Battle, Bellatrix managed to kill her cousin, Sirius Black, but was unable to kill Harry Potter. Voldemort then helped her to escape. She is still at large, a highly dangerous and evil witch.

Name: Bellatrix Lestrange

Age: 42

Description: A tall, dark-haired, sensuously beautiful woman with heavily lidded eyes

Dominant abilities: Curses, teleportation, torture

Traits: Highly sadistic, selfish, ruthlessly ambitious

Nature: Evil

Power: Very strong

Type: Classic/Wizard

Domain: Curses, transformation

Goal: To help Lord Voldemort take over the planet

Key equipment: Wand

Creator: J. K. Rowling

◈ Dark woods lurk behind Hogwarts School of Witchcraft and Wizardry. Could Bellatrix Lestrange be hiding in them, as her master Lord Voldemort once did?

Part Two

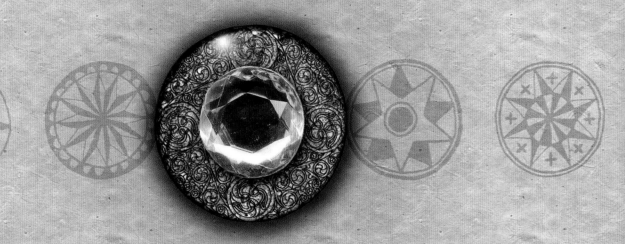

Wizards

8

The Way
of the
Wizard

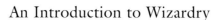

Wizards are dangerous and mysterious. They have mighty powers, casting spells with nothing more than a gesture and a word or conducting elaborate rituals that produce hidden results. They control the forces of the world but often stand back from it, alone and withdrawn. They are the ultimate image of mankind's desire to control his surroundings – willpower and wisdom made human.

An Introduction to Wizardry

Magic is as old as thought. It comes from the same ideas that created the earliest beginnings of religion in the minds of our earliest ancestors – the destructive power of fire, the awesome displays of fierce weather, or the exceptional luck in the hunt. It is fascinating to imagine that the forces of the universe can be controlled with either a thought or a word. Many of us would love to live in a world – a mysterious and exciting world hidden behind ours, that can reach out and save us – where men and women of power can perform such supernatural marvels … It's a tempting idea.

Of course, even within the world of the wizard, only a very special few have the potential to master the forces of magic. It takes willpower, intelligence, persistent effort and solid belief. If everyone could learn, then everyone would – wizards are rare, and that means that it is difficult to become one. Fictional and mythological wizards are usually born that way, with the power buried within. Harry Potter is a wizard by birth, and magic runs in his blood. Merlin, King Arthur's wizard, is not entirely human, and gets his power from elsewhere. Gandalf from *The Lord of the Rings* is a heavenly being in disguise. Luke and Anakin in *Star Wars*, Garion in the *Belgariad*, Will Stanton in *The Dark is Rising*, Rand in *The Wheel of Time* … over and over again, wizards are born to their power and grow up knowing nothing about it until it bursts out of them.

Wizards are usually thought of as crotchety old men wearing robes and pointy hats. That isn't always true, though. Wizardry goes beyond any simple description, and it isn't only found in fantasy – you also find it in modern fictional settings, in science fiction, in mythology, and in all sorts of other places.

✦ Far Left: A medieval wizard uses Heaven to subdue Hell.

✦ Left: The ghost of a dead woman is called back to life by a wizard.

There are even real historical people who have claimed to be wizards. There are no stereotypes that you can rely on. Circe of Greek myth and Baba Yaga of Russian folklore are female wizards, Harry Potter is a child (and Hermione, his friend, is a girl too), John Dee really lived in the sixteenth century, Rincewind, the Discworld wizard, only knows one spell, and Jedi Master Yoda isn't even slightly human.

In this book, we are going to take a detailed look at the world of wizards and wizardry. We will investigate all of the most famous wizards, both fictional and historical. That includes information about their lives, magical powers, interests and the worlds (or times) in which they lived. We will also look at the items and assistants with which wizards surround themselves, the places they like to live in, the organizations that they belong to, and the tools that they use in their magical work. First of all, though, we are going to consider what being a wizard actually means, how you can tell wizards from other types of magic-using people, and the different varieties of wizard that you might come across.

The Nature of Magic

The most important requirement for being a wizard is the ability to use magic. Without it a wizard is nothing much more than a stage magician. Magic is at the heart of a wizard's powers, but it manifests itself in many different forms, and may come from many different places. It is important to know what magic really is. Magic is the art of causing something to happen without going through the normal process that is required to make it happen. Everything that happens normally involves a chain of events, each leading from one to the next on the way to the result. That is called "causality", because each moment is physically caused by the one that happened before it. Magic cuts straight through that, providing you with a more direct way to achieve the result.

The science fiction writer Arthur C. Clarke once said that: *"In a sufficiently advanced society, technology is indistinguishable from magic."* He meant that if our science was good enough, we would be able to achieve seemingly magical results. That may be true, but it misses the point entirely. Magic is about causing effects by the power of your mind alone. If you use technology, you are not a wizard – you are a scientist.

Let's look at an example of that. Moving from place to place normally requires you to somehow travel from A to B. You have to use energy to move, or someone or something else – like a horse, a car or a plane – has to use energy to carry you. Wizardry could move you from A to B without energy being used. That is not possible in normal causality … and that is what makes it magic. If you use a scientific teleport device, there is a causal explanation – and an energy source – so it's normal causality, not magic.

✦ Right: A real wizard has no need for an audience …

✦ Far Right: … while a stage magician has to look flashy and mysterious.

★ Left: A wizard may cast
his magic by reading
spells from a book ...

Types of Magic

Magic comes in many different varieties, but spells are
the most traditional form. A **spell** is a set of words
that channels magic power and can either be spoken
or written. They may be in the wizard's own language,
they may be in a foreign, forgotten or secret language,
they may be in a special magical tongue, or they might
even be in no language at all. Spells can be as short as
one syllable, or can be so long that they take days to
speak. They might be sentences, commands, rhymes
or nonsense. They usually sound impressive, but even
that is not always the case. Spells work by shaping and
defining the wizard's desires and bringing them out
into the world. The very sounds of the spell somehow
key into the universal forces of magic and bring about
the desired result. Many wizards need to be holding a
wand or a staff in order to cast a spell – they help to
channel the spell's magic into the real world.

For many wizards, though, something extra is
needed. Some magic requires physical motions called
gestures. This may be in addition to a spell, but
sometimes just the physical action is enough on its
own. Gestures like this might be long and complicated,
or they might be as simple as the flick of a finger.
The actions involved in a magical gesture are thought
to bring the wizard into alignment with the magic he
– or she – is channelling. Magical items and **tools**
may also be required. A wizard may require particular
clothing, candles or fires, chalices, altars, knives or
daggers, a particular place or room, special herbs or

place in a special or magical location – a lonely hilltop, an underground temple, a forest glade – and require a number of different tools. They can get extremely complicated, and are usually ruined if they are disturbed. For that reason, most wizards prefer simpler spells when they are available.

Most magical effects fall into one of five different categories. Spells that change one thing into another, or change part of something, are spells of **transformation**. Typical transformation spells include changing lead into gold, turning an enemy into a toad, or shifting your appearance to look and sound like someone else. When something is summoned from another place or created out of thin air, the process is called **invocation**. This can include calling servants, creatures or monsters from other dimensions, casting a fireball at a rival, or cloaking yourself in an illusion. When feelings, emotions and other intangibles are changed or manipulated, it is known as **evocation**. This covers things like love spells, making people avoid a certain area, stopping time, or cursing someone to bad luck. Playing around with physical qualities – location, speed, weight, size, health and so on – falls under **manipulation**. This includes teleporting and moving objects around as well as curing disease or becoming invisible. Finally, **divination** deals with spells that look into other times and places, or ones that seek answers. This can involve making predictions, discovering who last held an object, learning someone's history, or spying on a distant place.

✦ Left: ... or may need special ingredients such as morning dew.

other magical substances, bells or instruments, assistants or sacrifices, or all sorts of other things. These are collectively known as tools, even though an assistant is a living being, and wands and staffs are so ubiquitous that they don't count.

A **ritual** is a piece of magic that requires one or more tools. Most rituals include spells, and often gestures as well. Rituals are as variable as everything else and may take months or just a moment to complete, but most last for an hour or two. They usually take

Other Wizardly Powers

There is more to being a wizard than just magic, however. There are a number of powers and abilities that wizards often possess that are magical, but do not really count as a spell that can be cast. These may be passive abilities that are always active for the wizard even if he or she is doing something else, or they may be specific skills that the wizard can use when he or she wants to. They are differentiated from spells in that they do not necessarily have a specific result – a spell makes something happen; other powers, on the other hand, may just be.

✦ Above Right: A wizard's ritual is far more impressive on the astral plane.

✦ Right: The Oracle of Delphi could predict the future.

Psychic ability is a good example. Many wizards are psychic in one way or another. They may get spontaneous glimpses of the future – unasked for, unexplained and sometimes even irrelevant. This can also manifest itself as knowing when they are in danger. Others can read minds or emotions, or at least feel the presence of other beings around them. A few can even tell which actions are going to give the best results, or even when something is going to prove to be a mistake. The Jedi's mind-control ability, for example, is a spell that requires a gesture to cause a result – the Jedi gestures and tells the victim what to think – but their power of perceiving surroundings through the Force is a psychic ability, because it is like a sixth sense, and it is always on. Some wizards have just one psychic ability, but others may have a whole range of different psychic senses and powers.

Astral projection is similar to psychic ability, but there are certain differences. It is a power that allows a wizard to step out of his or her physical body into an invisible shell of consciousness. This shell can then go to other locations at the speed of thought, and perhaps even to other times or dimensions. When in an astral form, most wizards can watch and listen passively, but can take no physical action. A few can cast spells from the astral shell, which makes them immensely powerful.

Some wizards are partly **immortal** in one way or another. This is usually limited. The wizard may be immune to ageing and disease but not to injury or attack – or vice versa. Even fully immortal wizards usually have one weakness or vulnerability that can be used to harm them, in the same way that a werewolf can only be harmed by silver. Ageless wizards mostly look old, but as always there are exceptions, and some immortals may appear young, even child-like. Similarly, a frail old wizard may well prove completely invulnerable to physical harm. There are even some wizards who regularly change their appearance, altering their apparent age, sex, country of origin and even species on a whim. Some go so far that they even forget what they originally looked like.

One of the greatest wizardly powers, however, is **knowledge**. Most wizards are well learned, with access to all sorts of information that those around them do not have. The term "wizard" itself comes from the derivative "wise". Often, a wizard will have a knowledge of certain chemical or physical processes that give him access to entirely natural powers – how to mix explosive powders, for example, or which herbs can be used to promote natural healing.

In the hands of someone intelligent and dedicated, almost any knowledge can be a powerful tool or weapon, whether it is the knowledge to bring about magical changes in the world, or the knowledge to bring about physical changes. To the unenlightened, there may seem to be no difference between the two – what does it matter if the wizard mixes two powders or waves a wand, if a ball of fire is the result? Sometimes, a wizard may be a scientist as well.

★ Below: Virgil's great knowledge gave him a reputation as a sorcerer.

Masters of Magic

Wizards are not the only people with access to the forces of magic. Although a wizard needs some sort of access to magical abilities to be a wizard, the reverse doesn't automatically hold true – having access to magic does not automatically make you a wizard. In fact, it is really all a matter of style. Wizards impose their will on reality and force it to conform to their spells and rituals. Other types of magically empowered people approach the universe in a rather different way, particularly witches, shamans and mystics.

It is common to assume that wizards and **witches** are just male and female versions of the same thing, for example.

✦ Right: Witches are in touch with nature and work with it.

The pointy hats that they both wear go a long way to making that an obvious assumption. It is not actually correct, though. The Harry Potter books aside, witches are not female wizards. Although most wizards are men and most witches are women, they approach magic – and the rest of life – in very different ways. Witches work with nature and the spirits of the earth. Their magic comes from long rituals that usually have several participants, and it works by summoning, persuading or controlling natural spirits and energies. Old wisdom – herb lore, the power of fire, knots and candles, minor curses and cures, the rhythm of the cycles and the natural times of power – forms the basis of their power, which is useful for everyday things. A witch can tell your future, make someone fall in love with you, dry up your cows, or go flying on a broomstick. A lot of witches' magic has to be done at specific times or in specific places: when the moon is full; at midnight on a Friday; naked around a bonfire; in a sacred grove at dawn; and so on. If you want to strike a bargain with the spirit of a forest, learn the future or have an enemy become ill and die, you need to go to a witch. The correct term for a male witch is a warlock (according to historical definitions); the correct term for a female wizard is actually still a wizard.

A **shaman** is another nature-based spell-caster. Unlike witches, shamen work alone, usually on behalf of one tribe or village. Their power comes from being able to access a special realm where spirits live, using a power a bit like astral projection. The first time a shaman enters the spirit world, he or she is adopted by one of a number of powerful spirits called totems. These totems usually represent a certain species of animal, and are named after it – Bear is strong and slow to anger; Raven is clever; and Spider is wise and patient. A shaman's totem reflects his or her true personality. Different parts of the world have different totem animals, but almost any living species can have a totem. Once the shaman has been accepted by the totem, the spirit realm is open. The totem acts as protector, guide and teacher. The shaman can read the future by calling on the totem to guide a particular type of divination, and can heal the sick by journeying into the spirit realm and correcting whatever is wrong with the patient's soul. He or she can also tell the village's hunters where to find food, and advise the chief on the things that are going to be important to the people.

Mystics gain access to magical powers through physical and mental exercises. These exercises are often extremely difficult, dangerous or uncomfortable, and it can take years and years of work to start gaining powers. Mystics normally have control over their own bodies, and also acquire a range of impressive psychic powers, but rarely have any skill at directly influencing others. Common feats include being able to slow ageing and stop disease, ignore poisons, the ability to harden the body to resist weapons or punch through stone, holding their breath for days on end, becoming blindingly fast in combat, or climbing seemingly impossible surfaces – all of which would be immensely dangerous tricks without magical powers. Some mystics are peaceful, and focus their powers into mental abilities and passive skills, while others, like the legendary monks of China's Shaolin temple, are devastatingly dangerous martial artists.

Magical powers can be found with other types of person as well. **Demigods** are the mightiest of heroes and villains, either the child of a union between a god and a mortal, or a fraction of a larger god crammed into a human form. Their powers are a natural result of their

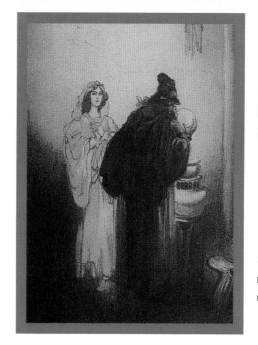

✦ Left: Mystics may be able to look out to other places and times for clients.

✦ Below: A shaman's ritual may involve the whole tribe in a frenzied dance.

divine blood, and need no spell or concentration to activate. Their abilities, while often spell-like, are not linked to magic in any way, and they dedicate themselves to furthering their divine interests. **Occultists** are normal humans who use complicated traditional spells and rituals to bring about fairly minor effects, such as luck in business or gambling, or to heighten someone's affection. Magic is not natural, instinctive or a core part of identity for an occultist; it's more like a job or a hobby. Some of the legendary occult rituals offer incredible abilities – the power to become invisible, to change shape, or to control the mind of another person – but many of these rituals are long lost. There are lots of types of occultist, and many people actually try using occultism to solve their problems.

Different Strokes

Just as there many types of people with access to magical powers who are not wizards, there are also several different categories that wizards can fall into. Different spell-casters have different interests, or channel their abilities into separate lines. They all share the common ground of wizardry – using the power of magic to force reality into doing unnatural or unusual things – but they have different skills. Some are so specialized that they cannot do anything outside of one narrow field, while for others, their specialization is more a question of style than of actual ability.

The main division of wizarding style is between sorcerers and ritualists. **Sorcerers** are wizards who use their powers almost spontaneously, with no ritual and almost nothing in the way of spell or gesture. Their magic tends to be strong, sudden and showy, rather than subtle or gradual. Sorcerers tend to be good at invocation and manipulation. If a wizard is frequently using magic without actually speaking a spell, or spends a lot of time on flashy magic such as casting fireballs, collapsing walls, flying or changing shape, he or she is likely to be a sorcerer. Sorcerers often neglect the usual trappings of wizardly life, and may appear to be a completely normal person, perhaps not even carrying a wand or staff. Despite the staff he carries, Gandalf is a typical sorcerer.

✦ Right: A ritualist in his underground temple, preparing a spell.

Ritualists are the opposite. These are the wizards who wear robes and hats, carry wands, and devote time and energy to each spell that they cast. Their powers are less immediate than those of sorcerers, but they make up for it in other ways. Ritual wizards can only cast spells that they know while some sorcerers can make it up as they go along. On the other hand, a ritualist's spell can create extremely complicated results, and may have several subtle, long-lasting effects. It takes a ritual to create a portable

manor house, filled with lavish rooms, dedicated servants and delicious foodstuffs, in which you can accommodate 20 people overnight when you are travelling and still fold up to the size of a matchbox and put in your pocket the next morning. For complex stuff, ritual is a must. Ritualists are particularly good at evocation and divination. Harry Potter is a ritualist, although most of his rituals are quite short.

There are various kinds of wizard who special- ize in certain areas, known as **domains**. **Necromancers** specialize in the dead. They can create zombies, skel- etons and other undead, talk to people who have passed away, predict the future or learn about the past, and use magic to destroy things and kill peo- ple. **Alchemists** work with equipment and ritual to create transformations, turning one thing into another. Their traditional aims are to turn lead into gold, and to gain eternal life.

Demonologists are skilled at summoning and controlling demons and other powerful beings. Their power usually consists of command- ing other beings to perform magical acts for them, and they may actually be powerless away from their

✦ Left: An unusually kindly old necromancer talks to this couple's deceased relatives to bring comfort.

magical slaves. Demonologists and necromancers are usually evil. **Elementalists** specialize in the control and manipulation of one or more physical substances. These are often the Greek classical elements of air, fire, water and earth, but can also be Chinese elements such as wood, stone or metal, or just about any other broad class of sub- stance. Elementalists can make their particular elements do just about anything, and can often summon their element as well – a water wizard could make it rain, part the sea, breathe water, or make a lake lash out at a boat. **High Mages**, finally, are concerned with the universe as a whole. Their magic is abstract and difficult to understand, and often relates to other magic, or to the balance of good and evil in the world. They can be immensely powerful, but do not usually stoop to interfere in day-to-day affairs.

9

Magical

Characters

Wizards become famous. It's almost inevitable. As their power grows, word of their incredible achievements spreads across the land. Whispers, rumours and travellers' tales combine to form legends, and the legends in turn become bedside stories. Sometimes the telling inflates the truth, and the wizard may find that his skill is dwarfed by his reputation. On other occasions, certain feats might be overlooked as too amazing to be true. Even reclusive wizards may still become known, their names attached to wild rumours by suspicious locals. Learning magic takes time and practice and most wizards are old, so it is amazing that the most famous of them all is a boy.

harry Potter

The creation of author J.K. Rowling, Harry Potter is the world's best-known wizard. From the moment he first appeared in 1997, his adventures have been thrilling fans all over the globe. With his award-winning books selling tens of millions of copies and a major Hollywood blockbuster backing him up, Harry's is the most prominent name in all of wizarding. His beginnings were humble, though.

BIOGRAPHY: Harry Potter is an orphan. His parents, James and Lily Potter, were murdered while he was still a baby. Their killer was the evil Lord Voldemort, mightiest of the Dark wizards. Voldemort tried to kill Harry as well, but special protections around the infant bounced the attack back at him. Voldemort was left dreadfully crippled, and Harry received a vivid scar on his forehead in the shape of a lightning bolt.

After the attack, Harry was given into the care of his aunt and uncle, Vernon and Petulia Dursley and their son, Dudley. Aggressively anti-wizard and resentful of the imposition, the Dursleys treated Harry appallingly, more like a slave than a family member. He grew up knowing next to nothing of his parents or even about magic. That all changed when he was invited to enrol at Hogwarts' School of Wizardry. He suddenly discovered the wizarding world, and found out that he was a celebrity, famed for surviving the evil Voldemort's attack.

Since that time, Harry has had several daring adventures with his friends Ron Weasley and Hermione Granger. In addition to being brave, resourceful and resilient, Harry is an excellent Quidditch player, his amazing broomstick control giving him a big edge in the frenetic airborne sport.

★ Far Left: Berlin fans celebrate Harry Potter.

★ Left: The movie world's face of Harry.

★ Below: Joanne Rowling, Harry's creator.

WORLD: In Harry's topsy-turvy version of Earth, wizards keep themselves very carefully separated from non-magical people, whom they refer to as "muggles". Wizardly activities are restricted so as to not risk alarming the general population, and most of the community lives inside magical areas that are invisible to muggles. Hogwarts School, with its towers, cellars, Great Hall and stone corridors, is an extremely magical place – so much so that even technology stops

✱ Below: All sorts of Harry Potter merchandise is available ...

✱ Bottom: ... but nothing beats the books themselves.

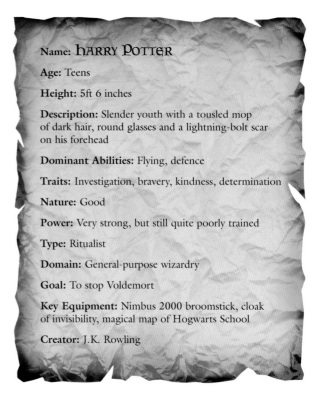

Name: HARRY POTTER

Age: Teens

Height: 5ft 6 inches

Description: Slender youth with a tousled mop of dark hair, round glasses and a lightning-bolt scar on his forehead

Dominant Abilities: Flying, defence

Traits: Investigation, bravery, kindness, determination

Nature: Good

Power: Very strong, but still quite poorly trained

Type: Ritualist

Domain: General-purpose wizardry

Goal: To stop Voldemort

Key Equipment: Nimbus 2000 broomstick, cloak of invisibility, magical map of Hogwarts School

Creator: J.K. Rowling

working within its boundaries. The headmaster, Albus Dumbledore, is an immensely powerful wizard, and a staunch ally of Harry's.

Throughout the books, wizardry is a hidden world, tucked just around the corner from mundane reality. Diagon Alley, a major shopping street for wizards, is located in London, but hidden behind an innocuous door. Platform 9¾, on King's Cross station, can only be reached by running through a solid barrier. The wizards themselves do all they can to keep hidden from the muggle world, and in fact have very little understanding of it.

As Hogwarts is a boarding school, Harry spends most of his time within its grounds. Each of the four Houses has its own tower, and rivalry for the annual House Trophy is as fierce as it is for the Quidditch Cup. The sinister house of Slytherin is famous for producing Dark wizards – Harry, naturally, belongs to

On the sign: Harry Potter

brave Gryffindor. The teachers and other adult figures never quite seem to know what's going on, with the exception of wise old Dumbledore, who always turns out to have known everything all along, so Harry and his friends are repeatedly left to thwart Voldemort's evil plans on their own.

MAGIC: Spells are activated by a short, pig-Latin invocation (*"Expecto Patronum"* for example), and require the use of a wand. Once out of the school system, wizards seek jobs in a number of different magical areas, and enjoy status according to career, wealth and family, much like the rest of us. Female wizards share an equal footing. Although they are sometimes referred to as "witches" in the books, they practise wizardry, not witchcraft. Wizards have wands and hats and blast things with spells, while witches have bonfires and nakedness, and conduct night-time rituals in secluded glades. Female wizards are a long-standing tradition, and the term should really be thought of as gender-neutral.

➤ Right: Gandalf the
Grey is at the heart of
The Lord of the Rings.

One man cast
a lingering spell
of awe and wonder,
of magical innocence
overcoming evil,
of simple courage
conquering fear
— he gave us the legend
that will live forever
in our minds.

J.R.R. Tolkien triumphed
with the perception that
a single dream is more
powerful than
a thousand realities.

Come to Middle-earth,
a world beyond the
furthest reaches of
your imagination.

J.R.R. tolkien's
"the Lord of the Rings"

A SAUL ZAENTZ PRODUCTION
A RALPH BAKSHI FILM
J.R.R. Tolkien's "THE LORD OF THE RINGS" Music by LEONARD ROSENMAN
Screenplay by CHRIS CONKLING and PETER S. BEAGLE • Based on the novels of J.R.R. TOLKIEN
Produced by SAUL ZAENTZ • Directed by RALPH BAKSHI

DOLBY STEREO

A Fantasy Films
Presentation

Released thru United Artists
A Transamerica Company

Gandalf

The Lord of the Rings, by J.R.R. Tolkien, is the book that created the entire fantasy genre. It has been consistently voted the best book of the twentieth century in reader's poll after reader's poll, and it is certainly one of the most influential. The genre of books that followed it is the second most popular on the planet (after romantic fiction, in case you were wondering). Its patterns and settings have become almost regulation for most works in the fantasy field. Gandalf himself strides through the book, a mighty and mysterious central figure with incredible powers tempered by near-infinite kindness and wisdom. In many ways, Gandalf is the archetypal wizard – the one who defines all the others.

BIOGRAPHY: Ancient and timeless, Gandalf is not actually human. Like the other Istari – the wizards of Middle Earth, the land that *The Lord of the Rings* is set in – he is one of the Maya, a spiritual being working for the forces of goodness, clothed in human form and mind. He is an old man with long white hair and a long white beard, dressed in robes and a mantle. He carries a staff that is the channel for his power, and also wears the Red Ring of Fire, a magical ring of incredible power that gives him command over flame and can kindle passions and miracles.

Gandalf has held a number of names over the centuries. His original name was Olórin, and he is known as Mithrandir by the elves. He arrived in Middle Earth during the Third Age, when Sauron, the ancient enemy, was starting to re-establish himself in the forest called Greenwood the Great. As Sauron's power grew, and Greenwood came to be known as Mirkwood, Gandalf and the other Istari came out of the west by boat. Gandalf had many powers of mind and hand, and travelled through Middle Earth talking to humans and elves, as well as to the animals and birds, gathering information.

Gandalf was the most vigilant of all the wizards, and suspected that the darkness in Mirkwood was due to Sauron regaining his powers. He drove the darkness out of the forest, but it returned, slowly. Gandalf went there again, came face to face with Sauron, and managed to escape with his life. He tried to persuade a council of the leaders of the free people to act against the enemy, but was stalled by the traitorous wizard who led the council, Saruman. Finally, it became obvious that action was necessary and Saruman could delay no longer, and Sauron was driven out of Mirkwood again. The enemy had regained his former powers, however, and fell back to his old kingdom of Mordor.

In the battles that followed, Gandalf's wisdom and power tipped the balance in favour of the free people. Saruman the traitor was cast down, and Sauron was destroyed for once and for all. With his work done, Gandalf left Middle Earth as he had come, by boat, and returned to the ancient lands of the west.

WORLD: In many ways, the land of Middle Earth itself is the real hero of Tolkien's opus. He saw his works as a history of what could have been rather than seeing himself as a writer of an epic adventure story, and he often paid as much attention to the world and its past as he did to the characters and plots. As a result, the history, geography and politics of Middle Earth are well known.

Middle Earth is a magical place. It is populated by a number of sentient species, the "Free Peoples" – humans, elves, dwarves and halflings – as well as several other species of intelligent creatures, ranging from fairly pleasant beings such as ents to evil monsters like orcs, half-orcs, trolls, giants and dragons. The Free Peoples are settled in a number of nations and regions. Humans occupy a number of different countries, and elves, dwarves and halflings all have various nations, enclaves and territories. Some of the monstrous species – most notably the orcs of Mordor – also have their own national areas. Middle Earth itself is not unlike Europe or America. It is large and mostly temperate in climate, with great mountains, huge plains, pleasant dales and vast tracts of forest hiding strange and ancient creatures. To the north, the land becomes steadily more polar, getting colder and bleaker; to the south, it becomes hot and sandy.

Magic is a common companion in Middle Earth. Although Gandalf and his fellow Istari are the only ones formally known as wizards, many elves also have access to magical abilities, and rare individuals of the other species also possess power. In addition, many

magical objects and items exist that can grant special abilities. The sword "Sting", for example, passed by Bilbo the hobbit to his nephew Frodo, has the power to glow with blue fire when orcs are nearby. The rings of power – three for the elves (including Gandalf's Red Ring), seven for the dwarves, nine for the humans, and one master control ring – are at the other end of the power scale, and are able to grant incredible powers. For most of the population, monsters, sorcery and the undead are things to be cautious

Name: GANDALF THE GREY, AKA MITHRANDIR, OLÓRIN, STORMCROW

Age: Thousands of years

Height: 6 ft

Description: Slender old man with long white hair and beard, big crooked nose, dressed in blue robes and carrying a staff

Dominant Abilities: Manipulating fire (offensive and defensive), wisdom

Traits: Resolve, determination, kindness

Nature: Good

Power: Incredibly strong

Type: Sorcerer

Domain: Elementalist (fire)

Goal: To help the Free Peoples to overthrow Sauron

Key Equipment: Staff, The Red Ring

Creator: J.R.R. Tolkien

of, rather than merely being a part of legend and rumour.

MAGIC: Gandalf is largely sorcerous in his use of power, leaving ritual aside. He is a mighty wizard, with huge reserves of strength and wisdom, and the knowledge to back it up and apply it. He is a particular master of fire, with a love of creating incredible firework displays. Although he rarely bothers with speaking spells, he can call upon them when required. Others in Middle Earth are more ritual-dependent. Tom Bombadil relies on – and responds to – spells; the elves tend to draw on long-established rituals to construct wondrous artefacts.

Yoda

A wizened little old alien whose comical appearance hides incredible power and wisdom, Yoda is one of the rarest of wizardly breeds – a science-fiction wizard. The original *Star Wars* films imprinted themselves on an entire generation who were thrilled by the blend of high-tech special effects, spaghetti western plots and fantasy-style magic and mysticism. The *Star Wars* series was created and conceived by producer-director George Lucas, and Hollywood found the whole idea so peculiar that it took him ten years to raise the money to produce the first one. Yoda belongs mainly to the second film of the original trilogy, *The Empire Strikes Back*. He has proved so popular, however, that he has featured in every *Star Wars* film since.

BIOGRAPHY: A mighty master of the Jedi religion and the being responsible for training new Jedi, Yoda was a powerful individual, both politically and spiritually. A senior member of the Jedi council in the old Republic, he was already more than 850 years old when he escaped the destruction of the Jedi at the hands of a traitor and fled to the jungle world of Dagobah. By using the planet's natural, dark emanations as covering camouflage, he managed to stay hidden from his enemies for more than 20 years.

In due time, Yoda's old friend and pupil, Obi-Wan Kenobi, managed to get Luke Skywalker to go to Dagobah. When he got there, Yoda took on the role of trainer one last time, and did his best to nurture the power inside the young man. Luke progressed rapidly

✦ Far left: Don't be fooled – Yoda may be sci-fi but he's still a wizard.

✦ Left: Master and pupil: training to be a wizard can be hard work.

under Yoda's expert tutelage, leaving before he could complete his training in order to attempt to rescue his friends. Already ancient beyond his years, Yoda managed to hang on to life long enough to greet a fully-developed Luke when he returned, before finally dying of old age.

Although he was small, green and wrinkly with droopy ears, spindly limbs and a walking cane, Yoda managed to be a convincing spiritual master. He combined patience with irritability, understanding with insistence, knowledge with power, and although one's abiding impression of him is of a kind being, he was still able to be frightening and awe-inspiring when the need arose. He also had an unusual way of phrasing his sentences, placing the subject at the end of a sentence, rather than its more common location at the

beginning – "Strong am I" rather than "I am strong", and "Luminous beings are we", rather than "We are luminous beings".

WORLD: In the old Republic, Yoda was largely based in the capital of Coruscant. An incredible world, Coruscant has been completely built up and built over into one gigantic city that covers the whole globe. Even so, the towers of the city shoot miles up into the sky, and they themselves are overlooked by a maze of floating platforms and suspended walkways and buildings. Coruscant is terminally short of space. The Jedi had a building to serve as their headquarters, but it was destroyed when they were betrayed. The Dagobah system was a significant change. The planet he settled on was a swamp world, heavily populated by wild creatures and other life forms but with no intelligent

✦ Below: Robe, staff and magic powers – Obi-Wan qualifies too.

species. As a planet strong in the darker side of the force – the natural cycle there is vicious and predatory – the planet's natural emanations masked his presence, strong in the light side, from his enemies.

For most of the population of the Empire/Republic, magic is a matter of superstition and mythology. Only those few people who ever come face to face with a Jedi or a Sith ever have the chance of seeing any magic in action. Most people rely on technology to help get through the day. Once the Empire took over and the Jedi were destroyed, knowledge of them was suppressed to discourage their resurgence, and the power of the magic available to them was largely forgotten.

MAGIC: Yoda is a master of the Jedi art, a fascinating blend of wizardry and mysticism. For the Jedi, magic stems from the Force, a flow of universal energy that moves through all things and binds them in a myriad of ways. Using the power of the Force, it is possible to move objects telekinetically, look into the future (and sense the present), control the minds – and bodily functions – of others, enhance yourself, and even manipulate raw energy. The Jedi originally served as the guardians of law and honesty, actively enforcing the rules and regulations of the Republic, and their power in the Force was used to enhance their abilities to serve as super-police. Their foresight made them blindingly fast in combat, because they could see the moves of their opponents before they happened, and physical enhancement added to their strength, speed and agility. In addition, their abilities to control minds and move objects added to their skill at enforcing law.

Spells and rituals play next to no part in Jedi magic. Although the old Jedi art had all the trappings of a religion, with rites of passage and celebration, and

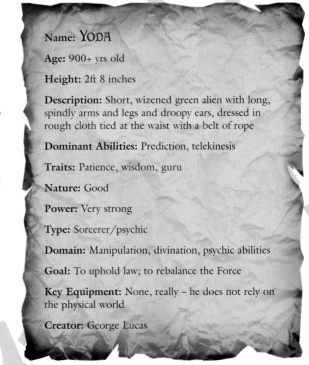

Name: YODA

Age: 900+ yrs old

Height: 2ft 8 inches

Description: Short, wizened green alien with long, spindly arms and legs and droopy ears, dressed in rough cloth tied at the waist with a belt of rope

Dominant Abilities: Prediction, telekinesis

Traits: Patience, wisdom, guru

Nature: Good

Power: Very strong

Type: Sorcerer/psychic

Domain: Manipulation, divination, psychic abilities

Goal: To uphold law; to rebalance the Force

Key Equipment: None, really – he does not rely on the physical world

Creator: George Lucas

formalized language and training, the magic itself is largely concentrated on gestures for channelling the power of the Force. In addition to the sorcerous component, Jedi also possess strong psychic powers, particularly when it comes to sensing physical surroundings and the minds of specific individuals, discerning the way that future events will play out, and feeling the flow of the Force.

The Jedi represent the light side of the Force and are collectively dedicated to law and justice, but their goodness is counterbalanced by the dark side of the Force as embodied in the evil Sith lords. The Sith are the opposites of the Jedi, dedicated to personal gain and power, but they share the same techniques, powers and even many of the quasi-religious rituals and formalities of the Jedi religion. After centuries in hiding, the Sith finally betrayed and destroyed the Jedi, hunting them down and killing them, and used their own powers to take control of the Republic, turning it into the Empire.

Rincewind

The unlikely hero of Terry Pratchett's first two humorous fantasy novels – and of several more further on in the series to boot – Rincewind is the Discworld's most inept wizard. He is a peculiarly fitting hero for the series of hilarious parodies and catalogues of disaster that make up Pratchett's work. Rincewind is one of the Disc's most enduring characters, almost seeming to represent the crazy world itself. With the series running in at more than 20 novels, two computer games, a role-playing game and numerous other items, it looks like he is going to be around a while yet.

BIOGRAPHY: Rincewind was born under the inauspicious constellation known as the "Small Boring Group of Faint Stars", a star-sign traditionally associated with onion-sellers and people who make chessboards. He grew up in the Shades, a particularly dangerous, smelly area of the city of Ankh-Morpork. As the city has a well-deserved reputation for being generally dangerous and smelly itself, the Shades is the sort of area that tourists stumble into by mistake, only to emerge several days later as dog-food. The River Ankh, which divides the metropolis into the old cities of Ankh and Morpork, is so full of sewage, pollution, mud and other rubbish that it is generally thought to slither rather than flow.

Despite this unlikely start to his wizarding career, Rincewind managed to get into the Unseen University, the greatest academy of the magical arts on the Discworld. Once there, his lack of any real magical talent was totally overshadowed when, on a dare, he opened a magical grimoire called the Octavo that held the eight Great Spells used by the creator to make the world. One of the spells escaped into Rincewind's head, and stayed there. Other spells didn't dare share his mind with a spell of that ferociousness. The finest wizards of the Faculty of Medicine were unable to remove it, leaving Rincewind magically castrated. Worst of all, whenever he was run-down, the spell would try to force him to speak, and no one knew whether or not that would unmake the world.

After graduation, Rincewind was still unable to perform magic, and scratched out a living as a petty translator until he met Twoflower, the Discworld's

★ Below: The chaos of the Unseen University, Discworld's premier establishment for magical learning.

first tourist. After initially trying to con Twoflower out of enough gold to set him up for life, Rincewind was persuaded, at sword-point, to act as a guide for the tourist. They stumbled through a number of cataclysmic adventures, including being attacked by an evil elder god, kidnapped by riders of imaginary dragons, and falling off the edge of the world in a golden fish, until Rincewind finally managed to banish the spell from his mind and Twoflower went home.

Even after getting rid of the great spell, Rincewind proved a failure as a wizard. Still unable to master even the most basic magic, he spent a period of time acting as an assistant to the university librarian, who had been magically transformed into an orang-utan some time before. After a brief period stuck in the dungeon dimensions, he was accidentally summoned back onto the Disc again by a careless demonologist called Eric. Other adventures naturally followed. Rincewind was last seen making his way in the lost continent of "Forecks", still cheerfully unable to muster any magical forces.

WORLD: The Discworld is magical in much the same way that the universe is really rather big. It is a physically impossible realm, brought into existence because an infinitely varied universe demands it somewhere. The Discworld itself is, as the name suggests, a flat, circular planet. It rests on the back of four great elephants, named Berilia, Tubul, Jerakeen and Great T'Phon. These mighty creatures in turn stand upon the back of Great A'Tuin, a gigantic star turtle swimming endlessly through the seas of space. A small sun,

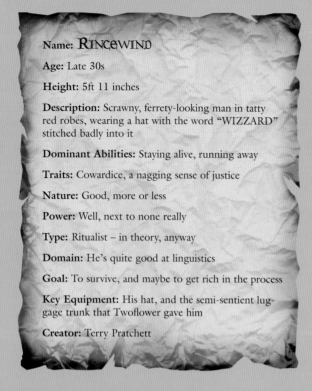

Name: RINCEWIND

Age: Late 30s

Height: 5ft 11 inches

Description: Scrawny, ferrety-looking man in tatty red robes, wearing a hat with the word "WIZZARD" stitched badly into it

Dominant Abilities: Staying alive, running away

Traits: Cowardice, a nagging sense of justice

Nature: Good, more or less

Power: Well, next to none really

Type: Ritualist – in theory, anyway

Domain: He's quite good at linguistics

Goal: To survive, and maybe to get rich in the process

Key Equipment: His hat, and the semi-sentient luggage trunk that Twoflower gave him

Creator: Terry Pratchett

✱ Below: The Discworld is so magical that wizardry is hardly worth the effort.

swords and special potions through to werewolves, gnomes and even sentient trees. The Disc's inhabitants don't believe in magic, in the same way that we don't believe in traffic – it's not a matter of belief, because it's all around you. It simply exists, and belief doesn't come into it. Discworld wizards tend to be a fairly complacent lot, more interested in their academic tenures and sorting out their next meal than in probing the secrets of the universe.

Unseen University, in Ankh-Morpork, is the most important seat of magical learning on the Disc. Its main building is a large, sprawling, gothic-style affair with all sorts of wings, towers, basements and annexes. The internal layout is somewhat unpredictable, and all sorts of surprises lie in wait for the unwary, particularly in the vicinity of the magical, high-energy research laboratories. The Great Hall, where meals are served, remains predictably stable.

MAGIC: Discworld magic is really rather hard work, and not usually considered worth all the effort. It can take months or years to memorize a spell prior to casting it, and once it's ready, the ritual involved may take hours of work, and require all

no more than a mile across, endlessly circles the disc, providing day and night to its inhabitants. On a planet like that, pretty much anything can happen.

Magic on the Discworld is so common as to be almost routine. Any number of petty soothsayers, hedge-doctors, witches, alchemists and priests can be found. All sorts of things are magical, from talking

sorts of unusual ingredients. Frankly, it's all just too much bother. Therefore, most wizards concern themselves with far more sensible pursuits than spell casting – lunch, for example. Rincewind, having had a great many adventures, is considered, well, a bit *peculiar* by the other wizards.

The Wizard of Oz

L. Frank Baum created one of the most enduring fairytales of the modern world with his prodigious series of books based in the land of Oz. Its most famous portrayal was in the 1939 film *The Wizard of Oz*. This was based primarily on Baum's book *The Wonderful Wizard of Oz*, published in 1900. In it, a young Kansas orphan called Dorothy and her dog Toto are transported – perhaps dreaming – into the magical fairytale kingdom of Oz. The mysterious Wizard who gives his name to the film rules this kingdom. *The Wonderful Wizard of Oz* was the first book Baum published about the kingdom, and he wrote 13 more books about the land between 1904 and his death in 1919, eight more than he had originally planned. Other writers took up where he left off, and there are now 40 works that are considered canonical (i.e. genuinely accurate) stories about the land. Despite being seen by many people as the definitive Oz story, the 1939 *The Wizard of Oz* film itself is just one of 17 different films based on Baum's works. It is the most respected of them all by far, however.

BIOGRAPHY: Oscar Zoroaster Phadrig Isaac Norman Henkle Emanuel Ambroise Diggs was born in Omaha, Nebraska in 1828, the son of a local politician. Almost from the first, the child felt weighed down by the burden of such a long and cumbersome name. Aware that his initials spelt out "ozpinhead", Oscar grew up calling himself O.Z., dropping the "P.I.N.H.E.A.D." part as an unreasonable slur on his intelligence. Perhaps because of resentment about his name, Oscar ran away from home while still a young man, and joined a circus. He learnt to do tricks – ventriloquism, stage magic and hot-air ballooning – and became a skilled sideshow performer. To make sure the audience got the right idea, he called himself

★ Left: The original book cover.

✦ Top: The Wizard and Dorothy (as played by
Judy Garland) prepare to set off.

✦ Right: Life can be a witch sometimes. The Wicked Witch
of the West and one of her fabulous flying monkeys.

a wizard, and stencilled his initials on his balloon and on other pieces of equipment.

One afternoon, a wind blew him and his balloon away from the circus and out over the desert. After a time, he arrived over the four countries of the Munchkins, the Gillikins, the Winkies and the Quadlings, each one ruled over by a witch. Oscar declared himself a wizard, and everyone deferred to him, already being impressed with his arrival from the air. He ordered the locals to build the emerald city at the point where the four countries touched each other, and declared himself the ruler of the land of Oz. He ruled Oz in peace for many years, eventually becoming old and homesick. When Dorothy arrived, blown in by a cyclone, he agreed to carry her back home again. The balloon proved beyond his control again, and he was blown off. Dorothy got home anyway, and Oscar eventually got back to Omaha.

Once there, he discovered that all his old friends had died or moved away, and he returned to Oz again. The land was now ruled by the rightful Princess, Ozma, and Oscar was made her official Wizard. Under tuition from the Good Witch Glinda, he eventually went on to gain a diploma from the Eastern Evian University of Magic, and become a genuine, bona fide spell-caster rather than a humbug wizard.

WORLD: The land of Oz is one of the faerie realms, and as such magic is a common and everyday part of life. All sorts of magical creatures and people can be found, so much so that people are divided roughly into "meat" and "non-meat" – people made of flesh and blood and bone, like Dorothy and Glinda, and people made of other things, such as the Tin Man and the Scarecrow. In addition to the evil witches of the West and East that Dorothy "liqui-dates", there are two evil witches, Mombi and Singra, who had ruled the North and South until the good witches Glinda and Locasta defeat and exile them. The evil Mombi goes on to cause much trouble throughout the series of books, as does Roquat the evil Nome King.

MAGIC: Wizardly magic in Oz conforms to stereotype fantasy patterns – there is a higgledy-piggledy mixture of spells, rituals, gestures and magical objects. A chant can make the Wizard pass through a closed door without opening it, but a spell is required to make him invisible, and herbs sprinkled on his head turn him temporarily to wood. In general, Oz magic is powerful but not cataclysmic. What it lacks in sheer firepower, however, it makes up for by being a major part of daily life.

Name: THE WIZARD OF OZ AKA OSCAR ZOROASTER PHADRIG ISAAC NORMAN HENKLE EMANUEL AMBROISE DIGGS

Age: 72

Height: 5ft 4 inches

Description: A kind-looking little old man with a bald head and wrinkled features, dressed in black velvet robes

Dominant Abilities: Ventriloquism

Traits: Kindly, helpful

Nature: Good

Power: None

Type: Charlatan

Domain: Circus tricks

Goal: To rule the land of Oz

Key Equipment: Hot-air balloon

Creator: L. Frank Baum

Abdul al-Hazred

The cycle of stories known as the Cthulhu Mythos were created by Howard Phillips Lovecraft, an American horror writer born in 1890. In these stories, he set out his terrifying view of the world as a tiny spot of pleasant light in a universe of dark evil. Humanity, according to Lovecraft, teeters on the edge of a gigantic abyss, which could reach up to engulf the Earth at any time. Everything we believe in is apparently false; the true lords and masters of Earth are supposed to be a collection of foul, monstrous Elder Gods, locked away from our reality for a short time, but ready to return "when the stars are right". Cthulhu itself is one of these vile deities. Lovecraft's work is still stark and disturbing, and it has been a major influence on our literature and film – not just in

horror, but in other areas as well. Throughout the stories of the Cthulhu Mythos, the one corrupting influence that crops up time and again is the *Necronomicon*. This evil tome of magic details Cthulhu and its fellows, and provides spells by which the servants of the Elder Gods can be called forth and compelled to do foul deeds. To read the *Necronomicon* is to be driven mad ... but the *Necronomicon* itself is a translation of an earlier manuscript, the *Kitab al-Azif*, written by the mad Arab, Abdul al-Hazred.

BIOGRAPhY: Abdul al-Hazred (or more correctly *Abd al-Azir*, "Worshipper of the Great Devourer") lived in the late seventh/early eighth centuries AD. Born in Sanaa in Yemen, he was a poet and philosopher who found a degree of artistic success and acceptance during the period of the Ommiade caliphs, some time around 700AD. Something of a student of magic, astronomy and early science, he toured around ancient Arabia looking for inspiration and secrets, and was accounted mad. He journeyed through the ruins of Babylon, and in the labyrinths beneath the Egyptian temple city of Memphis, before going out alone into the great southern desert – the *Roba al Khaliyeh* or "Empty Space" of the ancient Arabs, known more recently as the *Dahma* or "Crimson" desert. Many strange tales and marvels are told by the few who have penetrated into the desert and returned alive, stories of the jealously protective evil spirits who live there, and the lethal monsters that keep them company. Al-Hazred spent his time in the *Roba al Khaliyeh* listening to the spirits and the monsters, and exploring the region. He claimed to have visited the long-lost, evil city of pillars, Irem, buried beneath the shifting sands, and learned strange things in a hidden room. It was a nameless desert town that proved to be

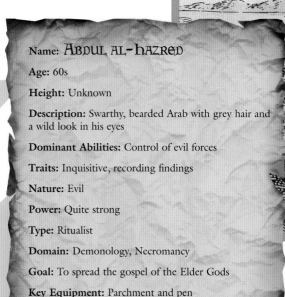

Name: ABDUL AL-HAZRED

Age: 60s

Height: Unknown

Description: Swarthy, bearded Arab with grey hair and a wild look in his eyes

Dominant Abilities: Control of evil forces

Traits: Inquisitive, recording findings

Nature: Evil

Power: Quite strong

Type: Ritualist

Domain: Demonology, Necromancy

Goal: To spread the gospel of the Elder Gods

Key Equipment: Parchment and pen

Creator: Howard Phillips Lovecraft

his greatest find, however. Beneath the ruins, he found documents detailing the horrifying secrets and legends of a race of gods far older than mankind. This work provided much of the information that went into the *Kitab al-Azif*. On his return from the *Roba*, he settled in Damascus, where he wrote the *al-Azif*. Shortly after its completion, according to his twelfth century biographer, Ebn Khallikan, he was seized by one or more invisible monsters in broad daylight in the middle of a bustling bazaar, and ripped to shreds as horrified witnesses looked on.

WORLD: The title of the *Kitab al-Azif* translates approximately into English as "the screeching of the desert demons", although Lovecraft normally rendered it more poetically. The fictional book may have actually been loosely inspired by the work *Kutu Kitab Katulu*, housed in the British Library. The mythology that the *al-Azif* portrays holds that the Elder Gods are locked away, but it does make some rather shocking allegations about a race of aliens who created humanity and the other animals. These creatures lived in gigantic cities now locked under the Antarctic ice sheet. Other occasional monsters apparently lurk in the hidden places of the earth as well, in lonely forests and quiet mountainsides, generally keeping out of the way of humanity. In general, though, true magic is very rare and more or less unknown.

MAGIC: Abdul al-Hazred's magic is dedicated mainly to the summoning, control and manipulation of the Elder Gods and their servants. The spells he lists in the *Kitab al-Azif* seem to be flawed, however, either through his madness or in their translation, as most attempts to work with the techniques in the *Necronomicon* seem to end in disaster. Some wizards, however, have been able to correct or fine-tune the formulae involved not only to summon and control monsters, but also to raise the dead and switch bodies with other people, gain eternal youth, and uncover all sorts of long-forgotten secrets. The most famous excerpt from the *Necronomicon* however is not a spell, but a warning of what Lovecraft alleged was still to come – "That is not dead which can eternal lie, and with strange aeons even death may die."

★ Right: Lovecraft sitting among his most famous creations.

Yog-Sothoth Knows the gate Yog-Soth gate

That is not de which can eternal And with strang even death may

H.P. Lovecraft
1890 ~ 1937

The Sorcerer's Apprentice

The story of the Sorcerer's Apprentice is genuinely
ancient. Although the character is most famous now
for the eight-minute feature segment in Walt Disney's
animated classic *Fantasia*, it has a long history.
The Disney section, originally from 1940, is animated
to accompany an orchestral scherzo of the same
name by Paul Dukas, premiered in Paris
in 1897. Dukas based his piece on *Der
Zauberlehrling*, a ballad-like poem written in 1796 by the German writer, Johann
Wolfgang von Goethe. This poem was in
turn based on *The Lie-Fancier*, a tale recorded
by the ancient Greek satirist, Lucian of
Samosata, in 150AD. Lucian himself is
thought to have been rewriting a story
that came out of ancient pharonic Egypt,
and may have even pre-dated it. As such,
the tale of the Sorcerer's Apprentice has an
ancient pedigree, and has remained largely
unchanged as it has passed down the centuries.

BIOGRAPHY: The original story of the Sorcerer's
Apprentice is almost as simple as the version retold
in *Fantasia*. A village boy goes to the castle of a local
sorcerer and asks for his help in getting some food for
the village. In return, the sorcerer takes the boy on as
his apprentice and starts teaching him magic. Tiring
of his chores one afternoon, the boy takes advantage
of the sorcerer's absence to use a spell he has seen his
master use. He uses the magic to animate a broom, so
that it will fetch pails of water for him from the well.
All works as planned, until the apprentice realizes that
he doesn't know how to stop the broom. The castle
quickly starts to fill with water. In desperation, the
boy chops the broom in two, but finds that both parts

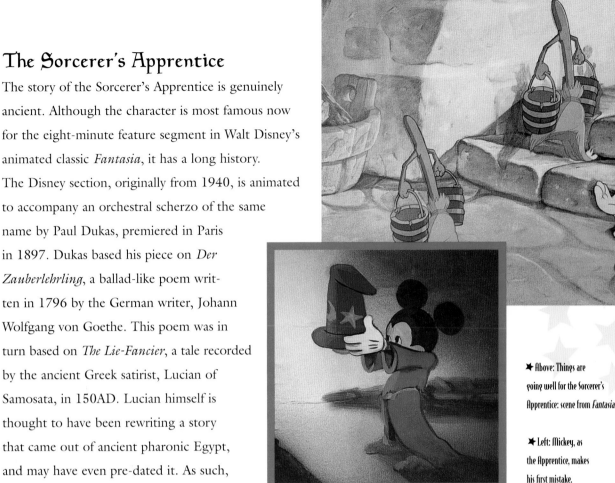

✦ Above: Things are
going well for the Sorcerer's
Apprentice: scene from *Fantasia*.

✦ Left: Mickey, as
the Apprentice, makes
his first mistake.

Name: THE SORCERER'S APPRENTICE

Age: Adolescent

Height: Unknown

Description: A boy, portrayed as Mickey Mouse by
Walt Disney

Dominant Abilities: Re-animation of objects

Traits: Mischievous, lazy, repentant

Nature: Good

Power: Low

Type: Charlatan

Domain: Manipulation

Goal: To put down what he has called forth

Key Equipment: Broom, bucket

Creator: Traditional story

continue the work, filling the castle twice as quickly as
before. Finally, just before the situation becomes totally
disastrous, the sorcerer returns, banishes the magic,
and sets everything right. Chastened, the boy returns
to his studies and duties properly, and in due time
learns all his master's magic. At that point, the sorcerer turns himself into a toad and leaves the area, hand-
ing the castle over to the new sorcerer, who can give
as much food to the village as is necessary.

WORLD: *The Sorcerer's Apprentice* is a fable, set
within a fairytale-like land. As such, the sorcerer and
his magic are part of reality, but stand outside everyday
events, representing a special solution to the problem
of hunger. Within the framework of the tale, magic is
a plot device used to represent the limitations of
knowledge. It is never really explored or explained; it

is just there to make the story work and to help it
carry its point effectively. The real message of *The
Sorcerer's Apprentice*, of course, is that a little knowledge can be dangerous – don't assume that just
because you can do something, that you should do it,
or that you can undo it once you have started.

MAGIC: The magic used to animate, and later
quieten, the broom is assumed within the framework
of the story to be a fairly simple spell, with limited
gestures and no real ritual of any significance. The
Apprentice knows more magic than just how to start
the broom, but either the crisis forces his knowledge
out of his mind, or it is of no real significance to the
situation he finds himself in, because he does not
attempt to fall back on it, and we never learn what it
might be.

Honourable Mentions

There are a great many wizards of all shapes and sizes who are worthy of further consideration, but sadly we don't have the room to go into them in the proper detail. They include mad, cackling **Tim the Enchanter** from *Monty Python and the Holy Grail*, who casts fireballs around convulsively and teleports himself from place to place; **Belgarath, Garion** and the brotherhood of immortal sorcerers from *The Belgariad* books by David Eddings; **Will Stanton** and **Merriman Lyon**, youngest and oldest members of the Circle of Old Ones who work for the Light in its endless struggle to stop the Dark from taking over the earth in the *Dark is Rising* sequence by Susan Cooper; super-powerful wizards **Pug** and **Macros** from Raymond Feist's *Riftwar* Saga; **Rand al-Thor** and the other **Aes Sedai** destined to break the world in Robert Jordan's *Wheel of Time* series; and diverse other worthies such as **Ningauble of the Seven Eyes** & **Sheelba of the Eyeless Face, Shimrod** scion of **Murgen, Rhialto the Marvellous; Raistlin; Arithon Prince of Shadow; Sir Adam Sinclair** and many more.

✦ Below: John Cleese as Tim the Enchanter.

10

Mythic

Figures

Mythic Figures
Important Legendary Wizards from Around the World

The myths and legends of the past play an important part in our world. All through history, humans have used thrilling stories of mighty heroes, villains and gods to make sense of the world, the universe, moral issues, and even birth, sex and death. A society's myths bind it together, helping to give it definition and character.

Important Legendary Wizards from Around the World

Because of this, although the modern world has moved away from traditional forms of storytelling, the myths and legends of the world continue to provide both inspiration and background. We now have television, cinema, CDs and computer games to tell us stories, but the people who actually produce our entertainment continue to draw imagery and tales from our myths, wrapping them up in modern forms. *Buffy the Vampire Slayer* would have been perfectly at home at an ancient Greek campfire, next to stories about Hercules or Odysseus.

Wizards are a vital part of myths and legends all around the world. Heroes are exceptional, by definition – that means that they need exceptional powers, and exceptional enemies. Sometimes the hero him- or herself is a wizard, calling on magic tricks to win the day, while other times a friendly wizard acts as advisor, providing enough help to make the task possible, but never enough to make it easy. Sometimes, it is the villain who is a wizard, using magic to cause all sorts of problems. Often, the wizards in legends remain nameless plot devices to make the hero look good, being just "a wizard". Some mythic wizards are much more than that, though. Their very names have power, and shout down to us through the centuries, carrying the old tales with them. The greatest wizard of all, the most famous, the most flawed, was Merlin.

✦ Left: Merlin amd Arthur claim Excalibur.

✦ Below: Buffy, as played by Sarah Michelle Gellar, is a true mythic hero.

Merlin

The myths and legends of King Arthur and the Knights of the Round Table form a vivid, colourful cycle of wonders and betrayals. The stories, set in the golden age of Arthur's rule of Britain, are a fascinating tapestry across time. Some come from the earliest Celtic accounts of Camelot some 1,500 years ago, while other elements were added when Britain became a Christian country. It was further expanded by French and German stories in early medieval times, and tied together into a great romance, *Le Morte D' Arthur*, by the fifteenth-century poet Thomas Malory. Merlin is a central figure of the myths, Arthur's wizardly advisor who helped him to conceive and form Camelot itself.

BIOGRAPHY: The most famous mythological wizard, Merlin (originally Myrrdin) was born after his mother, a Christian nun, was raped by a demon. At the moment of his birth, fearing that the child might take after its evil father, his mother snatched him up and plunged him into a fount of holy water. Although this wise treatment gave him a deep-seated love of the mortal world and the desire to help humanity out as much as possible, he also kept some of his father's qualities. This included the ability to change shape, a powerful driving restlessness that made him a wanderer, a mastery of the magical arts, and an extremely strong sexual appetite.

He was raised by the witch Nimue (sometimes Niniane or Viviane), a fellow shape-changer who fell in love with him as he became an adult. Merlin rejected her, however, and went out into the mortal world. The adult Merlin spent much of his time appearing as a wise old man. In this guise, he acted as a wizardly adviser to a number of early kings and warlords, including High King Vortigern and Uther Pendragon.

Whilst still a child, Merlin was found by soldiers working for Vortigern. The King was busily trying to build a fort on a rocky hillside in Wales, and the structure kept collapsing. Merlin was imprisoned underground and threatened with sacrifice if he did not tell the King what was going wrong. He dutifully explained to Vortigern where he was going wrong – the rock actually had objections to the castle, which needed to be overcome – and went on to prophesy his downfall, which indeed came to be. Next, working as the advisor of Ambrosius Aurelianus, Merlin was responsible for the creation of Stonehenge, erected in celebration of Amrosius' reign.

Uther Pendragon later demanded supernatural help from Merlin to become supreme ruler of Britain. Merlin refused, telling him that his ambitions would fail and that he would destroy his own line. Uther took no notice, and demanded the power to change shape. Merlin agreed, transforming Uther into the likeness of a rival, King Gorlois of Tintagel, the ruler of Cornwall. Uther was infatuated with Gorlois'

queen, Ygern, and once he looked like her husband, he immediately went to have sex with her.

Ygern became pregnant, and her son, the young Arthur, was raised in secret by Merlin. Partly as a result of Merlin's teachings, Arthur was able to pull Uther's sword from the stone his father had embedded it in, and unite Britain as King, fighting against the Romans. When the sword broke in a duel with a giant, Merlin guided Arthur to the Lady of the Lake. A hand rose out of the water holding the magical sword Excalibur, whose edge never blunted and whose scabbard stopped

★ Right: Arthur is
presented with his birthright.

★ Far Right: "Oh yesss, yess,
good." Nicol Williamson's
superb portrayal of
Merlin in *Excalibur*.

bleeding. Arthur was given the sword for the duration of his reign.

At other times, however, Merlin's demonic nature would exert a hold. Sometimes he would transform himself into an extremely handsome young man, and wander around the country seducing every girl he came across. At other times, he would disappear entirely from the mortal world. He particularly enjoyed spending time as a stream of water, a breeze, a cloud in the sky, or even just a thought, whispering through the world.

It was his lustful nature that eventually proved his downfall. Nimue, devastated by Merlin's rejection, decided to seek revenge on him. She changed herself into every shape she could imagine to trap him, and each time he was wary enough, and smart enough, to escape from her. Finally, she turned herself into a beautiful woman, and allowed him to seduce her. Merlin's lust blinded him to her true identity, and he made love to her. At the moment of ecstasy, when all his defences were down and he was fully distracted, she changed herself into a sphere of amber and engulfed him completely. Once he was trapped, she transformed into an oak tree. They remain locked together still.

WORLD: Merlin is primarily remembered for his place in the Arthurian myths. They are set in the middle of the first millennium AD, when the Romans occupying Britain were losing their grip on even their safest territories, and the country was reverting to a collection of petty territories ruled by warlord kings. Arthur united the country, defeating the Romans and various Viking chieftains, and bringing all the territories under his rule. He ushered in a time of justice, law and fairness for all the land, and ruled wisely from Camelot during a golden period. His wife Guinevere, who had an affair with Lancelot, his finest knight, later betrayed Arthur and the innocence of his reign was shattered. The quest for the Holy Grail followed, and finally the war with Morgan, Arthur's half-sister, and their son Mordred, which saw the end of the period, and Arthur taken away by the faeries of Avalon to sleep until the world needed him again. This was a period rich in supernatural occurrences; faeries, witches, shape-shifters and monsters were common in the land. The rituals of superstition guarded the common people against magic threats lurking in wait. Merlin, being only half-human, stood between the worlds of normality and of faerie, and acted as a protector of the people.

MAGIC: The styles and patterns of Merlin's magic have varied through the years with each different storyteller, so it is difficult to be certain exactly what

process he followed. Some accounts have Merlin speaking spells, while others indicate that his magic came from his mind alone. The most famous incarnation of Merlin in modern times was Nicol Williamson's frightening portrayal of the role in the classic 1981 movie *Excalibur*. This showed him as a strong, aloof man in a metal skullcap, almost alien in outlook and interests, sharing little in common with the mortals around him – his magic was accomplished with the aid of one versatile spell, the "Charm of Making". Whichever format is taken for Merlin's powers, he is consistently able to see into the future, change his form, talk with spirits and control the elements around him.

Name: MERLIN

Age: Immortal

Height: Varies

Description: As a wizard, he appears as an elderly man with long white hair and beard, carrying a staff

Dominant Abilities: Divination, transformation

Traits: Helpful, sympathetic, restless, driven, lustful

Nature: Good

Power: Very strong

Type: Sorcerer, mostly

Domain: Elementalist, particularly with respect to nature

Goal: To help humanity

Key Equipment: None in particular, but he did personally make the Round Table, cause Stonehenge to be built, and lead Arthur to Excalibur.

Taliesin the Bard

The tradition of sorcerer-bards is strong in Welsh folklore. Taliesin was the greatest of all the bards, blessed with all the knowledge in the world and a radiant, shining beauty. It is generally believed that the legendary stories surrounding Taliesin were created to flatter and honour a real man of the same name, who was court bard to the Welsh kings in the sixth century AD, and who is believed to be buried at a village that was named after him.

BIOGRAPHY: Caridwen was a witch, and with her husband, Tegid Voel, she lived in the middle of Lake Tegid in Penllyn, and they had three children. Their eldest child, Morvan ab Tegid, was a normal son. Their second child was a daughter, Creirwy, the most beautiful maiden in the entire world. Their third child, however, a son named Avagddu, was as ugly as his sister was lovely. Caridwen despaired for Avagddu, thinking that because he was so ill favoured he would never win acceptance in the world, and so decided to give him the gift of knowledge and wisdom. She set out to brew a potion that would contain all of the knowledge, inspiration and magic in the world, which she could then feed to her son. To create the potion she desired, the cauldron had to be stirred, boiling, without end for a year and a day, until finally three drops would be yielded that would contain all the world's wisdom.

Gwion Bach was the son of Gwreang of Llanfair, born in Caereinion in Powys. Gwion was captured by the witch Caridwen, and put to work stirring her cauldron. She also caught a blind man named Morda, and set him to feeding the fire beneath it. She threatened them with dire fates if the cauldron should stop boiling. While they toiled, she studied books written by ancient astronomers and, during the correct planetary times and alignments, went out to collect all sorts of charm-carrying herbs to add to her brew.

The cauldron continued to brew until one day, towards the end of the year, Gwion was slightly careless in his stirring. While Caridwen was off gathering herbs and speaking spells to prepare them, three drops of the enchanted brew splashed out of the cauldron and struck Gwion on the finger. Because they were so hot, having been boiled for nearly a year, he sucked his painful finger. As soon as the drops went into his mouth, he gained the power of the brew, and suddenly foresaw everything that was to come. Realizing that the witch meant to kill him and Morda after the year was up, and

✦ Right: Caridwen with her cauldron.

✦ Far Right: Taliesin plays to inspire the harts.

a piece of wood and hit Morda so hard around the head with it that one of his eyes fell out. He protested that she was being unfair by wounding him, because he was not to blame. Then Caridwen saw the truth of it – Gwion had benefited from her work, and so she went after him.

At first she ran after the boy, but when he saw her, he turned himself into a hare and sped off. She responded by turning into a greyhound, and chased him down. Before she could grab him though, he dashed to a river and turned into a fish. She transformed into an otter to pursue him, and he had to turn into a bird and fly away to escape her jaws. Even so, she became a hawk and shot after him, harrying him. Finally, terrified for his life, Gwion saw a heap of wheat on a bare floor, and dropped amongst it, turning himself into another grain of wheat. Caridwen saw him, however, and changed herself into a high-crested black hen. She scratched amongst the wheat until she found the grain that was Gwion, and ate him.

perceiving suddenly the great power and skill of Caridwen, Gwion fled off back towards his old home in Powys. The cauldron, meanwhile, split into two halves, because its contents were now poisonous without the three drops.

When Caridwen returned with the day's herbs, she found the cauldron broken, her hopes dashed and her year's work wasted, and she was furious. She grabbed

That was not the end, however. Having consumed the Gwion grain, she carried him with her for nine months, and finally gave birth to a child of radiant beauty, Taliesin. He was so beautiful that she couldn't bring herself to kill him after all, and instead she wrapped him in a leather sack and cast him out to float off to sea on 29 April, where the gods could decide what to do with him.

As luck would have it, he floated into the salmon weir of King Gwyddno Garanhir, which the king emptied every May eve. The king's son, Elphin, known throughout the kingdom for being unlucky, was emptying the weir that year. To Elphin's horror, the weir, which normally held a hundred pounds worth of fish, held only the leather sack. However, his luck was shown to have turned when he opened the sack and set Taliesin free. The child consoled him with a prophetic poem, foretelling fortune and honour for Elphin, and saying that he himself would be of more worth to the king's son than 300 salmon.

As he matured, Taliesin went on to become the greatest poet and bard that Wales would ever see. He had the gifts of prophecy and knowledge, understood science, and could use his songs and music to work all sorts of wonders. He could calm storms with a word, incite people to peace, love, bravery or frenzy, control the weather, bring fertility to plants and animals, open locks, travel through time and space and make himself invisible. The tales of his exploits include visiting a number of biblical figures – God in heaven, Noah in the ark, Jonah in the whale and Satan in his kitchen – as well as watching Romulus and Remus build the walls of ancient Rome, and guiding King Arthur into the underworld of Annwn to steal the Cauldron of Plenty, which could provide prosperity and immortality.

WORLD: The myths and legends of the Celtic peoples were greatly eroded by Christian influence. The Christians saw the Celtic myths as vile devil-worship, and did their best to convert the tales and legends into a framework that they felt better about. This combined with the Roman persecution of the Celts across Europe, means the myths that remain are mostly fragmented remnants of what would have once been a rich and powerful tradition. The underworld, Annwn, was a major feature of most stories. All the faeries, demons and goblins lived in this invisible realm, taking on characteristics and identities when they encroached onto the living world. For the people of the time, all sorts of threats apparently lurked just on the edges of normal life, and the rituals of superstition were all that kept the mischievous and malicious spirits away. Taliesin, with his magic and his songs, may have represented the power of knowledge.

MAGIC: Most of Taliesin's power lay within his music. It was through his songs or his playing that he was able to work most of the wonders that he did, and his prophecies, too, were always couched in verse, and usually sung. Against the usual run of this trend, his ability to change shape was spontaneous, requiring no active spell casting.

Name: TALIESIN

Age: Varies

Height: 6ft

Description: An extremely handsome young man with a radiant brow

Dominant Abilities: Evocation, divination, transformation

Traits: Creative, musical, just

Nature: Good

Power: Strong

Type: Magic channels mostly through song

Domain: General

Goal: To create works of beauty and help the weak

Key Equipment: His harp

The Yellow Emperor

The traditional creator of China's Daoist religion, the Yellow Emperor; is still respected and honoured as one of the great civilizing forces of the country. The forces of heaven and hell play a large part in traditional Chinese mythology, where every being, mortal or immortal, has a specific role to fulfil.

BIOGRAPHY: The Yellow Emperor, Huang Di, ruled China 5,000 years ago. He was the first of the mythic Five Emperors, a dynasty of wise sorcerer-rulers who steered China from barbarism and chaos into civilized order. Like his later brethren, the Yellow Emperor had the power to change his shape and appearance, and lived slightly outside time, so that he aged far more slowly than most mortals.

Even from the moment of his birth, the Yellow Emperor was knowledgeable and wise. He was born knowing mighty magic and was able to speak all of the languages of the world, as well as knowing everything that the people of Earth at that time knew. He devoted himself to bringing knowledge and enlightenment, and taught the people of China how to hunt, fish, farm and build roads. He then went on to invent a great number of different innovations based on the knowledge that he held, including the wheel, armour, weaponry, ships, the compass, coins, law and government. During his small amounts of spare time, he entertained himself by creating music, pottery, painting, poetry and other arts. His wife, meanwhile, discovered how to make silk, and his chief official created writing.

On top of everything else, the Yellow Emperor was in frequent communication with the gods in heaven. He was permitted to climb the holy mountain, Tai Shan, in order to speak with them through prayers

✦ Left: The Yellow Emperor, mythic creator of Daoism.

and sacrifices. He travelled up the mountain in an ivory chariot. This vehicle's driver was a green crane with a human face, and six dragons and an elephant pulled it. The chariot was followed by processions of phoenixes, snakes, tigers and wolves. When he reached the top of the mountain, the Yellow Emperor would take his place at the centre, and alter his shape until he had four faces, so that he could gaze out at the four quarters of the earth.

The Yellow Emperor's golden reign was calm and prosperous – apart from one short period when the rain god and the wind god rebelled against him – and he himself spent the years presiding over continual feasts and merry-making. For 15 generations, he ruled China wisely. Eventually, however, the endless feasts took their toll, and he started to become fat and slow. He immediately abandoned his luxury, and went to

live in a grass-roofed hut in the palace grounds, fasting and praying.

Eventually, he had a dream of a calm paradise where the inhabitants felt no pain, sorrow or longing, foreswore emotion, and lived revelling in the pure bliss of the spiritual state. When he woke up, he announced that he had discovered Dao, "the way."

His reign lasted for just one more generation, during which time he set forth the eight-fold tenets of Daoism, and invented healing, including Qi Gong and acupuncture. Finally, his work complete, the Yellow Emperor was honoured by being taken up to heaven, and his followers mourned him for 200 years.

WORLD: Back at its early beginnings, the Chinese

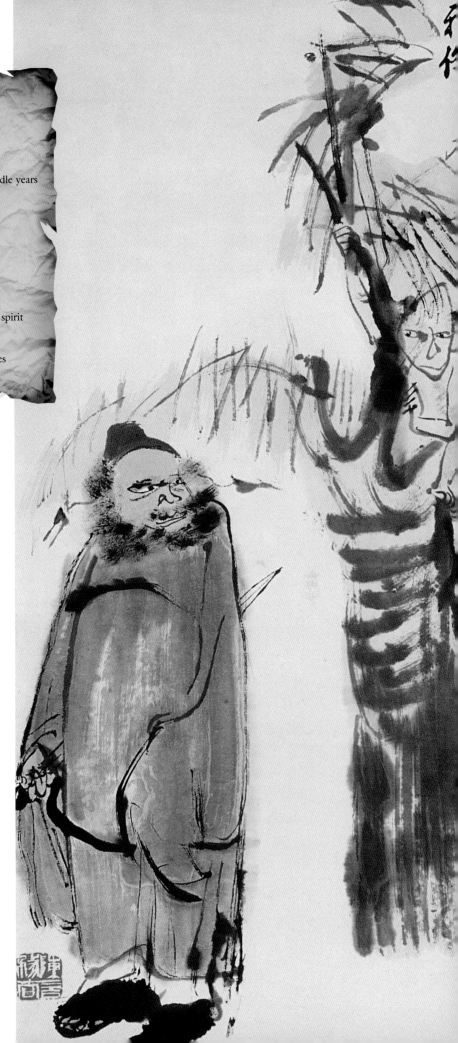

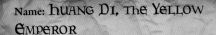

Name: HUANG DI, THE YELLOW
EMPEROR

Age: 400 years

Height: 5ft 7 inches

Description: An ascetic Chinese noble of middle years
in yellow robes

Dominant Abilities: Invocation, evocation

Traits: Ordered, wise, inventive

Nature: Good

Power: Extremely strong

Type: Ritualist

Domain: Demonologist, in principle if not in spirit

Goal: To bring order to the empire

Key Equipment: Magical chariot, yellow robes

empire was a broad mix of peasant smallholdings,
nomadic tribes and occasional bandit fiefdoms, with
very little in the way of internal structure. Technology
was almost non-existent, and the world was seen to
be populated by all manner of gods and spirits. The
Yellow Emperor brought technological advancement
and consistent internal government to the Empire. In
the minds of the people, that was far greater magic
than any of his sorcerous tricks. He remains one of the
greatest cultural heroes of Daoism.

MAGIC: Much of the Yellow Emperor's power
came from the rightful authority that he held as the
mandated lord of the people on Earth. As such, quite
a lot of his magic boiled down to having the right to
order spirits and godlings around. On other occasions,
he made use of the kind of convoluted ritual traditional to Chinese folklore, involving spells, complex gestures, written formulae on parchment, burning herbs,
bells and gongs, and other similar items.

Circe

Gods and goddesses were a familiar part of the daily routine for the ancient Greeks. They meddled continually in mortal affairs, passed on omens and warnings, pulled tricks on people, slept with them, sent them on quests, and generally manipulated them left, right and centre. Half-god heroes and villains, both humans and monsters, were to be found all over the countryside. In many ways, the divine world was there for everyone in much the same way that the adult world is there for young children – all around, but, somehow, you don't quite get to take part in it properly. This familiarity between gods and humans made them extremely intimate, which is perhaps why even now, 2,000 years later, they are still a vibrant part of our culture – as shows like *Hercules: The Legendary Journeys* and *Xena: Warrior Princess* attest.

BIOGRAPhY: One of the most notorious sorceresses of Greek legend, Circe was the daughter of a liaison between the Sun and Hecate, the goddess of black magic, who took the form of an ocean nymph to seduce him. Circe inherited stunning beauty and grace from her father, and great magical prowess – and a rather nasty streak – from her mother. Her double nature caused her continual problems, making her desire a normal life, but also forcing her to angry displays of magical power over petty issues. Like many children of a god, she had a huge appetite for sexual intercourse with mortals.

Circle fell in love with and courted an Italian prince named Picus, but he turned her down. When she realized that she would not be able to have him, she transformed him into a woodpecker. She next turned her affections to a minor sea god called Glaucus, but discovered that he preferred her half-sister, the lovely sea sprite, Scylla. Furious, Circe transformed Scylla into a hideous sea-monster; human from the waist up but below the waist she was left with 12 dog's legs and six snarling, fang-toothed heads on long, snaky necks. Circe actually went so

far as to marry the prince of the state of Colchis, but found the idea of giving up her powers to live in his harem too objectionable. She killed him instead, in an attempt to seize his throne. Her father, the Sun, rescued her from the furious subjects of Colchis, and gave her the floating island of Aeaea to rule in an attempt to keep her out of trouble.

Circe spent her time on Aeaea sitting at a loom in her palace singing a song – a song so beautiful that none could resist it. When sailors landed on the island,

Name: CIRCE

Age: Immortal

Height: 5ft 4 inches

Description: A beautiful young woman with long golden hair

Dominant Abilities: Transformation

Traits: Passionate, irritable, unreasonable

Nature: Self-centred

Power: Strong

Type: Ritualist

Domain: General, her focus on transformation aside

Goal: To find an equal partner

Key Equipment: Wand, loom, floating island

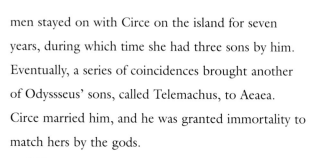

✦ Right: Circe sits in her beautiful gardens.

her song would bring them to the palace. Once a "guest" arrived, she would treat him to a generous feast, have sexual intercourse with him, and then transform him into a pig and leave him in her pens. Odysseus and his crew landed on Aeaea, but Hermes, messenger of the Gods, appeared to the hero and warned him of the danger he was in, giving him a herb, moly, to protect him. By the time Odysseus had finished with Hermes and crossed the island to the palace, all his men had been transformed. Circe gave him the standard routine – she welcomed him in, served him a feast, had sex with him, and then attempted to turn him too into a pig. The moly cancelled her magic, however, and she realized that Odysseus was protected by the gods.

Circe decided to obey his demands, and freed all her captive sailors from her spell. They then celebrated with a proper party for everyone – and no pig trans-formations – that seemed to last one night, but in reality kept going for months. Odysseus and the freed men stayed on with Circe on the island for seven years, during which time she had three sons by him. Eventually, a series of coincidences brought another of Odyssseus' sons, called Telemachus, to Aeaea. Circe married him, and he was granted immortality to match hers by the gods.

WORLD: The Greek myths are almost entirely set within a magical framework. The dividing line between the gods and mankind is extremely thin throughout them, and almost every tale features the supernatural. Unlike most mythologies, the Greek stories do not try to preach or set down religious lore, and they changed greatly over time, expanding and diversifying – more like an extended soap opera than a formal religion.

MAGIC: Circe's primary power lay in the ability to change a victim into another creature. She usually used a wand for this purpose, tapping the poor man with it. She also knew a wide variety of other spells and rituals, a legacy of her mother's power, but rarely made use of them – according to the major legends, anyway.

Honourable Mentions

Many of the wizards of mythology, both good and bad, remain as anonymous or shadowy characters in the background who guide the plot of the myth or move it along. There are a number of important wizards in world myth that deserve to be recognized, though. **Odin**, the all-father of Norse myth, was a god, but he deserves credit for the way he sacrificed an eye and spent ten nights crucified on the World Tree to learn the power of the runes and gain the mighty magic they represented. **Baba Yaga** was an evil Russian sorceress who lived in a hut that walked around on huge hen's legs and was surrounded by a skull-topped fence. The skulls' eyes glowed in the dark. She rode around the countryside in a giant mortar, using her pestle as an oar. Her teeth were knives and she could turn victims into stone with a glance. **Dido** the sorceress travelled to the northern African coast and founded the city of Carthage. **Cormac MacAirt**, King of Ireland, was raised by wolves and owned a magic cup that would divine the truth. **Faust**, a medieval wizard, sold his soul to the devil in exchange for all the knowledge and experience on earth. **Kao Guojiu**, a sage, found the Daoist inspiration to become one of the legendary Eight Immortals. **Enumclaw** and **Kapoonis** feature in the myths of the northwestern American coast. They were twin wizards who tamed the spirits of fire and rock, and gained mighty powers. To keep the rest of the world safe, Father Sky snatched them off the face of the earth and made them into gods, of lightning and thunder respectively. Other characters – such as the ambitious and sorcerous Grand Vizier of Arabic legend, the evil Wizard of the Baron Munchausen stories who kept his soul in a nut, and the necromantic wizards and zombie-masters of Chinese folklore – are common visitors to the cycles of mythology. Every mythic system has countless wizards and sorcerers of different types and forms who appear in one or two tales and vanish again, but we do not have the room to discuss them here.

✦ Below: Baba Yaga rides through the forest.

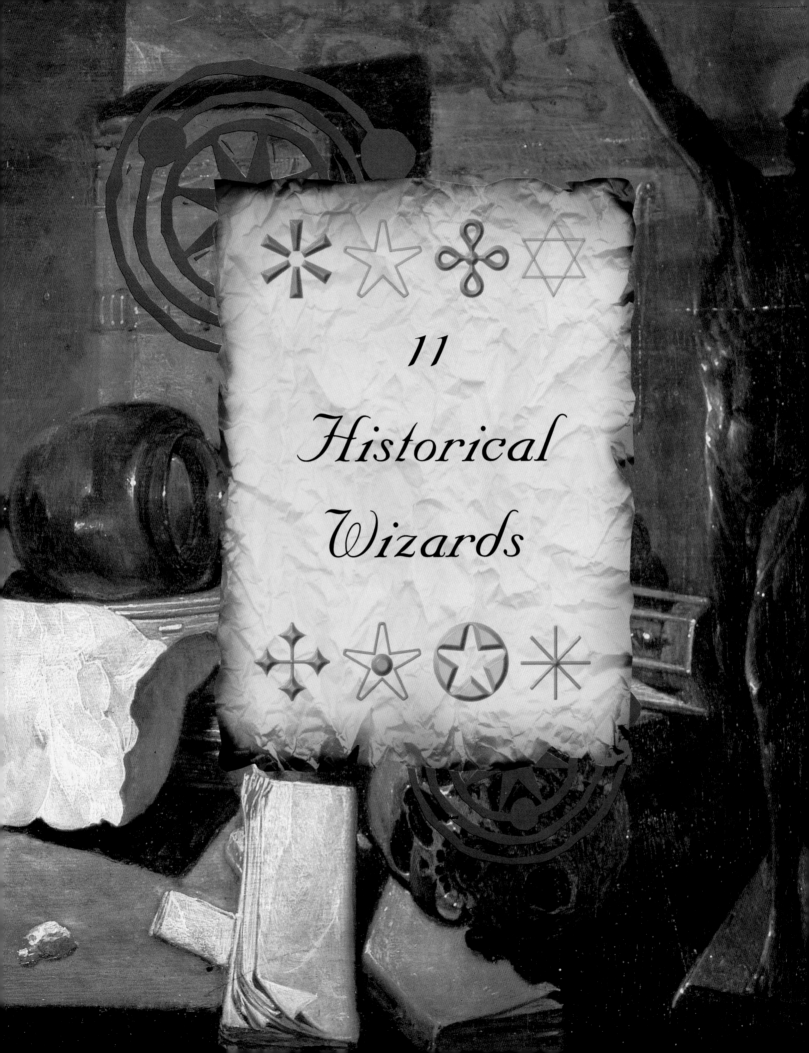

11
Historical Wizards

Down the centuries, the accusation of wizardry has blighted lives across the world. People have been tortured and killed on nothing more than a suggestion of arcane power, battles have been fought – and won or lost – because of it, and fortunes have been destroyed by it. The bottom line is that people the world over are scared of things that they do not understand, and anyone demonstrating uncanny abilities or knowledge is seen as a threat. The fear of inexplicable skills or powers is a constant factor in human history. Superstition, bigotry, jealousy and greed – all of these have made life extremely difficult for the groups and individuals that have been known for their rumoured wizardry. If there are any genuine wizards lurking in our world, they are well hidden – and, given the way that the rest of us have treated these historical cousins of theirs, you can understand why.

John Dee

One of the most notorious wizards in English history was the Tudor alchemist and court astrologer, Dr John Dee. He reached the height of his fame during the reign of Elizabeth I, and was known across Europe as a scientist, scholar and sorcerer. He enjoyed a period of considerable wealth and influence, but eventually fell from grace, and died nearly penniless. He left behind him a legacy of philosophical, wizardly, astrological and chemical writings and translations that remain important today.

BIOGRAPHY: John Dee was born in 1527 and educated at the Chantry School in Chelmsford. From there, he proceeded to Cambridge University and entered St John's College, before transferring to Trinity College. In 1547, aged 20, he made his first journey to Europe, and spent some time discussing a number of matters with assorted people in the various Dutch universities. The following year he travelled to the University of Leuven in Belgium, where he obtained his degree as a doctor.

In 1551, Dee obtained an introduction to the Court of King Edward VI, to whom he had already dedicated two of his books. He returned to court in 1553, when Mary Tudor gained the throne. By this time he was known as an astrologer, and was invited to prepare the Queen's natal horoscope for her. He also calculated a horoscope for the young Elizabeth, at that point still a princess.

Shortly after this time he began to experiment with magic. He quickly ended up in trouble, though, and was arrested on the testimony of a man called George Ferrys, who had accused Dee of cursing his children, killing one and blinding another. Other rumours accused Dee of trying to curse the Queen. His home was searched and he was brought to trial in front of the Secretary of State, but was cleared of all charges.

Astrology was a fascination that ran throughout society at the time, and anyone with a skill at casting horoscopes was in high demand. Dee's reputation ensured that his fame as an astrologer spread and he became quite a common figure at court.

When Elizabeth succeeded to the throne, her first commission for Dee was to name an auspicious day for her coronation. Shortly after she was crowned, she invited him to enter service in her retinue, and promised him a master's position at St Catherine's Hospital. On one occasion, when a wax effigy of the Queen was found lying in a prominent position outside a minor royal building with a large pin stuck through its chest, the general consensus was that someone was attempting to inflict disease or death upon the Queen. Dee was summoned, and his verdict was that it offered no danger to the Queen, which pleased her.

In 1570, Dee moved to the riverside London district of Mortlake, taking his library and research lab with him. The Queen occasionally stopped at his

★ Right: Edward
Kelley invokes the dead
at Walton-Le-Dale.

★ Background: Dee's
"Monas Hieroglyphia"
embodies the power
of the universe.

home to see his latest wonder or invention, and was said to be anxious for Dee to become her official court astrologer. He was an active alchemist at this time, and his search for the Philosopher's Stone may have had something to do with the Queen's eagerness to recruit him. He is said to have held discussions about the transmutation of metals with her in Westminster.

In 1581, Dee's wizardry really took off. He met up with a would-be medium and alchemist named Edward Kelley, who convinced him of his abilities. Kelley claimed to have found a pair of caskets containing mysterious red and white powders with which he was able to turn base metals into gold. Dee's diaries record Kelley using his powders to turn mercury into gold, and later pieces of brass, copper and other metal. This process is described as involving nothing more than adding Kelley's powders to the metal and then warming it in a fire.

Dee and Kelley travelled to Europe together to raise funds to work on the large-scale transmutation of base metals into gold. Although Dee returned to England in 1588, Kelley did not – he was imprisoned on and off by Emperor Rudolph of Prague, who wanted his secrets, and he died in 1595 after falling from a turret window whilst trying to escape. Queen Elizabeth, meanwhile, took pity on Dee's poverty and appointed him warden of the Collegiate Church in Manchester. Accusations of wizardry continued to harass him, however, and he had to defend himself further against accusations of devil worship and conjuring. He presented a petition to the James I on 5 June 1604, begging for a trial and exoneration to clear his name and to quieten the slanders that followed it. Dee died peacefully in 1608, aged 81, and was buried in Mortlake church, near his long-time home.

MAGIC: Although Queen Elizabeth's favour protected him to a certain extent, it was commonly said that Dee was a magician of dubious reputation. He openly practised the sorcerous art of divination, and held séances at which he claimed to raise spirits. His divination was conducted with the aid of an oval mirror made of black obsidian, which he claimed could conjure an image of a person into thin air. The mirror itself can now be found in the British Museum in London.

Dee's magical legacy has earned him a place of honour in modern occultism, too. In 1583, Dee and Kelley began a series of séance works with the black mirror. In this sequence of researches, Kelley entered a state of trance and worked with Dee to produce details of a special system of magic. This system, known now as Enochian magic, was based around the hierarchy of angels, their responsibilities, and their language, referred to as "Logaeth" (pronounced "Logah"). The Angelic spirits dictated several tables of letters to Kelley, along with instructions on how to use the tables to derive the names of all the various angelic spirits at all levels of authority. Specific words of Logaeth were dictated to Dee ("MRE", pronounced "Emm-Ree", meaning "with", for example), and letters were assigned numeric value, so that a word of a given numeric value was linked to all other words of the same value. This system of sorcery allowed for all manner of good spirits to be given sorcerous tasks to carry out on behalf of the wizard. Enochian magic is still practised by thousands of people world-wide today ... with unverifiable results.

✦ Below: Dee's laboratory in the Powder Tower is still preserved.

Name: DR JOHN DEE

Time Period: 1527–1608

Region: England, with journeys into Europe

Description: "[he] wore a long beard and was of dignified presence…"

Dominant Supposed Abilities: Divination, invocation, transformation

Traits: Learned, inquisitive

Nature: Fairly good

Magical Power: Weak

Type: Ritualist

Domain: Demonology, alchemy

Goal: To acquire wisdom

Key Equipment: The black "shewstone" mirror, wax tablets for scrying engraved with magical figures, multicoloured Enochian Magic tables, Logaeth manuscripts

The Knights Templar

One of the most famous and controversial groups in early medieval history, the Templars rose from very humble beginnings to become one of the richest and most powerful sects in Europe. Initially founded to protect pilgrims journeying to the Holy Lands between crusades, they swiftly grew in both influence and wealth. At the height of their power, several countries owed them a lot of money. Their reputation was tarnished with accusations of wizardry, however, and they were subsequently destroyed.

BIOGRAPHY: In 1095AD, the forces of Christianity in Western Europe launched their great First Crusade to "reclaim" the holy land of Palestine from its Muslim residents. By the time the war ended four years later, the holy city of Jerusalem had been captured, and the united force of the Crusaders created the Kingdom of Jerusalem. In 1118, a group of nine French knights created a monastic order based in Jerusalem dedicated to forsaking wealth and offering protection to various pilgrims and religious worthies visiting the Holy Land from Europe. The order's full title was "The Poor Knights of Christ and of the Temple of Solomon", shortened to the Knights Templar.

The order's most powerful ally was St Bernard of Clairvaux, a Cistercian Abbot and the chief spokesman for the united powers and churches of European Christianity – so influential that he was often known as "The Second Pope". Bernard prepared the order's codes of conduct and oath of poverty, oversaw their formation and, when the time was right, sponsored the Templars for full acceptance within Christendom as a fully sanctioned monastic order. When they won acceptance, the Templars gained the full support of the Pope and the collected kings of Europe.

Because the individual Templars swore to poverty and gave all their goods and lands to the order, the group quickly became rich. Most of the members came from minor nobility, and had substantial wealth to begin with. This all went to the order, along with the generous donations received from the rich pilgrims that they escorted. After the Crusades, the order relocated back to Europe, and their wealth gave them power. Pope Innocent II declared that the Templars were exempt from all authority other than that of the Pope, which meant that they were above any earthly law. They used this immunity – and their great wealth – to lend money for interest, a practice that was commonly illegal. The Templars became a leading financial

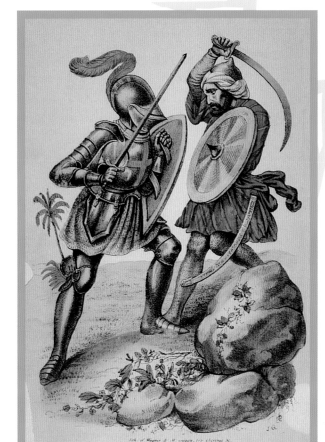

✦ Right: A Templar fights a heathen enemy.

✦ Far Right: The death of Simon de Montfort, who had been the scourge of the Templars.

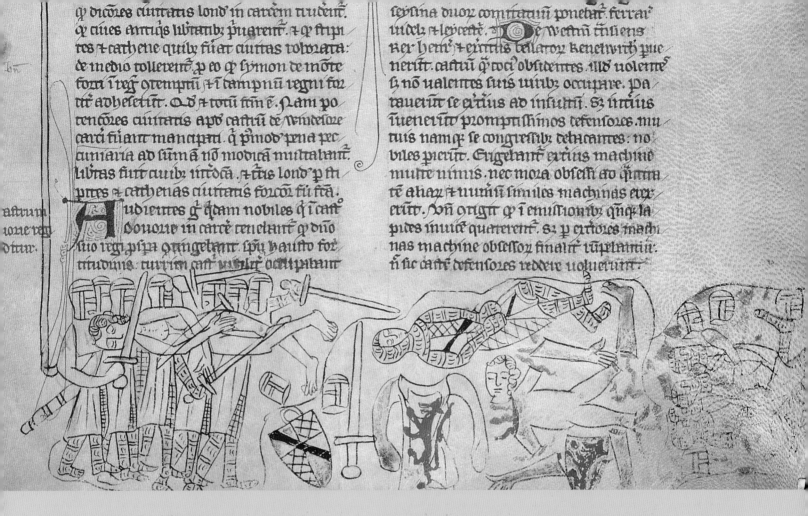

source for most of the European kings. In the process, they set up the structures and practices that later became the world's banking and finance industry, so now you know who to blame.

Almost from the outset, the Templars had been fairly secretive. They regularly held secret meetings, complete with rituals, at which the Order's business was discussed and decided. Exactly what went on remains uncertain, but people at the time were convinced that wizardry was involved. How else could the order's rise to power be explained? No nobleman wanted to believe that the Templars were simply better businessmen. By the start of the 14th century, the French crown owed vast debts to the Templars. The King, Philip the Fair – so-called for his hair, not his morals – conspired with the then Pope, Clement V. Clement resented the Templar influence, and the pair

agreed to destroy them. A rumour at the time claimed that Philip had received a vision from God that showed to him that the Templars would be responsible for the destruction of the Earth. There is no way to be sure, however, if Philip genuinely believed that he had seen such a sign.

On 13 October 1307, Philip ordered the arrest of all Templars on the charge of heresy, which fell under the authority of the Pope. This allowed him to take their money and torture them into confessions of their sorcery, which included worshipping demons, possessing occult powers, stamping on the cross, and performing illegal sexual acts. Clement V did his part by officially dissolving the order in 1312, removing their last shreds of protection.

MAGIC: Many of the Templars said, under interrogation, that they worshipped a disembodied head.

nchu.rrmr

This was known as the "Skull of Sidon". Legends from the time say that there was a Templar knight who was deeply in love with a Moorish woman. She fell ill and died, and, overwhelmed with grief, the knight made love to her one last time. After he had finished, a strange voice spoke to him telling him to return to the spot in nine month's time to collect his son. When he did return at the appointed time, he discovered a strange, bearded head sitting on the leg-bones of the woman's corpse. The head spoke to him, and told the knight to take it with him. If he did so, the head promised to grant him all manner of good things and wisdoms.

The head became his guardian, and used its devilish powers to bring him everything that he wanted. In due course, he passed the head on to the order, and it in turn made sure of their success.

Other reports state that the Templars performed

rituals in honour of a strange being called Baphomet, which had the head and legs of a goat, and the body and arms of a lush young woman. It was even said that Baphomet sat in on some of these rituals in person, accepting the adulation of the knights. It is certainly true that the Templars favoured round temples to worship in rather than the usual cross-shaped Christian churches, and that their circular churches frequently featured lots of carvings of strange faces looking down on the congregation from the walls. A particularly fine example, still open to the public, is the Temple Church in the City of London. Not content with this odd style of church, the Templars redesigned the Christian cross for their own rituals, too.

It was certainly commonly believed that the Templars had all manner of wizardly powers, in partic-

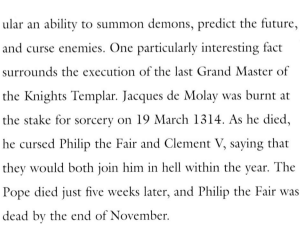

ular an ability to summon demons, predict the future, and curse enemies. One particularly interesting fact surrounds the execution of the last Grand Master of the Knights Templar. Jacques de Molay was burnt at the stake for sorcery on 19 March 1314. As he died, he cursed Philip the Fair and Clement V, saying that they would both join him in hell within the year. The Pope died just five weeks later, and Philip the Fair was dead by the end of November.

✦ Far left: Templars are put to death.

✦ Above: Jacques de Molay is burnt at the stake.

Name: The Poor Knights of Christ and of the Temple of Solomon, a.k.a. The Knights Templar

Time Period: 1118–1312 (although a number of people believe that some Templar groups survived in hiding and that they remain in existence today)

Region: Europe

Description: A religious order of warrior-knights who were thought to be wizards and sorcerers

Dominant Supposed Abilities: Divination, invocation

Traits: Rich, powerful, influential, bankers

Nature: Uncertain – they may have been innocent, and Philip's charges motivated purely by greed and jealousy

Magical Power: Fairly weak

Type: Ritualists

Domain: Demonology

Goal: To gain wealth and influence

Key Equipment: The Skull of Sidon, and, according to rumour, the Seal of Solomon, by which all demons could be commanded.

The Alchemists

Alchemy has long been thought of as a magical version of chemistry, in which muttering wizards cast brooding spells over crucibles and alembics in an attempt to discover the secrets of eternal life via the Fountain of Youth, and near-infinite wealth through a substance known as the Philosopher's Stone. Alchemists have been presumed to possess all sorts of different wizardly powers and abilities, even if they have so far failed to reach their ultimate goal. These arts have supposedly included talking with demons, brewing poisons and other dangerous potions, controlling the minds of others, predicting the future, and creating artificial life.

BIOGRAPHY/MAGIC: Despite the assumptions surrounding it, the art of alchemy has won the devoted research of hundreds of intelligent, well-educated people from all corners of the world for thousands of years. Looking at accounts of their lives, it is difficult to escape the conclusion that, despite the rumours, what the Alchemists were really after was the perfection of the human condition. They shared a common vision of humanity freed from disease and conflict, transmuted into the perfect likeness of divinity in a state of beauty and harmony. The ultimate subject of the alchemical transformation was not metal – it was the alchemist himself.

Alchemy as we know it was born in Egypt and was founded by an ancient Pharaoh, a sorcerer known to the Greeks as **Hermes Trismegistus**, literally: "The three times greatest messenger of the gods." He is thought to have lived around 1900BC, and was greatly renowned for his knowledge of the way that nature operated. Most of his works were destroyed at the command of the Roman emperor Diocletian in the third century AD. Of the surviving fragments of his books, the Tabula Smaragdina or "Emerald Tablet" is acknowledged to be the first and foremost

document to consider the art of alchemy.

The focus of alchemical research in the first millennium AD took place in the Arabian nations. Despite Diocletian's purge of ancient knowledge in 296AD, in which much irreplaceable material was destroyed, alchemy flourished. Alchemists such as **Zosimus the Panoplite** in the fourth century, **Morienus** of Alexandria in the fifth century, and the magician **Cedrennus** in the sixth century all left books, documents and records of their alchemical works and findings. In 750AD, Abou Moussah Djfar-al Sell, known as "**Geber**", or "Wise One", was born in Mesopotamia. He is generally held to be the greatest alchemist after Hermes Trismegistus and is said to have written over 500 documents, of which only three remain. He introduced several vital concepts to the art, and set the pattern of veiling alchemical works in allegory and mystery to protect the knowledge from profane eyes. It is his name that gives us the word "gibberish". Geber also recorded an Arabic version of some of the material in the legendary Emerald Tablet. **Rhasis**, a peer of Geber's, was an Arab who was famous for his practical displays of transforming base metals into gold.

Around the time of the Crusades, during the eleventh century, the main focus of alchemical research shifted from the Arabian countries to Spain, where the Moors had introduced it. A Spanish philosopher called **Artephius** wrote a book about immortality through alchemy in the twelfth century, claiming that he had lived for 1,000 years. As his time was coming to a close, he said the only thing he wanted was to give other scholars the chance to live as long as he had. By the thirteenth century, alchemists had spread all across Europe. **William de Loris, Alphonso**

★ Left: An alchemist surrounded by his equipment.

✦ Below: The successful alchemist must be at peace with the world.

the King of Castile, **Jean de Meung** and **Peter d'Apona** all left important books discussing and instructing on alchemy. D'Apona, a Paduan, was accused by the Inquisition of owning seven evil spirits, each one locked in a crystal jar, that taught him about art and science. He died on the rack. His friend, **Arnold de Villanova**, managed to escape execution, but his books were burned for the heretical suggestion that acts of faith and charity may be more acceptable to God than the Catholic Mass. **Roger Bacon**, born

in Somerset in 1214, is remembered as something of a medical, astronomical and scientific genius. He corrected the Julian calendar, discovered lensed glass (and invented spectacles), researched the telescope and predicted all sorts of much later inventions, such as steam ships, automobiles and planes. The ignorant said that he was a wizard in communication with devils, and he was imprisoned in 1279 and forced to foreswear science. He wrote only two or three alchemical works, but it is generally thought from his writings that he attained the Philosopher's Stone, and had to hide the fact to save his life.

Into the fourteenth century, many alchemists produced great volumes of work on the subject, often known at the time as "The Great Art" and "The Universal Science". **Albertus Magnus**, who died in 1314, gave up all his worldly possessions and wealth to study alchemy in a monastery. His pupil, **Aquinas**, spoke openly of their successes at transformation. The Majorcan **Lully** devoted himself to proving Muslim religion wrong and Christian doctrine right, and came to alchemy late in life. He found apparent success, and worked with King Edward II in England, transforming metal into gold to finance crusades against the Muslims he hated so much. Estimates say that he produced more than £50,000 worth of gold – an incredible feat. Edward, becoming greedy, tried to lock Lully up, but he escaped back to the Continent. Records suggest that he was eventually killed at the age of 150, by furious Asian Saracens whom he was trying to convert. Even at that age, he could apparently run and jump like a young man.

The legendary success of alchemists such as Lully caused problems through the fourteenth, fifteenth and sixteenth centuries, though. Charlatans, seeing the

Name: The Alchemists

Time Period: Technically 2000BC to the present day, but their heyday was 1100–1700AD

Region: Originally Arabia and Egypt, with a presence in China and Japan, but really mostly Europe

Description: An informal collection of men who dedicated their lives to researching the ability to turn ordinary metals into gold and silver

Dominant Supposed Abilities: Transformation

Traits: Scholarly, determined

Nature: Altruistic or greedy

Magical Power: Fairly weak

Type: Ritualists

Domain: Alchemy, naturally

Goal: To gain riches, immortality and the perfection of the soul

Key Equipment: A fortune's worth of laboratories, libraries, experimental powders and reagents, and other such material – alternatively, just the Philosopher's Stone, a crucible, and some lead

potential for good scams, conned all sorts of merchants and nobles out of gold and silver, for "research" or "multiplication". The problem got so bad that parliamentary acts and Papal decrees made the art punishable by death – even though **Pope John XXII** is said to have provided a lot of gold for the Vatican treasury by his mastery of it – and soon all alchemists were seen as fakes. Even clear, explicit, metallurgical treatises like those written by Isaac **Hollandus Sr** and **Jr**, a Dutch father and son, were ignored. **Sir George Ripley**, the Canon of Bridlington Cathedral, moved alchemy onto a spiritual domain, talking about the purification of the soul – but still provided gold for the Knights Hospitaller of St John with the aid of his Philosopher's Stone. **Thomas Charnock** claimed to have finally discovered the Stone himself, but not before his hair had become white with age.

Right: A well-stocked
alchemical laboratory.

Far Right, Top: The
boyish charms of the wickedest
man alive: Aleister Crowley.

Far Right, Below:
Nostradamus, who may
have foreseen all, but if
so he hid it a bit too well!

Thomas Vaughan, a Welsh alchemist, followed Ripley. In his book *Lumen de Lumine*, he focussed attention on physical, mental and spiritual reality. He also claimed to have created the Philosopher's Stone, saying at one point that he had to flee a foreign country when the purity of some silver he was trying to sell betrayed his skill as an alchemist; tales claim that he demonstrated his transformations, separately, to the kings of Bavaria and Prussia. **Alexander Seton**, a Scotsman, demonstrated his powers in almost ten different European countries before being imprisoned in Dresden for his knowledge. He was beaten, racked, burned, stabbed, and scalded with boiling lead, but refused to pass on his knowledge. He was finally rescued by a friend, but still would not pass the secret on. The famous alchemists **Michael Sendivogius, Botticher,** and **Paykull** all spent part of their lives in prison.

As the seventeenth and eighteenth centuries passed, interest in alchemy slowly gave way to other wondrous scholarly pursuits, such as the emerging sciences of chemistry, physics and medicine. **Jean Baptista Van Helmont**, who claimed to have touched the Philosopher's Stone, was also the first person to teach the chemistry of the human body. **Sigmund Richter**, who published an alchemical text in 1710, was a dedicated member of the Rosicrucian religion. **Helvetius**, a doctor, claimed to have had the power of the Philosopher's Stone demonstrated to him by a mysterious craftsman who came to visit him one afternoon. As science advanced, and understanding of the physical world grew, the idea of the transmutation of one metal into another became ever more unlikely and the alchemists, finally, passed into obscurity. If any of the few hardy souls still following the path have managed to create the Philosopher's Stone, their web sites are keeping very quiet on the matter.

Honourable Mentions

A number of important individuals have been noted for their reputations as occultists. Being an occultist is not quite the same thing as being a wizard – occultism draws on supposedly "real" magic rituals to influence events and people in a subtle manner. Science is fairly certain that there is nothing much in it. Whether it is science or the occult community that has it right, occultism has more in common with witchcraft than wizardry. Even so, it is worth mentioning a few of the mightiest seers, occult magicians, societies and other magical, real-world figures. **Aleisteir Crowley**, the self-styled "Great Beast 666" and "Wickedest Man Alive" was a subtle, intelligent and amoral occultist who was active in the first half of the twentieth century. He is widely regarded as the most powerful occult adept of modern times, a man claimed to be in touch with a number of spirits and demons, who was rumoured to have turned one of his acolytes into a camel, and who even founded his own religion, called

Thelema, which is still active today. Crowley first came to prominence in the **Golden Dawn**, an important British occult society from the turn of the twentieth century. **Michel de Nostradamus** is still famous for his series of obscure prophecies that seem to foretell the First and Second World Wars, the rise of the USA, and the collapse of our society in 2012. The **Etruscans**, situated in a coastal part of Italy, were renowned for being an entire nation of wizards, sorcerers and soothsayers. Their priests were said to be able to call down lightning in battle – that is until the Roman armies defeated and absorbed them. **James Murrell**, who lived in Essex in the nineteenth century, was known as "The Cunning Man" because of his supposed magical powers. **Michael Scot**, a nobleman from southern Scotland, was known in medieval times as a notorious demonologist. Accusations of wizardry have never been particularly difficult to come by …

12

Tools of
the Trade

Tools of the Trade

Wizardry is a complicated business. One requires a wide range of materials to be successful in the magical arts, and there is a whole range of items and pieces of equipment that the discerning wizard will never be seen without. In this chapter, we look at the physical objects that are traditionally associated with wizards. Not just what the various items are, but how and why they might be used, what sorts of variations you might encounter, and the sorts of magical properties that they themselves might possess.

Clothing

The first visible hint of a wizard's ability is normally the clothes that he is wearing. The traditional "uniform" of wizards all across the board consists of **long, baggy robes** that reach down to the ankles, topped off with a tall, pointy, wide-brimmed **hat**. If you want to tell the world that you are a wizard, robes and a hat are absolutely vital. The exact nature of the robes varies from individual to individual, though.

At the top end of the spectrum, glamorous wizards usually wear robes made of the most expensive materials, such as velvet or silk. These may be brightly patterned or plain, but tastefully understated **magical symbols** or runes are often worked into the design, usually in gold or silver thread. These mystical symbols are most commonly found along borders, seams and/or belts, but might also be patterned or tiled all over the robes. In some cases, the symbols have magic power themselves, and may be an important channel for the wizard's magical abilities. Particularly flashy wizards can have symbols that glow when they cast a spell or activate a magical power. Wearing certain sets of robes may be a specific requirement for the successful completion of a magical ritual.

Wizards who wear good quality clothing generally have tall, impressive hats. These are usually made from the same material as the robes, and follow the same physical and magical design patterns. Common colours for high-end wizardly clothing include black, midnight blue, gold, silver and dark green. Less commonly, good clothing can be made in bright colours – reds, blues, sea greens and yellows particularly – or might be in some abstract pattern, some of which seem to swirl and shift of their own accord. High-quality white robes are uncommon, and usually indicate that the wizard in question is evil.

At the other end of the scale, many powerful wizards choose to approach fashion from the bottom end of the market. Although robes remain standard, they tend to be fashioned from cheap, homespun wool or sackcloth fabrics, and range in colour from off-white, through various shades of greys and browns, to dull greens or blues at best. No robe of this sort is going to display magical symbols. Rather than the impressive pointed hats of their more ostentatious fellows, wizards of this kind may settle for a battered, **floppy hat** that looks as if it could have been tall and pointy at an early point in its career. Particularly die-hard wizards may do without the hat altogether, replacing it with a **cloth cowl**. These deep hoods may be built into the robes, but are more normally attached to stoles, which cover the shoulders and upper back and chest.

Wizards in this sort of clothing blend subtly into the population, and are free to roam around the countryside looking no more threatening than a harmless old vagabond. These characters are usually sorcerers or spell-casters rather than ritualists; ritual, by definition, requires all manner of objects and ingredients, and so does not suit travelling wizards very well.

✦ Far left: Circe uses her staff to good effect, turning Odysseus's men to swine.

✦ Below: A threadbare wizard.

✦ Background: Norse rune-masters preparing rune staves.

★ Above: The spirit
of a dead child is conjured
by sword and wand.

Chapter Twelve

the wand and away from it in a straight line, so that
the wizard has to be quite good at aiming the wand to
achieve the best results.

On some occasions, the wizard may need to make
certain gestures with the wand to activate the spell,
perhaps sketching patterns or symbols in the air.
Sometimes, gestures like these will leave behind visible strokes of light in the air, as if the tip of the wand
were a marker pen that could write onto the fabric of
reality itself.

In general, wands are no shorter than the length of a
human hand, and no longer than a forearm. They usually
taper slightly, from the thickness of a thumb at the base
to less than the thickness of a little finger at the tip. They
may be made out of almost anything. Although wood is
a common choice, they may also be made from metal,
bone, crystal or any other tough substance. Some are
tipped with a **gem** or other precious stone, while others
may have a metal or crystal **globe** set into the base. Many,
though, have neither. Most wands are carved, engraved,
burned or painted with designs, magical symbols or words
of power, but some – mostly the wooden variety – are
plain, and difficult to identify as magical. The traditional,

Wands

After a nice set of robes, the second most important
piece of a wizard's equipment is a powerful **wand**.
Unlike clothing, which is usually only there for display,
a wand is a vital ingredient for a lot of wizardly magic.

Wands serve a number of purposes in casting a
spell. They may act as a conduit, the channel through
which the wizard's magic can reach the outside world.
They may provide a focus, helping the wizard to con-
centrate on his magic and prepare his mind for the
rigours of casting a spell. They are also extremely useful for targeting a spell – the magic often shoots down

נ.ותךוסךק

✦ Opposite, Bottom: This medieveal alchemist is down on his luck.

✦ Far Left: A wizard helps her client to gaze through a mirror and into the future.

✦ Left: The grinning demonic head of an invocational staff.

always made out of wood, as bones are rarely long enough, metal would weigh too much, and crystal is too fragile. They are less commonly decorated than wands, but may still bear mystical symbols, or be carved into various shapes and designs. Because most staffs are used for walking as well as for casting a spell, they tend to be tipped at both ends with metal "**shoes**". This stops the wood splitting on rocks and stones. These metal shoes are generally plain iron, but they can be made of more exotic substances and engraved with

stage-magician's straight black wand with a white tip is not really associated with wizards, except in occasional Hollywood movies.

Some wizards prefer a **staff** to a wand. Although they serve the same purposes, staffs are around head height, are as thick as your wrist, and do not taper. They are almost

magical designs. Some staffs have ornate headpieces rather than a shoe at the top, and these **headpieces** can be extremely large and impressive, particularly when the staff is being used in a ritual. However, although there is no real reason for it, the majority of wizard's staffs are pretty plain affairs.

Cauldrons

An important piece of kit for any ritualist, the **cauldron** is much more than just a big pot. In ritual terms, a cauldron is a special vessel of transformation – things enter it in one form, and are removed from it in a different one. Usually this occurs as a result of heating, brewing or cooking ingredients. In the most typical use of a cauldron, a range of items and liquids are tipped into the vessel, it is heated for a period of time whilst spells and other ritual formulae are performed over it. At the end, a magical **potion** can be removed, either for immediate use or for later storage.

Cauldrons are more versatile than that, however. A good wizard can use a cauldron to turn all sorts of things into all sorts of other things. Typically, in the type of transformation associated with a cauldron, some quality or nature is added to the base ingredient. Water and herbs are turned into a magic substance when a potion is brewed, for example. In other cases, the symbolism is more obscure. Some stories tell of dead people being placed into cauldrons and coming out alive. Others refer to the cauldron almost as a source of rebirth – a normal person is placed within it, and exits it, a short time later, wiser and more powerful than before. There are also tales of a magical cauldron that could duplicate everything that was placed within it – you could put a gold coin into it, and take two out; put in two, and you would take out four. In a similar vein, some cauldrons are never-emptying, so that the food they produce, usually a bland broth or gruel, can feed an infinite number of people.

Some of the most sophisticated wizardly uses of cauldrons are associated with the transformation of energy. A few wizards, for example, have cast spells into an empty cauldron and made it come out of a different cauldron. Others have used the cauldron to apply a spell to a local area. For example, a wizard might cast a spell of water into the cauldron in order to create a huge thunderstorm, or he or she might heat the cauldron up to make an enemy army's weapons melt.

Cauldrons have also been used to distil incredibly large concepts down into consumable potions and **philtres** – the sum of all human knowledge, the knowledge of magical power, spiritual perfection, and so on. These are typically things that the wizard himself does not possess; somehow the use of the cauldron, through the appropriate ingredients and spells, can capture the essence of these concepts from the world, and simmer them down into something the wizard can use.

The ingredients that go into cauldrons vary wildly from wizard to wizard. Some potions require a range of mundane **herbs**, oils, waters and so on. Others are more exotic, and demand strange, noxious or **magical substances**, such as three hairs from the head of the King's bastard son, soil from a graveyard gathered under the light of the full moon, powdered unicorn horn stirred with a dragon's scale, or three ounces of sunbeams.

Whatever is going to be placed within it, a cauldron is a fairly standard item. They are usually black, made of iron, and shaped like a slightly squashed ball that's had the top cut off. A lip surrounds the opening at the top, to help prevent spillage onto the fire underneath. They have three or four legs, spaced symmetrically, so that a fire can be lit underneath them, and they also have a semi-circular handle that spans the top of the opening when lifted up, so that they can be hung up above a fire-pit if necessary. Most stand to about waist-height, but they can come in any size, from tiny ones you could hold in the palm of one hand to cauldrons big enough to fit in five or six people comfortably. They are hardly ever decorated. Both wizards and witches make extensive use of cauldrons.

Ritual Weaponry

There are a number of key tools that are frequently required during a magical ritual. They represent different elemental forces and qualities, and are known as elemental weapons, despite the fact that only one is actually any use in a fight.

The **sword** represents the element of air, and, by association, is linked to the mind, knowledge, logical thinking, control and coldness. Ritual swords are used to compel certain types of behaviour or to tame unruly spirits, and to invoke mental skills and faculties. Ritual swords are often quite ornate and stylized. The blade is normally engraved with magic symbols, and the hilt is often complicated. The pommel may also hold a gem, crystal or special orb. Ritual swords have sharp blades, but despite this they are not usually much use in battle, as their weighting tends to be wrong, and the hit unwieldy.

Chalices, cups and **grails** represent the element of water. This is associated with emotions, feeling, psychic abilities, influence, transformation and love. In rituals, chalices are usually required to look into the future, the past or distant places, serve as a mini

cauldron by aiding in transformation, and can be used to influence the feelings of other people. Cups are, as the name suggests, shaped as simple, flat-bottomed beakers – in other words, there is just a flat base that separates the liquid in the cup from the surface that it is standing on. Chalices and grails are more advanced, with a round-bottomed liquid bowl supported by a stem. All three can be totally plain or extremely ornate, and are generally made of clay, pottery, wood, gold, silver or crystal.

Seals – mystic designs engraved in wax or stone, drawn onto parchment or on the floor, or made out of precious metals – are linked to the element of earth. They embody growth, fixing, channelling, linkage, protection and the shaping of power. In rituals, they are often used to specify the exact details of the results that the magic is supposed to produce. They may also be used to lock the wizard away from hostile forces or beings, or to increase the power of the ritual concerned. The most famous seal is also one of the most simple, the double-circle chalked onto a floor for wizards to stand within when casting spells. Others are considerably more sophisticated, if no more powerful – they may be created from exotic ingredients or with the aid of unusual equipment, specially prepared using elaborate rituals, or even devised through supernatural inspiration. They can appear as small parchment illustrations, pieces of ornate jewellery (generally gold, silver or platinum), designs scrawled on floors, or even as table surfaces, wall-hangings or obelisks.

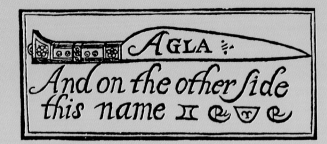

AGLA

And on the other side this name

✦ Above: A ritual knife to compel the element of earth.

✦ Below: The magical head of a Celtic sword.

Wands also double up as elemental weapons. They represent the element of fire, and therefore also energy, power, force and direction. They have already been detailed. A few other objects are also staples of ritual process, but do not necessarily embody a specific wizardly element. **Lamps** and lanterns embody wisdom and applied knowledge, guiding the wizard out of ignorance and safely to his destination. Ringing a **bell** indicates boundaries, beginnings and ends, and helps power to manifest itself – providing a climax to different stages of the ritual. Sources of flame, both indoor ones such as **candles** and braziers and large-scale conflagrations such as outdoor **bonfires**, provide a gateway between the worlds of flesh and spirit. There are plenty of other odd, assorted tools involved in ritual, but they are less ubiquitous. According to the famous fantasy author, Terry Pratchett, every wizard has at least one **stuffed alligator** hanging from the ceiling, too – but he's probably lying.

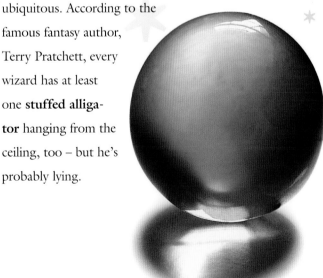

Sacred Spaces

In addition to the various items of equipment commonly associated with ritual magic activity, most wizards require the versatility offered by entirely larger facilities. Many rituals and spells have to take place within some sort of specially consecrated area. The magic circle seal is a good example of the sort of sacred space which can be constructed almost anywhere at a moment's notice, but other types are less convenient. An **altar** is a vital requirement for a lot of ritualist wizards. At its simplest, an altar is a large block, generally made of wood or stone, on which different implements may be placed. Even these roughest representatives possess inherent power, though, gained either through specific enchantments and preparations, or just through repeated magical use down through the centuries.

More complex altars may include indentations to hold candles or incense burners, to provide a built-in bowl for fluids, or even guttering through the centre of the block to drain away the blood from a sacrifice. Others can include compartments beneath the main surface, either obvious or hidden, in which the wizard may store ritual equipment. Although plain-looking altars are quite common, they can also be extremely ornate. They may be made of expensive or unusual materials, such as marble, sheet slate, crystal, fired clay, or semi-precious stone. They might also be inlaid with precious metals, including gold, silver and bronze. Some are carved or worked into extremely fanciful shapes, decorated with carvings or figurines, painted with a range of abstract, religious or magical designs, or, if they belong to an evil wizard, inset with implements of restraint and torture, such as spikes and shackles. Altars may also form part of a larger **shrine** to a particular god, spirit or demon.

Sometimes though, an altar alone does not suffice. Some spells and rituals actually require a specific **temple**, or another special-purpose room, for the working of magic. Locations such as these have been painstakingly prepared for the purpose of casting a spell and have often been purified and empowered over weeks, months or even years of dedicated effort. It may be that the spell in question simply will not work if it is not cast within the temple, or that the temple plays an important part in modifying or control-

✦ Far Right: A magician in his sacred temple.

✦ Below: Dee's famous wax tablet helped him contact good spirits.

ling the spell – or the forces and beings that it calls up.

Most good wizardly temples include an altar as part of the design, along with a complicated seal or other magic circle. The seal may be in the centre of the room as a focus for energies, or it may be around the altar, to offer protection and enhancement to the wizard. It may be drawn or painted onto the floor, but is more likely to be inlaid in metals. Temples are rarely subtle. Tall, flaming braziers often mark strategic points around the room's seal, but, if these are missing, burning brands may be set into the walls to provide light in their place. If the wizard habitually works with a specific god or spirit, the being will have a statue or other shrine near to the altar, which may also hold a lectern for a book. The walls will commonly be decorated with plush drapes, perhaps bearing magical symbols, and the floor may have mosaic designs. Doors are likely to be thick, with locks and a bar on the inside so that the wizard can make sure that there are no distractions.

In general, altars and temples seem to be associated more with evil wizards than with good ones. They are certainly linked with the idea of worship, because they are almost all associated with a particular being, or group of beings. The fact that the wizards that use them always seem to be evil may be some sort of comment on the nature of religion, particularly the worship of non-standard gods. Whatever the reasons, good wizards do not generally seem to have temples, and only a few use altars.

Laboratories

A must for the more experimentally inclined wizard, a magical **laboratory** is where the research for spells and alchemy take place. Laboratories tend to be concentrated into one room, usually big and rectangular. Labs are always kept out of the way of the rest of the building, partly for secrecy and partly in case something goes wrong. Many of them are in the basement, where noises and lights from experiments are going to be slightly subtler. Others are at the top of the structure, and have windows or panels in the roof so that the wizard can use direct sunlight and moonlight in his work. Labs usually have a plain, easy-to-sweep floor made of either stone or wood, with all manner of charts, diagrams, chalkboards and mirrors on the walls.

There are several items, naturally, without which a laboratory cannot possibly be considered to be complete. **Benches** are a must. Labs require all sorts of physical equipment, and that needs to be put somewhere, so most of them are crammed full with as many benches as the wizard can fit in there. **Alchemical apparatus** is another staple. Even wizards who would never dream of trying to find the Philosopher's Stone are going to have flasks, pipes, retorts, beakers, burners, alembics, crucibles, dishes, jugs, fraction and distillation columns, bubblers, droppers, stands, taps, clamps and any number of other bits of glassware. This is traditionally all linked together by glass or rubber tubes in a series of tottering configurations, with various brightly coloured liquids slowly winding their way around the maze.

✦ Below: A well-stocked laboratory ...

✦ Right: ... and a more magically ordered one.

Clear **work-surfaces** are almost as important as benches of equipment, and the wizard may have a **dissecting slab**, a **reading stand** and a **writing desk** as well. A source of water is generally available. Truly flashy wizards may have large pieces of obscure **electrical equipment** humming and crackling away in the background, such as a Van Der Graff spark generator or a Jacob's Ladder, usually attached to dials, levers and big, chunky switches of the Frankenstein variety.

Less common may be a specially constructed **magical seal** for experimental spell-craft that keeps all assorted energies and magical mishaps locked within it. Some powerful wizards have large growth **vats** and tanks, made of crystal or metal, in which they create servants, reanimate the dead, combine living beings and otherwise tinker with life itself.

Locked **cabinets** turn out to be full of all sorts of specimens, ingredients, reagents and other interesting materials associated with the wizard's research.

It is extremely rare to find an ornately designed laboratory. Wizards who want an impressive lab almost always go for extra content, rather than decorated walls or inlaid magical sigils (seals).

LE QUADRUPLE

ORACLE

DES DAMES ET DES DEMOISELLES

TABLE DU DESTIN

PAUL BERNARDIN, LIBRAIRE-ÉDITEUR
53, QUAI DES GRANDS AUGUSTINS, 53

Libraries

Books play an extremely important role in wizardly life. Many of the greatest wizards developed their powers from the information contained in books, either right from the very start, or as part of a broader process of training and learning. Books embody knowledge, and knowledge is a wizard's stock in trade. From time to time, every wizard needs to refer to books for some purpose or other – learning a new spell, researching signs, portents or prophecies, verifying or recalling a specific piece of information, identifying a mysterious item, being or phenomenon, or otherwise checking something out. Because it is never possible to be sure what information you are going to need, most wizards hoard books compulsively, collecting as many as they can get their hands on, about almost any subject. That means that they quickly accumulate extensive **libraries**.

✦ Far Left: A French manual of magical spells and techniques.

✦ Left: Apollonius, Greek philosopher and magician.

There isn't an incredible amount you can do with a room full of books other than put them in bookcases. The construction of the bookcases and the room itself can vary, of course, and the number of books concerned will play a large part in determining layout, but in general most libraries are pretty similar. Small collections of books can be held in a study, where bookcases line the walls, and the room itself usually holds one or more comfortable chairs, and perhaps a writing desk. Larger collections, though, require the bookshelves to be standing free on the floors of the room or rooms, and the only real scope for variation lies in the contents of the books themselves. Prophecies, spells and rituals, monstrous and magical beings, spirit lore, superstition, history and scientific knowledge are the most common topics of books in wizardly libraries. Some libraries are incredibly grand affairs made out of marble, with carpet laid between the bookcases to soften the impact of the floor, while others are more modest, with wooden floorboards. They may take up one small area, or sprawl through every room of a castle, mansion or labyrinthine tunnel complex, but they are still libraries – and that means loud noises and naked flames are extremely unwelcome.

13
Magical
Societies

Magical Societies

Groups and Social Structures

Wizards rarely get on with each other. Partly, it seems to be the nature of the job. Most wizards need to spend long years in near-isolation learning the arts of magic, which must leave them with a number of social issues. The few, mostly sorcerers, who come by their powers by accident, often resent their abilities, and that resentment extends to other magical beings. But there are other factors to consider, too.

Groups and Social Structures

Wizards are extremely powerful compared to normal people. Often, only other wizards are able to pose a genuine threat to them – and it is difficult to relax around potentially threatening people. Wizards are competitive as well, keen to show off the results of all the hard work they have put in, or to demonstrate how great their natural talent is. That adds to the strain of associating with others. In other words, between their social difficulties, paranoia and professional jealousies, it is astonishing that any wizard even manages to be on the same continent as another without resorting to fireballs.

Some wizards, however, actually operate in groups, societies and organizations. These mostly exist to teach new wizards, but can also be formed for the purpose of achieving an important common goal, to provide each other with protection, or to provide a useful opportunity to trade techniques and equipment.

The Istari

J.R.R. Tolkien's masterwork *The Lord of the Rings* was the book that founded the modern genre of fantasy fiction. Its characters, locations, races and histories set the pattern for the revolution in fantasy fiction that followed, and it is still widely regarded as one of the greatest pieces of modern English literature. In a poll conducted by a major British newspaper towards the end of 1999, it was selected as the most important book of the twentieth century. Whether or not it deserves such praise, it is without doubt an extremely significant work, and the new film series based upon it looks certain to be a major blockbuster.

Tolkien saw his writing as an exercise in recording a fictitious history. The sheer detail he crammed into his work is astounding. This, as much as anything else, gives his writing its power. It also means that when he died, he left a great legacy of information about his world, commonly referred to as Middle Earth after the continent most of his tales are set upon.

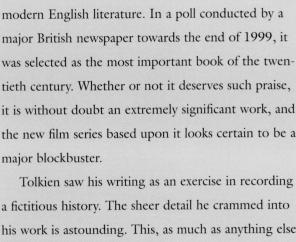

✦ Far Left: Gandalf sits by a brook enjoying his own company.

✦ Below: Middle Earth – the ultimate hero of *The Lord of the Rings*.

of the mortals, and this contribution was considered to be the maximum degree of acceptable intervention.

There were five Istari wizards, commonly named Saruman, Gandalf, Radagast, Pallando and Alatar. Saruman the White was the leader of the group, and largely dictated strategy. He was also the strongest of the Istari. Each wizard had extensive duties to undertake across the lands of Middle Earth, so they were widely dispersed and had little in the way of regular contact.

At the height of their influence, the western Istari formed the heart of the White Council, also known as "The Council of the Wise". This was a hybrid, strategic council that led the fight against Sauron, and was chiefly comprised of several of the Istari with various mortal leaders: Saruman, Gandalf and Radagast from the Istari, and Galadriel of Lothlorien, Elrond Halfelven, Cirdan, Deleborn, Gildor and Glorfindel from the mortals. Many of the elven members of the White Council possessed magic powers, but they were not classed as wizards in their own right.

The power that Sauron held, combined with the distractions and the powerful temptations of life amongst the mortals, led to the corruption of most of the Istari. Alatar and Pallando journeyed into the southern and eastern realms of Middle Earth with Saruman, but only he returned, and they dropped out of the chronicles of recorded history. Radagast became obsessed with the flora and fauna of the realm, and foreswore his quest in favour of dedicating himself to the study of the natural world. Saruman appeared to remain steadfast, but lusted after Sauron's power, and eventually he himself became evil. The leader of the White Council as well as of the Istari, Saruman used his authority to hide his corruption, and subverted the

········ Chapter Thirteen

The greatest wizard of Middle Earth was Gandalf the Grey, discussed in detail in Chapter Two. He was one of a brotherhood of wizards known collectively as "Istari". They were of a race of good spirits, Maiar, who agreed to take on human form so that they could help the mortals of Middle Earth to overthrow Sauron, the most powerful evil force at liberty at that time.

The Istari left their realm in the west, and journeyed to Middle Earth in order to both support and coordinate the struggle against Sauron. The powers of good had long vowed not to interfere in the domain

Council by disguising his true intent as excessive caution. While the people of Middle Earth struggled to resist Sauron's forces against Saruman's delaying tactics, and the Council held meeting after meeting to try to work out how to progress, Saruman used the time to search for the One Ring, the magical item that would allow him to seize ultimate power.

Of the five Istari, Gandalf alone remained true to his calling. He was instrumental in Sauron's downfall, and also stripped Saruman of his power. With Sauron defeated and Saruman dead, Gandalf left Middle Earth and returned to the isles of the West. The once-mighty Istari brotherhood was reduced to just Radagast, with both Pallando and Alatar having shared uncertain fates.

In the final analysis, the Istari's loose structure seems to have been one of the main reasons for its collapse. Right from the outset, Pallando and Alatar apparently divorced themselves from Istari authority and abandoned their mission. With no requirement for regular meetings and with no central base of operations, the informality of the Istari brotherhood encouraged independent action, which undermined the wizards' cohesion. Lack of any clear oversight or

The ISTARI

Wizard	Colour	Fate
Gandalf	Grey	Vanquished evil and returned home
Saruman	White	Became evil and waas slain
Radagast	Brown	Became diverted
Pallando	Blue	Missing
Alatar	Blue	Missing

✦ Far left: Gandalf stands at the gate ...

✦ Below: ... and at your bedside.

✱ Badger, lion, serpent and eagle, the house animals of Hogwarts School.

The Four Houses

House	Head	Colours	Animal	House Ghost
Gryffindor	Prof. McGonagall	Scarlet/Gold	Lion	Nearly Headless Nick
Hufflepuff	Prof. Sprout	Yellow/Black	Badger	The Fat Friar
Ravenclaw	Prof. Flitwick	Blue/Silver	Eagle	The Grey Lady
Slytherin	Prof. Snape	Green/Gold	Serpent	The Bloody Baron

Hogwarts Staff

Current Staff	Duties
Binns, Professor (deceased)	History of Magic
Dumbledore, Professor Albus	Headmaster
Filch, Mr Argus	Caretaker
Flitwick, Professor	Charms; Ravenclaw
Hagrid, Mr Rubeus	Care of Magical Creatures; Gamekeeper
Hoocah, Madame	Flying; Quidditch
Lupin, Professor Remus	Defence against the Dark Arts
McGonagall, Professor Minerva	Transfiguration; Gryffindor; Deputy Headmistress
Pince, Madame	Librarian
Pomfrey, Madame Poppy	School Nurse
Sinistra, Professor	Astronomy
Snape, Professor Severus	Potions; Slytherin
Sprout, Professor	Herbology; Hufflepuff
Trelawney, Professor Sybil	Divination
Vector, Professor	Arithmancy

Former Staff	Duties
Grubbly-Plank, Professor	Care of Magical Creatures
Kettleburn, Professor	Care of Magical Creatures
Lockhart, Professor Gilderoy	Defence against the Dark Arts
Moody, Mr Alastor "Mad-Eye"	Defence against the Dark Arts
Quirrell, Professor	Defence against the Dark Arts

peer pressure allowed Saruman the leisure to become corrupted by power and Radagast to go native. Close scrutiny from fellow wizards is an important survival trait for any wizardly society.

Hogwarts School

In the world of the Harry Potter books, wizardry is surprisingly well structured. The collected wizards of Earth have their own complete culture, separate from the normal (muggle) world, and which comes with its own structure built into it. Quite a large percentage of the adult wizards in Britain seem to work for the

Ministry of Magic, a large government department that oversees all things magical. Others work for the wizarding bank, Gringotts, play in one of the professional Quidditch leagues, serve as journalists, or run their own small businesses, catering to their fellows. The tightest-knit group, however, are the collected teachers of Hogwarts School of Witchcraft and Wizardry.

Hogwarts was founded more than 1,000 years ago by four great wizards – Godric Gryffindor, Helga Hufflepuff, Rowena Ravenclaw, and Salazar Slytherin. Alarmed by the way that muggle people were reacting to the wizards of the time, the founders built the school – a sprawling castle set in extensive grounds – in such a way as to hide it from the world. Only a wizard can find it, it doesn't appears on maps, and mundane technology does not function within its walls. To normal people it looks like a trashed old ruin set in a patch of wasteland. The four founders had very dif-

ferent ideas on what made a good student, and for several years after the founding, they each hand-picked their own students according to their preferences – Gryffindor preferred loyalty and bravery, Hufflepuff valued kindness and diligence, Ravenclaw wanted insight and intelligence, and Slytherin sought shrewdness and ambition. As the school grew, the founders divided the school into self-named houses embodying the virtues they preferred, and automated the process of selection by creating a magical Sorting Hat that would assess a child and assign him or her to the most appropriate house. The Sorting Hat is still in use today.

The four houses dominate the basic structure of Hogwarts. Each one has its own dormitory tower for pupils, complete with common room, bedrooms, and an animated painting that acts as the tower's guardian. The houses also have patron ghosts, specific symbols and colours, and are headed up by a member of staff, who is responsible for his or her pupils' well-being. Lessons are taught to collected house groups as well. The four houses compete at excellence throughout the year in a number of academic and sporting disciplines, attempting to outdo each other by earning House Points. The house with the greatest number of points at the end of the year is considered victorious, and holds the House Trophy for the following year.

Because the Sorting Hat actually makes allowances for a person's character when selecting their house, the four houses actually function as four small wizardly societies united under a single umbrella. Rivalry is common, and Slytherin and Gryffindor are particularly hostile to each other. The needs of the staff and pupils at the school are taken care of by a small battalion of house elves – magical creatures that live to cook, clean and do other mundane chores. Meals are taken collectively, in the grand dining hall. The castle itself is a warren-like building, crammed with the sort of secret passages, missing stairs, suits of armour and grand, sweeping staircases that can be expected in a school of magic.

At the heart of Hogwarts School is its immensely wise and powerful headmaster, Albus Dumbledore. He is personally responsible for recruiting the school staff, and the longer-serving members are all immensely loyal to him, despite an assortment of interpersonal differences. Dumbledore is widely regarded as the most powerful wizard alive, and is said to be the only living being that scares Lord Voldemort, the greatest of the Dark Wizards. Dumbledore has a skill for finding value in even the most unlikely characters, and employs a number of people considered dubious by the wizarding world at large –his judgement is usually proved sound.

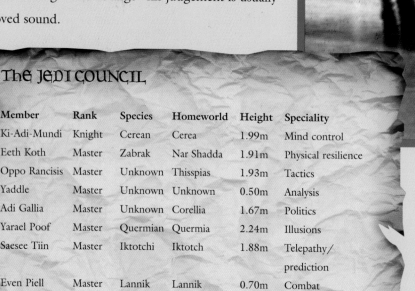

The Jedi Council

Member	Rank	Species	Homeworld	Height	Speciality
Ki-Adi-Mundi	Knight	Cerean	Cerea	1.99m	Mind control
Eeth Koth	Master	Zabrak	Nar Shadda	1.91m	Physical resilience
Oppo Rancisis	Master	Unknown	Thisspias	1.93m	Tactics
Yaddle	Master	Unknown	Unknown	0.50m	Analysis
Adi Gallia	Master	Unknown	Corellia	1.67m	Politics
Yarael Poof	Master	Quermian	Quermia	2.24m	Illusions
Saesee Tiin	Master	Iktotchi	Iktotch	1.88m	Telepathy/ prediction
Even Piell	Master	Lannik	Lannik	0.70m	Combat
Depa Billaba	Master	Chalactan	Coruscant	1.64m	Insight
Mace Windu	Master	Human	Unknown	1.88m	Negotiation/ fairness
Yoda	Master	Unknown	Unknown	0.66m	Training
Plo Koon	Master	Kel Dor	Dorin	1.88m	Extrasensory perception

The Jedi

Basically serving as a wizardly police force during the days of their glory, the Jedi are a society united by their common goals and moral codes.

Their purpose was to uphold law and justice within the old Republic in the Star Wars universe, and they did so with an impressive blend of wise

compassion and relentless fury. The ruling body of the Jedi, based in the Temple building on the Republic's capital city-planet, Coruscant, was the Jedi Council of the 12 greatest Jedi. The Council consisted of five permanent members on a lifetime membership, four long-term members who served until choosing to step down, and three limited-term members who had a specific time on the council. This mix of membership helped to ensure that the council remained balanced. With the Council keeping stable control, the Jedi were a powerful, united force.

Part of the long-lasting success of the Jedi lay in their training. Infants who were found to have potential for great strength within the Force, from which Jedi draw their powers, were recruited for training at a very early age. The implication is that very young children were separated from their family and friends before they were old enough to have formed very strong bonds, and raised compassionately within the Jedi order. The order itself therefore came to stand as both mother and father to its members, effectively bringing them into its family as a way of creating solid bonds of loyalty, obedience and affection. It is a technique that groups have used throughout human history.

The strong moral code of the Jedi further helped to keep the group together. The Jedi were the guardians of law and order, sent to arbitrate disputes, enforce Republic laws and catch serious criminals. Their powers gave them advantages far beyond those of more mundane police forces – they had the ability to influence minds, sense truths and perceive the past and future, all of which made it very difficult to deceive them or to hide from them. If a person was in the wrong, they would be found out and their crime would be dealt with appropriately. The strong sense of moral rightness that pervaded the entire Jedi order – that they were the exemplars of goodness and virtue – went a long way to blunting competitive disagreements between individuals. Jedi Council sanctions against disobedient or unruly members added a little overt encouragement for citizens to behave and to be nice to each other.

The final glue that kept the Jedi together came from the nature of the Force itself. The Force has two sides, wildly opposing poles of goodness and evil. These poles, the Light Side and the Dark Side, exert an attracting power on people who are attuned to the Force. It is impossible to remain neutral; any individual will be either drawn to the Light or to the Dark.

While a solid grounding in Jedi training ensured that all members were firmly settled within the Light side, it always remained possible to turn someone from one side to the other, snapping them from good to evil or vice-versa. The danger of indulging oneself in negative emotions and selfish desires was extremely real – being anti-social would pull a new Jedi towards the Dark Side, with disastrous results. Very few people are prepared to risk being egotistical, greedy or spiteful when they know that

being so may cost them their soul. With their very powers reinforcing their sense of moral superiority, their fear of disappointing their superiors, and their indoctrination from a very young age, the Jedi were an immensely disciplined and united force for good. In the end, of course, their discipline – and the self-assured complacency that it created – was turned against them.

Followers of the Dark Side of the Force, the Jedi's evil counterparts, are known as Sith. Evil wizards are notoriously bad at cooperating with each other, so it should come as no surprise to learn that there are only ever two Sith, Master and Apprentice. Their relationship is never solid, either; the Apprentice frequently plots to overthrow and replace the Master, even as the Master seeks to abuse and oppress the Apprentice. Even so, the power of the Dark Side can be seen in the way that the Sith managed to destroy the Jedi, who considerably outnumbered them, take over the Republic, and found the Empire.

Honourable Mentions

Even though they are the exception rather than the rule in the magical world, there are a number of other important wizardly societies. The **Unseen University** is the premier establishment for magical learning in Terry Pratchett's Discworld. Unlike the genteel civility of Hogwarts, however, Unseen University's wizards are a fractious bunch, full of petty dislikes and political undercurrents. Promotion of an underling within the university's structure has frequently been gained at the cost of the superior's life, and representatives of the different schools of the university have often resorted to killing each other. Despite the occasional outbursts of anarchy, though, the university seems to be now functioning well under the leadership of one of its strongest Chancellors for years, Mustrum Ridcully, who brooks very little nonsense amongst his staff. **The Academy of Tsurani** magicians on Kelewan in Raymond E. Feist's novels is another teaching institution, but, interestingly, it also serves to shackle wizards to a certain extent. They are taught that they have to work for the benefit of the Tsurani Empire without meddling in politics, and the Academy itself is compelled, under threat of military action, to enforce the Empire's will upon its individual members. In David Edding's *Belgariad*, the **Brotherhood of Sorcerers** is a genuinely cohesive collection of extremely powerful wizards, and their sorcerous foes, the Grolims, are equally structured – but both groups are quasi-religious, held together by their fight to promote the gods that they support. In the *Dying Earth* of Jack Vance, the **collected wizards of the 21st Aeon** – approximately the 210th Century AD – form something like a rather vicious social club, in which they gather to show off to each other, and go some small way to keeping each other in line through group and peer pressure. Despite these mild successes, though, the fact remains that wizards are more inclined to working alone than together.

✦ Below: The usual chaos of Unseen University.

14

The Dark

Side

The Dark Side
The Evil Face of Wizardry

Wizards make excellent villains. They possess great power by virtue of their magical arts, so they already have a head start when it comes to ambition and control. It doesn't take much for the power that they hold to overwhelm their nobler side. In addition, the ways and needs of magic are frequently strange, so evil wizards are able to be cryptic, subtle or unsettlingly peculiar in a way that perhaps an evil warlord could not. Normal people tend to distrust wizards anyway, so alienation and resentment are common motivations. The overall result is that some of the most enduring evil characters have been wizards of great skill and power.

Darth Vader

Darth Vader is one of the most enduring evil characters of the past 30 years. Like several other characters from the first trilogy of Star Wars films, he captured the public imagination in a way that few characters have ever managed, and he is still an immediately recognizable, even iconic figure. His success is due to a number of elements. His physical presence was incredible – encased in black armour, standing over two metres tall, and constantly accompanied by the "urrrh-huhh" noise of his breather unit, he was like no character seen before. His voice, as characterized by the great James Earl Jones, was immensely threatening. Even his vicious, relentless nature made him captivating. He remains one of the greatest dark wizards we have seen to date.

BIOGRAPHY: Vader started life as Anakin Skywalker, a child of prophecy who is thought to have been the result of an immaculate conception on the part of the Force. He was born on the desert planet of Tatooine. His mother, Shmi, was a slave, and the boy Anakin inherited her lack of status. They were sold to a Toydarian junk-dealer named Watto while Anakin was still extremely young, and it was here that the boy learned a wide range of mechanical and technical skills. He was freed from his slavery by Jedi Master Qui-Gon Jinn following a wager on a race. Jinn recognized the young boy's potential and astonishingly high power in the Force, and took him back to the Jedi Temple on Coruscant for evaluation for training.

The Jedi Council could see Anakin's power, but their vision was clouded regarding his future. Sensing danger in him, they refused to train him. Following Jinn's death at the hands of the Sith Apprentice, Darth Maul, the Jedi Knight Obi-Wan Kenobi invoked an ancient privilege of the order to secure the right to train Anakin himself, as Jinn had wished.

Once he was inside the Jedi order, Anakin quickly became famous for his skill, power, recklessness and impatience – an uneasy blend for a Jedi. He had frequent nightmares, which Kenobi was unable to settle effectively. Finally, on a mission to find a missing Jedi, Anakin came up against an assassin, Ke Daiv. His repressed emotion surged out of him, and he unleashed his rage and

✦ Far Left: Morgan Le Fay prepares mischief.

✦ Below: Would you trust this boy with a used light sabre?

frustration to kill the man. Once opened, these emotions proved impossible to control. Furious with Kenobi for the slow pace of his training, Anakin forced a duel with his master. Despite the power of the Dark Side within him, he lost the fight and was very severely wounded. Only his fury and outrage kept him alive. Various cybernetic enhancements were required to save his life, and the moment that the metal fused to his flesh, Anakin Skywalker became Darth Vader, and turned to the Sith.

As the Sith Master, Palpatine, seized political power within the Republic and began the chaotic revolution that would replace it with the Empire, Vader rose to power. He and his agents hunted down and killed the Jedi, with only a few – such as Kenobi, Yoda and Vima-Da-Boda – managing to escape the purge. Vader himself was particularly merciless, and personally slew many of the top Jedi.

Despite his prominence, Vader was not much of a politician. He tended to ignore affairs of state, preferring an active life in the Imperial armed forces. He also made good use of his excellent engineering skills, overseeing the design and initial construction of the Empire's most effective short-range spacecraft, the Sienar Fleet Systems T.I.E. Advanced Starfighter. Many Imperial navy officers bitterly resented Vader's privileges, considering them unearned. His management style did him no favours, either – his sudden fits of pique were feared throughout the fleet, and he was well known for slaughtering unfortunate, long-serving officers for petty mistakes. Unsuccessful assassination attempts did not lighten the Dark Lord's nature.

When the Rebel Alliance rose up against the Empire, out of the trampled ashes of the Republic, Vader was put in charge of the Super Star Destroyer "Executor", and tasked with suppressing it. He man-

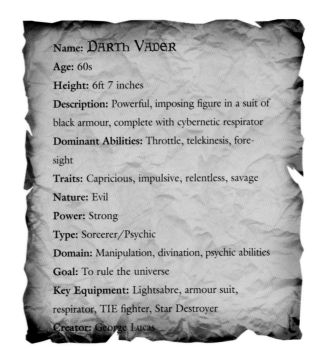

Name: DARTH VADER

Age: 60s

Height: 6ft 7 inches

Description: Powerful, imposing figure in a suit of black armour, complete with cybernetic respirator

Dominant Abilities: Throttle, telekinesis, foresight

Traits: Capricious, impulsive, relentless, savage

Nature: Evil

Power: Strong

Type: Sorcerer/Psychic

Domain: Manipulation, divination, psychic abilities

Goal: To rule the universe

Key Equipment: Lightsabre, armour suit, respirator, TIE fighter, Star Destroyer

Creator: George Lucas

aged to locate the rebel's headquarters, and finally killed his old master, Kenobi, in a duel. Vader was unable to finish the rebellion, however, because the space station that was to destroy the secret base was itself blown up before it could do so. This was achieved by the first of a new generation of Jedi, his long-hidden son, Luke Skywalker.

The rebels fled, and Vader followed, harrying them from hideout to hideout. Eager to stamp out any potential Jedi resurgence, Vader set a trap for Luke, but did not manage to capture him. Luke eventually returned to confront him again, and, following a titanic battle, managed to reawaken his compassion. Vader turned back to the Light Side and killed his Sith master, the Emperor, receiving mortal wounds in the process.

Vader/Skywalker died shortly afterwards, but having been redeemed by his son, he was able to take his place within the Force alongside his old friends.

WORLD: Vader lived in a period of anarchy and darkness that he himself was largely responsible for

creating. It could be suggested that his fall into evil was an inevitable result of his flawed training, but the potential for fear and impatience was always within him. The old Republic had been a stable force for order and justice for thousands of years, and although it was fairly corrupt, it was still largely benevolent. The Empire which replaced it was cruel and repressive, and this suited Vader perfectly. Within its auspices, he was not only free to indulge himself in the petty malice and bloodthirsty viciousness that he enjoyed, but he was actually rewarded for it.

MAGIC: Qui-Gon Jinn believed Anakin Skywalker to be the chosen one who would bring balance back to the Force, which he indeed was. Unfortunately for the Jedi, balance comprises of both Light and Dark. For millennia, the Sith – and the Dark Side of the Force

– had been weak and suppressed. Jinn fondly imagined that the chosen one would do away with the remaining corruption and cruelty, and usher in a golden period, but he was greatly mistaken as to the nature of balance. As the chosen one, Vader rebalanced the Force into a tool of both good and evil in equal measures. The Jedi paid for Vader's foolishness not only with their lives, but with the lives of billions of innocent people as the Republic crumbled. Vader typically relied on a relatively small number of his powers. His preferred technique for punishment – and persuasion, through fear – was a form of physical influence that closes a victim's airways, choking him to death. This was his favourite method of execution for his unfortunate subordinates. In battle, he preferred to focus on his superb combat skills and Force-boosted reflexes, calling on his telekinetic

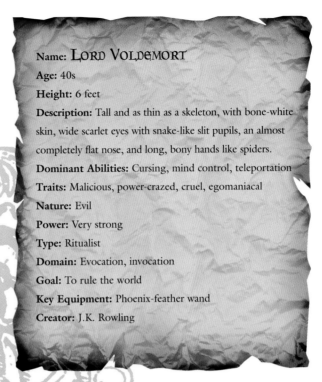

Name: LORD VOLDEMORT

Age: 40s

Height: 6 feet

Description: Tall and as thin as a skeleton, with bone-white skin, wide scarlet eyes with snake-like slit pupils, an almost completely flat nose, and long, bony hands like spiders.

Dominant Abilities: Cursing, mind control, teleportation

Traits: Malicious, power-crazed, cruel, egomaniacal

Nature: Evil

Power: Very strong

Type: Ritualist

Domain: Evocation, invocation

Goal: To rule the world

Key Equipment: Phoenix-feather wand

Creator: J.K. Rowling

➤ Far Left: King's Cross plays host to platform 9 ¾.

➤ Left: The chronicles of Voldemort's return.

powers to provide an edge where necessary. He could also sense individuals around him, read minds and, to a limited extent, foresee the future.

VOLDEMORT

It is said that a strong hero needs a strong enemy to bring out the best in him. If that is true, then Harry Potter is destined to become extremely strong indeed, because his arch-enemy, the evil wizard Lord Voldemort, is immensely powerful and very dangerous indeed. He is so terrifying to the rest of the wizarding world, in fact, that hardly anyone dares speak his name – referring to him as "You know who", in case saying "Voldemort" would bring them to his attention.

BIOGRAPHY: Tom Marvolo Riddle was the son of a witch and a normal muggle man. His mother did not reveal her true powers to her husband until after she was pregnant, and he promptly deserted her in disgust. She died in childbirth, leaving young Tom alone in the world. He grew up in a muggle orphanage, loathing every moment of it. He quickly came to hate his father, and all muggles by association. He swore that he would get his own back on his father for deserting him and for stranding him in the

orphanage. At the age of 11, Riddle was invited to enrol in Hogwarts School of Witchcraft and Wizardry, and he entered into House Slytherin.

During his time at Hogwarts, Riddle uncovered legends that the founder of House Slytherin had hidden a secret chamber inside the school which could only be opened by his descendant and spiritual heir. Riddle managed to gain access to the chamber and befriended the evil monster inside. He then used it to kill pupils at the school who had one or two muggle parents, known offensively as "mudbloods". When the school came close to being closed as a result of the killings, Riddle panicked thinking that he might have to leave and go back to the orphanage, and framed a fellow student, Rubeus Hagrid. Hagrid was expelled for letting a monster loose, and Riddle remained at the school.

Riddle hid his evil side and eventually graduated from Hogwarts at the top of his year, both well liked and respected. He promptly returned to his father's family home, a manor in the village of Little Hangleton, and murdered him. For good measure, he also killed his father's parents, who were living in the house. The method of death remains a mystery, although they were said to look as if they had died of sheer terror. Riddle framed the gardener – who was let off for lack of evidence – and left. His bloodlust wasn't diminished, though.

Riddle possessed great power and ability, and his openly anti-muggle stance won him a number of enthusiastic supporters amongst the traditionalist, pure blood wizard families. He took the name of Lord Voldemort, an anagram of his full name, and started gathering acolytes and followers, whom he named Death Eaters. He took control of a large number of other wizards by using a specific curse that gave him complete power over them. When he had built up a cadre of Death Eaters, he launched a terrorist campaign against mudbloods and muggle-friendly wizards in the wizarding world, and against muggles themselves out in the mundane world.

His ultimate aim was to seize power in the magical world. The Death Eaters' secrecy, brutality and power protected them, and Voldemort continued to grow in strength from the dark magics he was learning and the lives he was taking. More people flocked to his banner, some out of evil ambition and others out of fear and self-preservation. The wizarding security forces, shot through with spies and traitors, were powerless to apprehend the Dark Lord. Many wizards and muggles were murdered during the years of Voldemort's power, often in a spectacularly brutal fashion. The wizardly world was paralysed with terror.

Harry Potter proved to be Voldemort's downfall. For uncertain reasons, Voldemort was desperate to kill the Potters. The infant Harry and his parents, James and Lily, went into hiding, assisted by Professor Dumbledore, but a supposed friend betrayed them. Voldemort tracked them down, killed James and Lily, and then turned his power on the baby. Something astonishing happened though; when Voldemort tried to kill Harry, his magic rebounded and he himself was blasted. Physically wrecked and stripped of his powers, Voldemort fled. His movement collapsed, and most of his Death Eaters were arrested and put into prison.

Although not many people know it yet, Voldemort is now fully restored, thanks to the actions of one of his old servants, a cowardly wizard named Peter Pettigrew. He has summoned his remaining Death Eaters to his side, and wants revenge on Harry, Dumbledore and the rest of the magical world. With his powers back at his command, he is in a strong position to attempt to obtain it.

WORLD: During the time of his power, Voldemort horrified the wizarding world. He had loyal agents (whether voluntary or involuntary) throughout the Ministry of Magic and other organizations, and was able to stay several steps ahead of his enemies. Effective opponents in the fight against him were murdered in their beds, or if they themselves were out of reach, their families and friends were slaughtered brutally. Muggle-friendly wizards were also killed, as almost anyone whom Voldemort took a dislike to could be. Most wizards were starting to view his victory as inevitable, because there seemed to be nothing that could be done to stop him. Fear and paranoia ruled the wizard community. Harry Potter's unwitting defeat of Voldemort guaranteed him immediate and ever-lasting fame.

MAGIC: Voldemort has a wide range of techniques at his disposal. His magic is both powerful and deadly, and he uses it without any pity or scruples. He is a particular master of the Avara Kedavara curse, which strikes an enemy dead and cannot be countered, and of the Imperius curse, which lets him control the mind and body of another person.

Another technique he frequently uses to instil fear is the Dark Mark, a symbol of a snake wrapped around a skull, which he is able to conjure to hang tens of feet high in the air over the site of an atrocity, to warn other wizards that he has done terrible things at that location. Voldemort is also a "Parselmouth", a wizard who is able to speak Parseltongue, the language of snakes.

Morgan Le Fay

Once a student of Merlin, Morgan le Fay was a major enemy of King Arthur's rule in the court of Camelot. She was a sorceress and shape-changer, and her name indicates supernatural blood – "le Fay" means "the fairy", an indication that she was not completely of the mortal realm. She is first encountered in the tales that were penned early in the twelfth century by Bretonian minstrels in what is now France.
Before she became part of the Arthurian cycle, she may have been a water nymph from Breton folklore. She is now a central part of the Arthurian cycle, the evil sorceress who helped seed King Arthur's downfall.

BIOGRAPHY: Morgan was a student (and perhaps lover) of Merlin, and learned a large amount of her magical skills from him over the course of their association. She is linked to various dark Celtic goddesses, and is characterized by her strong associations with winter, warfare and the harshness of nature. She ruled a castle near Edinburgh, which was populated

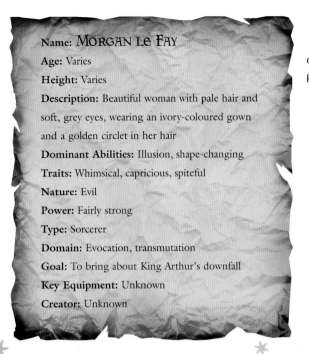

Name: MORGAN LE FAY
Age: Varies
Height: Varies
Description: Beautiful woman with pale hair and soft, grey eyes, wearing an ivory-coloured gown and a golden circlet in her hair
Dominant Abilities: Illusion, shape-changing
Traits: Whimsical, capricious, spiteful
Nature: Evil
Power: Fairly strong
Type: Sorcerer
Domain: Evocation, transmutation
Goal: To bring about King Arthur's downfall
Key Equipment: Unknown
Creator: Unknown

✦ Below: Morgan Le Fay casts away the scabbard of Arthur's sword Excalibur.

MORGAN LE FAY CASTS AWAY THE SCABBARD

appear at Arthur's birth as good fairies, and give him a number of gifts that include strength, longevity and political power. The more commonly known Morgan, however, is a schemer and plotter who pushes the king towards destruction time and again. She is responsible for revealing the secret of Lancelot and Guinevere's affair to the collected knights of Camelot, for example. Having invited Lancelot to her home and attempted, unsuccessfully, to seduce him, she encourages him to paint a mural. His passion for Guinevere proves so strong that the secret of their love becomes obvious from the mural, which she shows to subsequent visitors as a way of causing trouble.

Morgan also played a part in the birth of Mordred, Arthur's son. In some tales she herself is the mother (and, as the daughter of Gorlois and Ygern of Cornwall, is also Arthur's half-sister), but more commonly she is just responsible for the boy's upbringing. She teaches him to disdain his father and trains him in the arts necessary to attack Camelot – ultimately successful, as Mordred fatally wounds Arthur. She also sends the Green Knight to challenge Camelot, frighten Guinevere and test both Arthur and Gawain, the son of King Lot of Orkney.

Paradoxically, although Morgan is King Arthur's enemy during his life, she becomes his guardian and healer in death. When he is fatally wounded by Mordred in the battle of Caemlyn, Morgan and her sisters arrive to take Arthur to Avalon in a magical boat. There, the legends say that he was healed, and he remains there still, waiting for the time when he will be called upon again in his country's greatest need.

WORLD: Morgan is best remembered now for the time she spent interacting with Arthur at Camelot. In many tales, she herself spent much time at the court, pretending to be just another beautiful innocent young

by maidens, had wings which allowed her to fly, and could change her shape, in the manner of most Celtic wizards, into almost any other earthly form. She also ruled the island of Avalon, the blessed isle, where she dwelt with her eight sisters (also sorceresses), Cliton, Gliten, Glitonea, Mazoe, Modron, Moronoe, Thitis and Tyronoe. Her father, the old King of Avalon, had been Avallach, and Morgan may have had a consort on the isle for a time by the name of Gingamor.

In her very earliest forms, Morgan is not particularly evil. Although she tests people, she and her sisters woman, and using her guile to spread malicious rumours and cause other sorts of trouble. At other times, she stayed in Avalon and worked from there, or – particularly when she was bringing up Mordred – lived in the mortal world, secluded from the daily comings and goings of court.

MAGIC: A combination of natural fairy sorcery and Merlin's teachings in ritual gave Morgan a broad and powerful base for her magic. She specialized in enchantments and control of the weather, and spinning illusions and glamours to deceive and enchant. She assisted Mordred in battle by summoning a great fog that hid his armies, and her acts from Avalon show that paradoxically she must have had a great skill in healing. Like most shape-shifters, she seems to have been a largely changeable person, often performing very contradictory actions.

Dishonourable Mentions

Regrettable as it is, there is no shortage of other evil wizards whose prominence and malice is such that they too deserve recognition for their dark ways. **Saruman the White**, in J.R.R. Tolkien's *The Lord of the Rings* series, is the head of the Council of the Wise, the leaders of the free races in Middle Earth. A spiritual being who has taken on a physical form in order to lead the fight against the evil Lord of Darkness, Sauron, Saruman ought to have been beyond reproach... Sadly, Saruman was obsessed with gaining the strength to rule Middle Earth as its tyrant. His greed, corruption and hidden evil nearly led to the utter destruction of the free races, and it was down to Gandalf, the most vigilant of the wizards, to strip him of his powers. Although he was allowed to live, Saruman's ingrained malice proved to be his downfall shortly thereafter, when he was brutally murdered by his traitorous follower, Wormtongue. Saruman had simply pushed the

man too far. According to the non-fiction works of Andrew Collins, an evil wizard known as the **Black Alchemist** is not only real, but is alive and active in Europe today. His goals are unclear, but he is apparently able to corrupt the power of the land, set magical traps for psychic sensitives, summon (or create) spirits, and control the minds of others. Sometimes seen as a wizard, **Baron von Frankenstein** certainly managed to bring the dead back to life with the aid of his semi-alchemical techniques – and paid the price for his insane crimes against nature. Evil wizards, of course, feature anonymously in many stories. Plenty of them feature a maliciously unpleasant old sorcerer, bent and hunched over a staff or lurking in a hilltop castle and terrorizing the local population. These beings are often strange and frightening, and may keep their soul hidden in a foreign object, such as a stone or a nut. In one representative story, a Baron Munchausen tale, the evil wizard is holding a beautiful princess captive, and turns the heroes who try to save her into stone statues. A similar character can be found in a number of *Arabian Nights* tales, where the wizard is often a villainous **Grand Vizier,** the over-ambitious and frequently murderous assistant to the Caliph.

INDEX

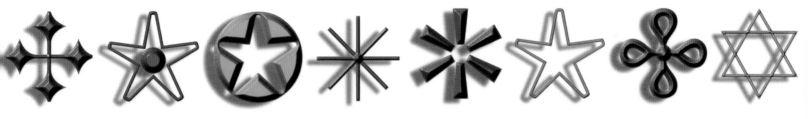

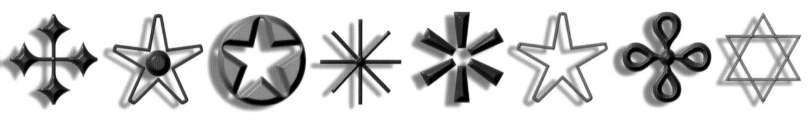

Picture Credits

The publishers would like to thank the following sources for their kind permission to reproduce the pictures in this book:

6 Corbis/Araldo de Luca; 8 Picture Desk/Kobal Collection; 10 Getty Images/ Paul & Lindamire Ambrose/Taxi; 11 Mary Evans Picture Library; 12 Mary Evans Picture Library; 13 Bridgeman Art Library/©Savely Dezso/Private Collection/Archives Charmet; 14 Corbis/Roger Tidman; 15 Topfoto.co.uk; 16 Mary Evans Picture Library; 18 Mary Evans Picture Library; 19 Mary Evans Picture Library; 20/21 Rex Features/Sipa Press; 22/23 Corbis/The Cover Story; 24 Getty Images/Photographers' Choice; 26 Bridgeman Art Library/ Private Collection; 27 Rex Features/20th Century Fox/Everett; 29 Corbis/ Tibor Bognar; 31 Getty Images/Photographer's Choice; 32 Rex Features/ Richard Sowersby; 33 Rex Features/Mike Webster; 35 Rex Features/Everett Collection; 36 Picture Desk/Columbia/Kobal Collection; 41 Rex Features/ Everett Collection; 42 Moviestore Collection Ltd; 44 Mary Evans Picture Library; 46 Mary Evans Picture Library; 47 Bridgeman Art Library/Private Collection/Archives Charmet; 49 Mary Evans Picture Library; 51 Corbis/ Images.com; 53 Mary Evans Picture Library; 55 Mary Evans Picture Library; 56 Topfoto.co.uk; 58 Picture Desk/MGM/Kobal Collection; 59 Corbis/ Academy of Natural Sciences of Philadelphia; 60 Topfoto.co.uk; 61 Topfoto. co.uk/Fortean; 62 Corbis/Michael Busselle; 65 Topfoto.co.uk; 66 Mary Evans Picture Library; 67 Corbis/Bettman; 69 Bridgeman Art Library/Chateau de Versailles, France, Lauros/Giraudon; 70 Corbis/Bettman; 71 Mary Evans Picture Library; 73 Topfoto.co.uk; 75 Corbis/Bettman; 76–77 Mary Evans Picture Library; 78 Llewellyn Worldwide Ltd/Wicca for a New Generation by Silver Ravenwolf; 79 Corbis/Historical Picture Archive; 80 Rex Features/Kevin Carlyon; 81 Corbis/Patrick Ward; 82 Alamy Images/Superstock; 84 Getty Images/Botanica/Rita Maas; 85 Mary Evans Picture Library; 87 Mary Evans Picture Library; 88 Getty Images/Mark Lewis/Stone; 89 Topfoto.co.uk; 90 Topfoto.co.uk; 91 Corbis/Clay Perry; 93 Corbis/Archivo Iconografico, S.A.; 94 Corbis/Wolfgang Kaehler; 95 Mary Evans Picture Library; 96 Getty Images/Jeremy Walker/Image Bank; 97 Topfoto.co.uk/Derek Mitchell; 98 Picture Desk/Kobal Collection; 100 Bridgeman Art Library/Collection of the Royal Shakespeare Theatre; 101 Topfoto.co.uk; 102 Topfoto.co.uk/Doug Houghton; 103 Topfoto.co.uk; 105 Rex Features/Rick Falco; 106 Corbis/ Christel Gerstenberg; 107 Created by Daystar for JaguarMoon CyberCoven, used by permission; 108/9 Corbis/Sygma; 110 Corbis/Sygma; 111 Topfoto. co.uk; 112 Bridgeman Art Library/Peabody Essex Museum, Salem, Mass.; 113 Topfoto.co.uk; 114 Rex Features/SNAP; 116 Topfoto.co.uk/The Arena PAL Picture Library; 118 Topfoto.co.uk/The Arena PAL Picture Library; 119 Photos12.com/Collection Cinema; 120 Photos12.com/Collection Cinema; 123 Bridgeman Art Library/Musée des Beaux Arts, Pau, France, Giraudon; 124 Bridgeman Art Library/Birmingham Museums and Art Gallery; 126 Mary Evans Picture Library; 127 Topfoto.co.uk; 128 Corbis/Richard M. Abarno; 129 Getty Images/Image Bank/David Epperson; 132 Corbis; 134 Art Archive/Eileen Tweedy; 135 Mary Evans Picture Library; 136 AKG–Images; 137 Advertising Archives; 138 Mary Evans Picture Library; 139 Images Colour Library; 140 AKG–Images ; 140 Mary Evans Picture Library; 141 AKG–Images ; 142 Christies Images; 143 Images Colour Library; 143 Mary Evans Picture Library; 144 Heritage Images; 145 Christies Images; 146–47 Christies Images/HultonDeutsch; 148 Popperfoto; 149 Popperfoto; 150 Carlton; 150 Popperfoto; 151 Popperfoto; 152 Advertising Archives; 154 Artists UK/Alan Lee (http://www.artistsuk.net); 155 Artists UK/Alan Lee (http://www. artistsuk.net); 156 Kobal Collection/Lucasfilm/20th Century Fox; 157 Kobal Collection/Lucasfilm/20th Century Fox; 158 Kobal Collection/Lucasfilm/20th Century Fox; 160 Artists UK/Josh Kirby (http://www.artistsuk.net); 161

Artists UK/Josh Kirby (http://www.artistsuk.net); 162 Artists UK/Josh Kirby (http://www.artistsuk.net); 163 Christies Images/Bettmann; 164 Ronald Grant Archive; 166 Images Colour Library; 167 Images Colour Library; 168 Images Colour Library; 169 ©Walt Disney; 169 ©Walt Disney; 170 AKG–Images; 171 Moviestore Collection; 172–73 Christies Images/Richard T. Nowitz; 174 Mary Evans Picture Library; 175 Kobal Collection/Wolf, Jerry/ 20th Century Fox Television; 176 Hulton/Archive;
177 Mary Evans Picture Library; 178 Images Colour Library; 179 Kobal Collection/Orion/Warner Bros; 180: "The Witch has just made a new spell!", illustration from "The Goat as Big as an Elephant" from *New Fairy Tales*, pub. By J.M. Dent and Sons, 1955 (w/c) by Doreen Baxter (b.1910), Bridgeman Art Library/Chris Beetles Ltd., London; 181: *The Bard*, c.1817 (oil on canvas) by John Martin (1789–1854), Bridgeman Art Library/Yale Center for British Art, Paul Mellon Collection, USA; 183 Mary Evans Picture Library; 184 Werner Forman Archive; 185 Werner Forman Archive; 187 AKG–Images; 188 AKG–Images; 189 Mary Evans Picture Library; 192 AKG–Images; 190–91 AKG–Images; 193 Images Colour Library; 193 Werner Forman Archive; 194 Fortean Picture Library; 194 Images Colour Library; 195 Fortean Picture Library; 196 Fortean Picture Library; 197 AKG–Images; 198 AKG–Images; 199 Images Colour Library; 200 Images Colour Library; 201 Christies Images; 202 Christies Images; 203 Christies Images; 204: *The Alchemist* from a book on the philosophers stone, (manuscript) *Tractatus Alchymicae Germanick Splendor Solis*, 1589, Bridgeman Art Library/British Library, London, UK; 205 Images Colour Library; 206 Artists UK/Dan Woods (http://www.artistsuk.net); 207 AKG–Images; 207 Fortean Picture Library; 208 Artists UK/PeterPracownik (http://peterpracownik.com); 209 Fortean Picture Library; 210 Mary Evans Picture Library; 211 Fortean Picture Library; 211 Mary Evans Picture Library; 212 Fortean Picture Library; 212 Mary Evans Picture Library; 213 Fortean Picture Library; 213 Mary Evans Picture Library; 215 Christies Images; 216 Fortean Picture Library; 216 Fortean Picture Library; 214: *The Witches in Macbeth*, c.1841–2 by Alexandre Gabriel Decamps (1803–60), Bridgeman Art Library/Wallace Collection, London UK; 217 Mary Evans Picture Library; 217 Werner Forman Archive; 218 Werner Forman Archives; 219 Fortean Picture Library; 220 Images Colour Library; 221 Images Colour Library; 222 Fortean Picture Library; 222 Mary Evans Picture Library; 223 Fortean Picture Library; 223 Mary Evans Picture Library; 224 Artists UK/Roger Garland (http:// www.lakeside –gallery.com); 226 Artists UK/Roger Garland (http:// www.lakeside –gallery.com); 227 Artists UK/Alan Lee (http://www.artistsuk. net); 228 Moviestore Collection; 229 Moviestore Collection; 230 Mary Evans Picture Library; 230 Mary Evans Picture Library; 230 Mary Evans Picture Library; 231 Mary Evans Picture Library; 232 Kobal Collection/Hamshere Keith/Lucasfilm; 233 Kobal Collection/Hamshere Keith/Lucasfilm; 233 Kobal Collection/Lucasfilm/20th Century Fox; 235 Artists UK/Josh Kirby (http:// www.artistsuk.net); 236 AKG–Images; 238 Fortean Picture Library; 239 Kobal CollectionKobal Collection; 240 Kobal Collection/Lucasfilm/20th Century Fox; 242 Christies Images/AFP; 243 Carlton; 243 Fortean Picture Library; 245 Fortean Picture Library; 246 Hulton/Archive; 247 Ronald Grant Archive; 254–55 Mary Evans Picture Library